THE OTHER
JOHN UPDIKE

ALSO BY DONALD J. GREINER

The Notebook of Stephen Crane (Editor)
Comic Terror: The Novels of John Hawkes
Robert Frost: The Poet and His Critics
American Poets Since World War II: Ammons through Kumin
(Editor)
American Poets Since World War II: Levertov through Zukofsky
(Editor)

THE OTHER JOHN UPDIKE

Poems/ Short Stories/ Prose/ Play

Donald J. Greiner

University of South Carolina

OHIO UNIVERSITY PRESS
ATHENS, OHIO

Library of Congress Cataloging in Publication Data

Greiner, Donald J.
    The other John Updike.

    Bibliography: p. 267
    Includes index.
    1. Updike, John—Criticism and interpretation.
I. Title.
PS3571.P4Z684   813'.54   80-22377
ISBN 0-8214-0585-3
ISBN 0-8214-0612-4 pbk.

As Always
this book is for Ellen
and for

Jan and Lee
Judy and Bob
Kathie and Risher

Acknowledgments

Acknowledgments are a pleasure to write. George L. Geckle, Chairman, Department of English, University of South Carolina, and Chester Bain, Dean of the College of Humanities and Social Sciences, provided the release time necessary for research and writing. Jane Thesing, Assistant Reference Librarian, Cooper Library, University of South Carolina, cheerfully tracked down information about the first printing of some of Mr. Updike's material. My graduate assistants, Carol Treacy, Caroline Bokinsky, and Michael Adams, checked references with accuracy and energy. Benjamin Franklin V, colleague and friend, read the manuscript and listened to the complaints of the struggling author.

I am grateful to be a member of the Department of English at the University of South Carolina, a department which supports and appreciates scholarship.

Donald J. Greiner
18 February 1980

Contents

Preface

The phrase "the other John Updike" refers not to a hidden side of the author's personality but to a substantial segment of his achievement which is generally overlooked. Although Updike the novelist has been a renowned figure on the American literary scene since 1959, Updike the short story writer, poet, essayist, and dramatist lacks recognition. This situation might not matter if the tales, poems, essays, and play were a minor part of his career, a kind of busy-work designed to fill the time between publication of his latest novel and preparation for the next. But such is not the case for an author who in addition to nine novels has also published, as of this writing, five collections of stories, four books of poems, two large books of prose, and one closet drama. Updike takes his non-novel writing seriously.

In offering the first sustained study of the other Updike, I hope to suggest a shape to his accomplishment thus far and to discuss his changing use of techniques, moods, and subjects. I am not arguing that his lesser known work is more important than the novels (or vice versa), but I would like to encourage attention to a body of art which merits examination.

I am aware that readers who attempt to keep up with the long career of John Updike face a time-consuming task: He is among the most prolific of contemporary American authors. To read the canon of a writer of such seriousness and sensitivity requires energy and enthusiasm. I also understand that readers who attempt to write about the long career of John Updike face the possibility of reply: He apparently does not take kindly to some evaluations of his work. To comment on the achievement of an author with spirited opinions causes uncertainty and hesitation. The record is clear. Updike does not like many reviewers, journal editors, and, one assumes, academic critics.

Updike's best known put–down of literary commentators was voiced in November 1971 during a mock interview between his character Henry Bech and himself. Confessing that he found reviews "humiliating" and reviewers so much cleverer than the author, he despaired of the way "all the little congruences and arabesques you prepared with such anticipatory pleasure are gobbled up as if by pigs at a pastry cart."[1] The implication that reviewers with a new book are like pigs at a dessert table became so well known that Updike was asked about it even seven years later when interviewed on the Dick Cavett Show.[2] There is more commentary just as pointed if not as well publicized. In "The Dogwood Tree: A Boyhood," originally published in Martin Levin's *Five Boyhoods* before being collected in *Assorted Prose*, he laments book reviews by "one of the apple–cheeked savants of the quarterlies or one of the pious gremlins who manufacture puns for *Time*."[3]   And then there is the foreword to *Picked-Up Pieces* in which Updike describes critics who reveal too much of the plot as "blabbing, and with the sublime inaccuracy of drunken lords reporting on a peasants' revolt."[4]   Finally, discussing Witold Gombrowicz's *Ferdydurke*, he sympathizes with the Polish author's diatribe against literary criticism: "If a harsh Providence were to obliterate, say, Alfred Kazin, Richard Gilman, Stanley Kauffmann, and Irving Howe, tomorrow new critics would arise with the same worthy intelligence, the same complacently agonized humanism, the same inability to read a book except as a disappointing version of one they might have written, the same deadly 'auntiness.'"[5]

Updike's distaste for critics is not at all masked. Confronting such witty but barbed statements, the commentator wonders if he should put down his pen, abandon the desk in the study, and transfer his admiration for the work of John Updike to the cocktail party or the classroom. And yet one sympathizes with the upset author. So many of the published commentaries on Updike discuss not what he does write but what he should. A typical lukewarm response to one of his books might go like this:

A sensitive, even startlingly acute handling of vocabulary and prose rhythms, but his fiction, both tales and novels, is too lightweight, too much involved with the business of memory and the nuances of private feeling, and thus it lacks the exploration of weighty matters which art of high seriousness demands. In an age which suffers from apocalyptic vision, sensitive readers find it difficult to give full attention to stories about leaves, museums, and the complexities of wife—wooing. With the 1970s and probably the 1980s so ungraspable, why, they ask, read the work of a man who often recalls the 1950s?

Some answers to this query will be forthcoming in the following chapters, but for the moment the questioner might note Tony Tanner's observation that Updike only "seems on first reading to stand quite apart from his contemporary fellow writers."[6] His work is not "visibly" experimental, and his general subject matter—New England suburbia and the American middle class—is disdained by his peers as a "desert of unreality." But, Tanner argues, careful reading shows that Updike's prose at its best is "edged with dread" of death, decay, nothingness, and waste which brings him into an "unexpected relationship" with an author like Thomas Pynchon.[7] Professor Tanner is convincing, but one point to emphasize is that Updike is a significant author not because his themes resemble Pynchon's or those of any other contemporary writer but because he has something to say and he says it uncommonly well.

Norman Podhoretz and John W. Aldridge vehemently disagree. Their negative opinions are not so much the issue as is the apparent relish with which they attack Updike. A reviewer who has harshly criticized *The Centaur* and *Of the Farm* in what even he admits is "a profoundly negative review," Professor Aldridge is a leading spokesman for the group of critics who insist that Updike has nothing to say. Although he seems to approve of *Bech: A Book*, Aldridge suggests that Updike's career since *The Poorhouse Fair* follows a line of steady decline: "...one has watched him over the years making that familiar agonizing descent from the position of Everybody's Brilliant Young Writer to a position of some insecurity and ambiguity, which the large popular success of such a book as *Couples*—known in certain uncharitable circles as 'the thinking man's *Peyton Place*'—did little to improve."[8] Reading such an unsympathetic comment, one hardly knows what to say except to remark that Aldridge must surely be a ringleader of that uncharitable circle. When he detects what to his mind is a weakness, he presses home: "...one is struck by the disparity between the complication and the pretentiousness of his symbolism and the thinness or irrelevance of the dramatic situation which presumably his symbolism is intended to illuminate.... Evidently, Updike learned from Joyce all the wrong lessons."[9]

Updike's response to this kind of carping reflects his sensitivity to the responsibilities inherent in the task of reviewing books. Singling out Aldridge (and Podhoretz) by name, he writes, "Do not accept for review a book you are predisposed to dislike, or committed by friendship to like.... Never, never (John Aldridge, Norman Podhoretz) try to put the author 'in his place,' making of him a pawn in a contest with other reviewers."[10] Podhoretz apparently hopes to usurp Aldridge's leadership in the circle of Updike disparagers.

The first sentence of Podhoretz's essay establishes the tone: "I have been puzzled by many things in the course of my career as a literary critic, and one of them is the high reputation of John Updike."[11] This is an essay by a man with an axe to grind, a point to prove, instead of a desire to analyze an author's work. From the first word, "I," one suspects that Podhoretz is more interested in selling himself than in presenting his subject. Thus one is not surprised, although doubtless he hopes one will be, when he argues that Updike's prose style is not extraordinary but "bloated like a child who has eaten too much candy," or that Updike has "no mind at all."

Podhoretz tries to convince the reader that his assessment is "balanced." He has, he assures us, done "his best to keep up with Updike" and to understand why so many people he "respects" enjoy Updike's fiction. Yet despite his good efforts, he decides that everyone he respects is wrong: Updike's short stories "disgust" him as "all windup and no delivery" and the "verbal pyrotechnics" alternately bore and exasperate him. The problem, announces Podhoretz, is that the rhetorical virtuosity does not serve sophistication and knowledge but rather masks callowness, cruelty, and sentimentality. The cruelty is shown in *Rabbit, Run* when Janet accidentally drowns her baby, a scene which leaves a "bad taste" in Podhoretz's mouth. The callowness is exposed in the sex scenes of the same novel, and the sentimentality is illustrated in the short stories.

Most of Podhoretz's attack is reserved for *The Centaur*, Updike's latest novel at the time the essay was published. Deciding that Updike's prose does nothing but strain self-consciously to call attention to its brilliance, Podhoretz takes him to task for violating verisimilitude in a description of pain, and for exchanging precision for "razzle-dazzle." He concludes that Updike is a popular author with little to say, a limited emotional range, a penchant for "a rather timid nostalgia," and a "mandarin and exhibitionistic" prose style. In a list of inflated literary reputations, says Podhoretz, Updike's name belongs near the top.

No wonder Updike sees pigs at pastry carts. Faced with such ill-tempered commentary, he can do little except jokingly allude to Podhoretz in one of his own books. Only those familiar with Podhoretz's campaign against Updike in *Commentary* will catch the mild retaliation in *Bech: A Book*. Updike explains: "to be candid, the bibliography was also a matter of scoring off various grudges, a way of purging my system. I've never been warmly treated by the *Commentary* crowd—insofar as it is a crowd—and so I made Bech its darling. Norman Podhoretz has always gone out of his way to slam me, and this is my way of having some fun with him."[12]

Calmer versions of the Podhoretz—Aldridge position usually boil down to the opinion that Updike's writing is all style and little content. One example will illustrate for the moment. Insisting that Updike could not sustain a ten-minute conversation with Rabbit Angstrom, D. Keith Mano writes, "Great issues aren't at issue in Updike's fiction. When ignorant armies clash by night, his people are somewhere else on the beach, skinny dipping perhaps."[13] Yet Mano apparently approves of some of the canon. He calls Updike "the sweet lonesome singer of Protestant mediocrity," "a middle class realist," and an author who by all standards should be unread. Yet he admits that because of "frankness and deft style," Updike is appreciated by millions. Mano's version of the left-handed compliment illustrates a general opinion that is a kind of rallying cry for those who are either not yet sure about Updike's achievement or just do not like it: "He plumps for no ideology: that would be an abuse of the author's position. In fact, John Updike, out of kindness or acedia, has very little to say. And no one writing in America says it better."[14]

As his published opinions of Podhoretz show, Updike does not shrink from retorting to "apple-cheeked savants and pious gremlins." He calls John Aldridge, for example, "a man with quite coarse critical perception and he was quite crass about the book" (*The Centaur*). He goes on: "There is no way a critic can get you to say what he might have wanted to say. That's one of the rubs between critics and authors. Critics really are often disappointed that the book they have to review is not the book they would have written if they had had the same topic."[15] No author can satisfy every reader. "There's a 'yes–but' quality about my writing that evades entirely pleasing anybody. It seems to me that critics get increasingly querulous and impatient for madder music and stronger wine, when what we need is a greater respect for reality, its secrecy, its music. Too many people are studying maps and not enough are visiting places."[16]

One of those who puts aside maps and mad music is Richard Locke. Asking if any contemporary American authors are consistently publishing distinguished books, if any are good enough for us to turn to and discover something about who we are, he answers that Updike, among several others, is such a writer. Updike has been with us since the late 1950s, reminds Locke; it is time we noticed. Yet Locke does not bow in praise of the entire career. The poems, he believes, are charming, witty, and clever, no more than they pretend to be. *Assorted Prose* is uneven but impressive because of "Hub Fans Bid Kid Adieu" and the reviews. The short stories are only tune-ups for the novels. Too many of them shift from the characters and scenes to call attention to the author himself and his versatile style: "When you're reading them you go along willingly, but when you look back they tend to melt together in a reverent hush of lyrical lissome linguistic curlicues. It is this that so excites the ire of Updike's critics."[17] Locke does not like the short stories which have what he calls a "sugary Olinger mist." Reserving most of his praise for the novels, he compares Updike the miner with Mailer the mountain climber as the two American authors most successfully writing today about human and cultural dilemmas.

As the following chapters will show, I value the short stories, essays, and many of the poems more than Locke does. Still, I do not think that Updike would invite him to the pastry table. Locke's largely appreciative remarks appear in the same issue of the New York *Times Book Review* which carries the mock interview between Updike and Henry Bech mentioned earlier and republished in *Picked-Up Pieces*. Although Updike's comment about reviewers being cleverer than he is ironic, the lament about unappreciated style, structure, and nuance is not. So many critics despair over his refusal to tackle "big" issues that they gobble up his subtleties on the way to their deadlines. Even the anonymous author of the appreciative, well-known *Time* cover story on Updike mistakenly observes, "The larger fact is that, however valid his own objectives and achievements, he has ignored the mainstream of contemporary Western fiction."[18]

This opinion is questionable, but Updike is aware that his work seems different to those who have in mind a limited definition of "mainstream." He views the artist as a "middleman between the ideal world and this, even though our sense of the ideal—and I'm speaking really of our gut sense, regardless of what we think we believe—is at present fairly dim."[19] As a middleman, he generally avoids the dramatics of apocalypse and shock. Suffering and disaster do occur in his writing, but usually not in the context of specific social or political issues: "My message has not been the kind that is especially congenial to my time. In a time concerned with urban and political issues, I've dealt with suburban, or rural, unpolitical man."[20] The "big" issues of his day are relegated to a subject matter which is often small, domestic, and concerned with the mystery of the quotidian and the magic of telephone poles. Economic and political questions are generally peripheral to his interest in the crises of home, school, and small town, what he calls "the despair of the daily." "One suspects that it's good to be alive, that there is much more beauty around us than we ever notice, that existence is charged with goodness. Yet even though one isn't willing to die, life still, day by day, often seems monotonous and long. Our goals, once we reach them, bore us."[21]

The interminable boredom of the well-to-do middle class is a primary topic in Updike's short stories after *Pigeon Feathers*. Moving his characters from Olinger to Tarbox, he shows with special attention to detail how an argument with a wife, or an assignation with a mistress, or even a journey to a foreign land does little to change circumstances and people. Once attained, the goal recedes to the horizon, and the desperation of domestic boredom settles in among the comfortable houses and groomed lawns. People frustrated by a combination of affluence and disappointment often turn to memory. In Updike's fictional world, the domain of memory is normally personified in the town of Olinger where families hold on and where first loves are won and lost. The usually implied but persistent contrast between current disappointment and past desire, between, as it were, Tarbox and Olinger, charges Updike's short stories with emotion which some readers believe degenerates to sentimentality. Sentimentality is not to be confused with nostalgia. Updike's stories often communicate a sense of longing, a nostalgia for other circumstances and other loves which may now be recovered only in fiction. He explains, a "writer begins with his personal truth, with that obscure but vulnerable and, once lost, precious life that he lived before becoming a writer."[22] The key word is "precious," for yesterday is extremely valuable in his tales. The occasional charge of sentimentality and the resulting dismissal by some reviewers quickly turning pages must rankle him. Stories like "In Football Season" are as far away from teary sentimentality as the latest slick best seller is from greatness.

This problem is discussed obliquely in "The Bulgarian Poetess" when Henry Bech describes his fictions to a group of Bulgarians. Bech explains that he writes of people "whose actions were all determined, at the deepest level, by nostalgia, by a desire to get back, to dive, each, into the springs of their private imagery."[23] When Bech mentions that his book was badly received, one listener implicitly criticizes method and tone: "Fiction so formally sentimental could not be composed in Bulgaria. We do not have a happy history."[24] The Bulgarian confuses nostalgia for sentimentality, and non-violent fiction with happy circumstances. But Updike's stories are more often than not about loss, loss so imperceptible and yet so severe that pain and desire revolve around memory and guilt. When asked if his characters are moved by love, Bech again stresses nostalgia as a basis for his fiction: "Yes, very much. But as a form of nostalgia. We fall in love, I tried to say in the book, with women who remind us of our first landscape. A silly idea."[25] The idea is not at all silly, as readers of "Leaves" and *Of the Farm* know. Updike is, among other things, our current master of nostalgia, not the brand which suggests that past days were better, but the nostalgia which lacerates a character with memory of the painful loss of something desired that paradoxically often hurt him when he had it. His definition of nostalgia should be kept in mind when reading the following chapters: "What is nostalgia but love for that part of ourselves which is in Heaven, forever removed from change and corruption?"[26] The desire for love and the inevitability of loss define the center of his stories about the past.

In this sense he touches the experience of most readers. Just as Updike implies that the critic's essential service is to recommend, so he suggests that one of the author's duties is to remind. His homage to E.B. White is to the point: "White has figured in my life the way an author should figure, coming at me from different directions with a nudge, a reminder, a good example."[27] Updike's nudges often urge the reader toward the narrowing doors of memory where the persistence of desire might find fulfillment. The opening sentence of "In Football Season" establishes a mood which is typical of many of his tales: "Do you remember a fragrance girls acquire in autumn?" Reminding the reader by a direct appeal to his own past, Updike calls attention to the universality of the emotions which he generates. Not every story is so explicit in its appeal, but the tone of recall—the nostalgia, the nudge—invites the reader to examine his own experience. The past may be gone and is thus without change, but it always exerts pressure on the present. Acknowledging that pressure is a kind of moral responsibility, Updike explains, "My books are all meant to be moral debates with the reader, and if they seem pointless—I'm speaking hopefully—it's because the reader has not been engaged in the debate."[28]

Norman Podhoretz and John Aldridge would not even have us try, but many others have joined the debate. Most of the critical attention given Updike has focused on his nine novels to date and on the cycle of stories titled *Bech: A Book*. His current popular reputation rests largely upon his stature as a novelist, particularly as the author of the award-winning *The Centaur* and of the best seller *Couples*. A reading of some of the critical books on Updike—of Alice and Kenneth Hamilton's *The Elements of John Updike* (1970), Rachael Burchard's *John Updike: Yea Sayings* (1971), Larry Taylor's *Pastoral Patterns in John Updike's Fiction* (1971), Robert Detweiler's *John Updike* (1972), Joyce Markle's *Fighters and Lovers* (1973), and Edward Vargo's *Rainstorms and Fire: Ritual in the Novels of John Updike* (1974)—shows that except for some of the short stories, especially those before *The Music School*, the rest of Updike's achievement is not discussed in detail. The poems, if they are mentioned at all, either are only acknowledged to exist or are discussed briefly as acceptable examples of light verse. The long collections of prose normally are not referred to and surely are not examined. The play, *Buchanan Dying*, is ignored. Yet the collected stories, poems, prose, and play total (as of January 1979) twelve volumes, a substantial part of any author's canon and a segment of Updike's achievement which deserves to be explored.

The following chapters attempt to do just that. Space does not permit discussion of every poem, story, and essay. If I have omitted someone's favorite, I can only apologize. In addition, I have not discussed *Bech: A Book* because it is clearly a unified cycle of tales, more of a variation on the novel than a collection of stories. Relevant opinions of other critics are duly noted in order to illustrate the reception and reputation of the books. Hoping to avoid an invitation to join Updike's pigs at the pastry cart, I have tried to discuss not what he should write but what he does. I should much prefer to meet him for a round of golf, a sport which I find just as mysterious and maddening as he shows it to be in his short stories and essays. In lieu of that opportunity, I offer this study.

Notes to the Preface

1. John Updike, "Bech Meets Me," *Picked-Up Pieces* (New York: Knopf, 1975), p. 12.
2. The interview was broadcasted on PBS on the nights of December 14 and 15, 1978.
3. John Updike, "The Dogwood Tree: A Boyhood," *Assorted Prose* (New York: Knopf, 1965), p. 175.
4. Updike, "Foreword," *Picked-Up Pieces*, p. xvii.
5. Updike, "Witold Who?," *Picked-Up Pieces*, p. 305.
6. Tony Tanner, *City of Words: American Fiction 1950-1970* (New York: Harper and Row, 1971), p. 273.
7. Tanner, pp. 275-276.
8. John W. Aldridge, "An Askew Halo for John Updike," *Saturday Review*, 27 June 1970, p. 25.
9. Aldridge, p. 26.
10. Updike, "Foreword," p. xvii.
11. Norman Podhoretz, "A Dissent on Updike," *Doings and Undoings: The Fifties and After in American Writing* (New York: Noonday, 1964), pp. 251-257.
12. Frank Gado, "Interview with John Updike," *First Person: Conversations on Writers and Writing* (Schenectady, New York: Union College Press, 1973), p. 105.
13. D. Keith Mano, "Doughy Middleness," *National Review*, 30 August 1974, p. 987.
14. Mano, p. 988.
15. Gado, p. 106.
16. Jane Howard, "Can A Nice Novelist Finish First?," *Life*, 4 November 1966, p. 82.

17. Richard Locke, review of *Rabbit Redux*, New York *Times Book Review*, 14 November 1971, p. 2.

18. "View from the Catacombs," *Time*, 26 April 1968, p. 68. Even more difficult to understand is the following comment by D.J. Enright: "John Updike is a remarkably skilled writer, but to me he seems hardly an author at all. He is less a maker than a dismantler, though the magic of his style has won the admiration of a number of critics with whom I tremble to disagree." What can one say except that criticism gives way to cleverness? *See* "Updike's Ups and Downs," *Holiday* (November 1965), 162.

19. Eric Rhode, "Grabbing Dilemmas," *Vogue*, 1 February 1971, p. 185.

20. Rhode, p. 184.

21. Howard, p. 76.

22. Updike, "Why Write?," *Picked-Up Pieces*, p. 38.

23. John Updike, "The Bulgarian Poetess," *The Music School* (New York: Knopf, 1966), p. 228.

24. Updike, "The Bulgarian Poetess," pp. 228-229.

25. Updike, "The Bulgarian Poetess," p. 229.

26. Updike, "More Love in the Western World," *Assorted Prose*, p. 287.

27. Updike, "Remarks on the Occasion of E.B. White Receiving the 1971 National Medal for Literature," *Picked-Up Pieces*, p. 437.

28. Updike, "One Big Interview," *Picked-Up Pieces*, p. 502.

POEMS

The Carpentered Hen (1958)
Telephone Poles (1963)
Midpoint (1969)
Tossing and Turning (1977)

The Carpentered Hen
and Other Tame Creatures

"Distance brings proportion."
—"Tao in the Yankee Stadium Bleachers"

Ask the student in the hallway or the literate man in the library
to name John Updike's first book, and he will probably answer
The Poorhouse Fair (1959). Those who try to keep up with the
rapidly changing scene of contemporary literature may name *The
Same Door* (1959), but in either case the title mentioned will refer
to one of Updike's books of fiction. This response is understandable,
for John Updike is generally accorded the stature of major American
novelist. The relative fame of *Rabbit, Run* (1960), the National
Book Award for *The Centaur* (1963), the best-seller status of *Couples*
(1968), and the critical praise for *The Coup* (1978), not to mention
the enduring reputation of the short stories in *Pigeon Feathers*
(1962), all testify to his importance to American fiction. When
Updike publishes a novel or a collection of tales, most major journals and many general readers respond.

Such is not the case with his poetry. Only literary specialists
know that Updike's first book is a volume of poems, *The Carpentered Hen and Other Tame Creatures* (1958), and that it is the first
of, at this writing, his four poetry collections.[1] The dust jacket
blurb announces that the volume "charts a nice course between
playfulness and sobriety." The book does just that. An antic mood
prevails as Updike expresses his observations in a tone bouncing
back and forth between tenderness and wit. A collection of fifty-

five poems on topics ranging from basketball to the humanities to instructions for a son, *The Carpentered Hen* begins with an epigraph from Boethius' *The Consolation of Philosophy*:

When she [Philosophy] saw that the Muses of poetry were present by my couch giving words to my lamenting, she was stirred a while; her eyes flashed fiercely, and said she, "Who has suffered these seducing mummers to approach this sick man? Never do they support those in sorrow by any healing remedies, but rather do ever foster the sorrow by poisonous sweets. These are they who stifle the fruit-bearing harvest of reason with the barren briars of the passions: they free not the minds from disease, but accustom them thereto."

The dichotomy is clear. Poetry serves the imagination, but only Philosophy expresses reason. Updike, however, does not heed Philosophy's complaint. Many of his poems suggest his distrust of the assault of the rational upon the imagination. In *The Carpentered Hen* especially, he has more fun with the senses than with reason. The book is a delight to read. Yet the reader must look out for irony in the juxtaposition of Boethius and these witty poems, for to read Updike's poetry as merely light verse is to make a mistake. Always lurking beneath the gaudy surface of the puns and play is a deep respect for language. He explains his position in several essays which the reader should consult as an introduction to his volumes of poetry.

Updike discusses the joyous artificiality of language in his review of Max Beerbohm, first published in 1964 and then collected in *Assorted Prose* (1965). In the foreword to *Assorted Prose*, he admits that his ideas may be questionable but that he is nevertheless persuaded of their value:

The theory of rhyme set forth in "Rhyming Max" is possibly totally wrongheaded; though on rereading it I was, curiously, persuaded anew. Mr. Walter Berthoff, a professorial friend, suggested to me on a postcard that pronounced meter and rhyme are dancelike; and perhaps there is a rigidity which is not comic, the rigidity of ecstasy, of rite. But rhyme, I would say, with our present expectations of language, aspires to this intensity vainly.[2]

Rhyme, for Updike, is an agency of comedy. Partaking of rigidity and regularity, it has the mechanical property which Henri Bergson identified as comic in his essay on laughter. Updike explains in

"Rhyming Max": "By rhyming, language calls attention to its own mechanical nature and relieves the represented reality of seriousness. In this sense, rhyme and allied regularities like alliteration and assonance assert a magical control over things and constitute a spell. When children, in speaking, accidentally rhyme, they laugh, and add, 'I'm a poet/And don't know it,' as if to avert the consequences of a stumble into the supernatural."[3]

Thus Updike accounts for his joy in light verse, in the puns, unexpected rhymes, and poems, like "Mirror" and "Pendulum," which are arranged typographically to illustrate theme. The prose writer's duty is to avoid rhymes and "verbal accidents" which might interfere with his response to impersonal reality, but the author of comic poetry has a different mission. As Updike defines light verse, it is "an isolated acolyte" which "tends the thin flame of formal magic and tempers the inhuman darkness of reality with the comedy of human artifice. Light verse precisely lightens; it lessens the gravity of its subject."[4] The technique of his poetry does not mean that he is a mere entertainer, although pleasure is a primary goal. His first volume of poetry is much closer to seventeenth-century lyrics with their delight in verbal facility and unexpected conceits than to the opaque density often associated with twentieth-century poets. Indeed, he is on record as saying that "of my own poems, 'Nutcracker,' with the word 'nut' in bold face, seems to me as good as George Herbert's angel-wings."[5] In Updike's light verse, playful surfaces often lead to consideration about language itself. We read, laugh, and conspire with the poet to deny the seriousness which would judge such humor as insignificant.

Updike credits Charles Stuart Calverley with introducing modern light verse, and he argues that it "calls into question the standards of triviality that would judge it.... The conceits and figures by which men have agreed to swear and live are tripped up by metrics, flattened by the simple inopportuneness of rhyme."[6] Updike's early poems thrive on the unexpected. Surprising rhyme joins regular pattern to challenge pretentiousness and to give joy. As countless readers have pointed out, his narrator in the short story "Dear Alexandros" (Pigeon Feathers) laments the joylessness of contemporary literature, and he even implies that both he, as a foster parent, and the Greek boy are identified by numbers as if the impersonality results from a national literature which communicates depression rather than delight: "Your nation should be very proud of producing masterpieces which the whole world can enjoy. In the United States the great writers produce works which people do not enjoy, because they are so depressing to read."[7] The poems in *The Carpentered Hen* are not depressing to read. Celebrating little things and delighting in verbal patterns, they illustrate uncommon pleasure in common objects.

Praising W.H. Auden's light verse, Updike defines his own poetry: "a man who, with a childlike curiosity and a feminine fineness of perception, treats poetry as the exercise of wit."[8] Updike is fascinated by the way things work, from washing machines to the intelligence of headline writers and magazine editorialists, and his poems reveal an ability to see magic in the mundane. Poetry for him is no idle affair designed to fill the time between novels and short story collections: "I began with light verse, a kind of cartooning in print, and except for one stretch of a few years, in which I wrote most of the serious poems in *Telephone Poles*, I feel uncertain away from rhyme, to which something comic adheres. Bergson's mechanical encrusted upon the organic. But the light verse poems putting into rhyme and jaunty metrics some scientific discovery have a serious point—the universe science discloses to us is farcically unrelated to what our primitive senses report—and I have, when such poems go well, a pleasure and satisfaction not lower than in any other form of literary activity."[9] He goes on to say that light verse dies when making two words rhyme no longer seems wonderful.

Needless to say, for all of the attention Updike now receives for each new book, *The Carpentered Hen* went virtually unnoticed upon publication in 1958. A short comment by Louise Bogan in the *New Yorker*, a magazine for which Updike had worked for two previous years and which might be expected to mention the collection, typifies the reception. Giving the book only one general paragraph, Bogan calls *The Carpentered Hen* "wildly original" and "charmingly perceptive," a volume of light verse which is not ephemeral because of the underpinnings of "neat thinking" and "sturdy observation."[10] Most of the commentary came after the canon was well established, but even now Updike's poetry is generally ignored. Those who mention it do little more than acknowledge its existence. Rachael Burchard, for one, does more. Reading from a religious perspective to discuss what she calls Updike's "yea sayings," Burchard interprets the poems as the "cries of the searcher," of the man who questions rather than answers.[11] One of the best studies is by Elizabeth Matson. Dividing the poems in *The Carpentered Hen* and *Telephone Poles* into four categories, she analyzes them in terms of Word Play, Social and Literary Criticism, Philosophy, and Description. Updike himself might wince at such formal divisions, but he would be pleased with the general discussion which argues that the lightness of the poems does not diminish the intelligence or the "frighteningly perceptive" sensitivity.[12]

Matson makes a good point when she dismisses the notion that Updike's comic verse is on a par with Ogden Nash's clever ditties. In the first place, many of Updike's poems are not comic or light, especially those published after *The Carpentered Hen*. Unperceptive readers have judged later collections by the first. More important, however, is the distinction between Nash and Updike. As Matson points out, Nash explains the joke. His light verse rarely invites the reader away from surface pleasantry toward more serious considerations, many of which in Updike reflect the conceits and puzzles common in seventeenth-century verse. In Updike's best poetry, there is a sense of distance, a detachment created by the intellectual approach which often results in subtle imagery and ambiguous tone. Comic surface masks serious intent, and the reader does a double-take after his initial grin as he determines the point of attack.

It is too easy to dismiss Updike's poems by quoting lines from "Thoughts While Driving Home" published in *Telephone Poles*:

> Was I clever enough? Was I charming?
> Did I make at least one good pun?
> Was I disconcerting? Disarming?
> Was I wise? Was I wan? Was I fun?

His poetry is clever, and it does give the impression of a confident young man showing off an enviable verbal facility. But most of the poems are not word exercises performed by a wise child who knows he is the best. Later collections show his distrust of reason, his wariness of science, his concern for the social age, his autobiographical roots, and his puzzlement over death. Word play is nevertheless nearly always part of the fun in the early poetry which all begins with *The Carpentered Hen*.

Generally rhymed with verbal acrobatics to induce a smile, couched in traditional stanza and metric patterns with amusing twists, and usually occasional, these early poems often include an author's note explaining the occasion of composition. The explanations are different from the footnotes and glosses sometimes appended to the work of difficult poets, for these details of inspiration, as it were, normally heighten the laughter. The incongruous juxtaposition between serious prose statement and comic poem adds to the fun. Journalistic inanity is exposed while creative joy is celebrated. Rigorous analysis can threaten the texture of Updike's first book, but walking the line between ignoring and dissecting the poems, and mindful of Philosophy's pout in the epigraph, the reader may discern why the ditties and lyrics are a worthy beginning to Updike's canon.

A case in point is the first poem in *The Carpentered Hen*, "Duet, with Muffled Brake Drums." The title pun on drums is amusing enough, but the statement of occasion widens the grin: "50 Years Ago Rolls met Royce—a Meeting that made Engineering History—advertisement in *The New Yorker*." Honoring brake drums that do not squeak, Updike suggests with tongue in cheek that the designers of the most expensive passenger car in the world deserve equal recognition. At the same time, he pokes fun at the pompous clichés of highly financed advertising. Meetings that "make" various kinds of history are a dime a dozen. Why equate them with the outrageous expense of a Rolls Royce?

Thus by the time we get to the first line of the poem, Updike has taken us through three changes of mood: Punning title to serious but pompous gloss to comic opening stanza:

> Where gray walks slope through shadows shaped like lace
> Down to dimpleproof ponds, a precious place
> Where birds of porcelain sing as with one voice
> Two gold and velvet notes—there Rolls met Royce.

The elegance, the style, the sheer expense of such a setting are all evident, but the cost is great in another sense. Lifelessness may have joined wealth to suggest sterility. The motionless ponds and porcelain birds, later united in the third stanza to a "well-lacquered sky," call to mind the perfection of art rather than the blemishes of life. One need only read Updike's story "Packed Dirt, Churchgoing, A Dying Cat, A Traded Car" in *Pigeon Feathers* to know the kind of transportation he reveres. He laughs as much at the manufactured image of Rolls and Royce as a branch of automotive royalty as he does at the ridiculous advertisement of their product which suggests that they knew they had history in their grasp at the first meeting:

> A graceful pause, then Rolls, the taller, spake:
> "Ah—is there anything you'd care to make?
> A day of it? A fourth at bridge? Some tea?"
> Royce murmured, "If your afternoon is free,
> I'd rather, much, make engineering history."

The poem is amusing, the occasion light, the skill evident. Assonance and alliteration are displayed throughout, especially in the first lines, and the iambic pentameter rhythm goes bouncing along as if Updike were taking a ride in the first Rolls Royce down that gray walk sloping through shadows. By the time we reach the last lines, we hold on to our hats as we jostle from three regular four-line stanzas into a five-liner with nine caesuras. Mr. Rolls may indulge in a "graceful pause" before speaking to Mr. Royce, but the pauses of nine caesuras are not as smooth. Neither, suggests Updike, is engineering history.

The second poem is not humorous. "Ex-Basketball Player" has no pun in the title or statement of occasion to touch the reader's funny bone. A somber piece of social observation, it is part of the long tradition of comment on loss of youthful prowess couched in the metaphor of past athletic glory. A.E. Housman's "To An Athlete Dying Young" stands behind Updike's poem. Housman's unnamed athlete and Updike's Flick Webb are "runners whom renown outran," but unlike the fate of Housman's young hero, Flick Webb is not yet forgotten. He occasionally dribbles an inner tube for laughs, but "most of us remember anyway."

Updike's approach to this traditional topic is different. Rather than directly lament Flick's fate or warn future athletes to pass on while the laurel crown still shines, he describes Flick's predicament dispassionately. Images and word choice rather than statement and emotion suggest the mood. The first word "Once" tells the tale. A long time ago Flick Webb was good, but like the avenue which runs past the high school, he is "cut off" only a few blocks down the street. His scoring record may still stand, and his hands are even now fine and nervous, but it is a long way from high school glory to pumping gas. His name foretells the paradox of his fate: Natural motion inextricably entangled.

Published before *Rabbit, Run* but after "Ace in the Hole" (first published in 1955 before being collected in *The Same Door*), the poem reflects those two fictions as portraits of a life forever stalled for an adolescent unprepared to meet the humdrum dailiness of adulthood in a boring small town. Many of Updike's poems have similar connections to the fiction and thus should not be dismissed as merely light. Readers may look at "Ex-Basketball Player" and recall a line from *Rabbit, Run*: "They've not forgotten him; worse, they never heard of him." A similar fate awaits Flick. How does one live with only a scrapbook? The question affects not only athletes but also many of Updike's adolescents. William Young, for example, in "A Sense of Shelter" (*Pigeon Feathers*), does not want to leave the high school where he sees himself as a king even if denying the world means losing the girl.

Updike captures the poignancy of the forty-point performance which no longer matters:

> He was good: in fact, the best. In '46
> He bucketed three hundred ninety points,
> A county record still. The ball loved Flick.

The past tense sets the scene. The ball no longer loves Flick, and a lug wrench does not care. He still "stands tall" and thus should have more than his ironic stature "among the idiot pumps" whose rubber hoses hang "loose and low," but Flick's fate is partly his own affair: "He never learned a trade." Updike's metaphors are precise. Pointing out the way the author and probably Flick view the scene in terms of basketball jargon, the metaphors also suggest the incongruity between the glory of the past and the dead end of the present. Flick does not belong here, but basketball degenerates to pinball, and the possibility for applause now rests with stacks of Necco Wafers. "Kind of coiled" in a netherworld between the cigars of adulthood and the candy-flavored drinks of adolescence, he just sits and nods. Note the pun on "tiers" in the last stanza:

Off work, he hangs around Mae's luncheonette.
Grease-gray and kind of coiled, he plays pinball,
Smokes those thin cigars, nurses lemon phosphates.
Flick seldom says a word to Mae, just nods
Beyond her face toward bright applauding tiers
Of Necco Wafers, Nibs, and Juju Beads.

Updike has always been interested in the challenge of athletics and the twilight of glory. In addition to "Ace in the Hole" and *Rabbit, Run*, one thinks of references to weekend pick-up games in the domestic tales of suburban Tarbox, "In Football Season" (*Olinger Stories* and *The Music School*), "The Slump" and "The Pro" (*Museums and Women*), and especially of the astonishing tribute to Ted Williams, "Hub Fans Bid Kid Adieu" (*Assorted Prose*). Knowledgeable about the sports because he has played them, Updike understands the difficulties of success and the poignancy of diminished prowess. When Flick Webb graduates with his forty-point games relegated to the paste of scrapbooks, Ace and Rabbit push through the locker room to take his place. The paste does not dry before the crowd roars to greet the new hero. The mutability of heroism is a theme of "Tao in the Yankee Stadium Bleachers," a better poem than "Ex-Basketball Player."

The first sentence is the key: "Distance brings proportion." Sitting in the bleachers, the poet views the players and thousands of fans as if he were watching a command performance. He imagines baseball stars of the past, and he quotes appropriate passages from Eastern philosophy: The uninhibited man is invulnerable; the swamp will find all, including this stadium; the dead rule longer than any king. Distance brings proportion. So, too, Hans Wagner gives way to Yogi Berra who in turn bows to Mickey Mantle. Small boys who purchase cups of ice in the bleachers will become old men who remember Mantle's home runs and who see "a personal mutability" in the changing rosters:

The Inner Journey seems unjudgeably long
when small boys purchase cups of ice
and, distant as a paradise,
experts, passionate and deft,
wait while Berra flies to left.

Updike uses the ephemeral glory of sports to illustrate the tenuousness of man's threescore and ten. Everyone flies out, and the swamp overtakes the stadium. "Ex–Basketball Player" and "Tao in the Yankee Stadium Bleachers" are not comic ditties relying upon verbal pyrotechnics and wit to earn their keep. Like many of his lyrical meditations in prose, these poems reflect Updike's observations of a social scene which is rapidly changing as he himself moves from young adult to middle age. The seeds of a poignant contrast between past and present which he cultivates so effectively in fiction to express a sense of diminishment and loss are present in these early poems. The short stories may be more effective in detailing the pain of memory, but this consistent theme in the Updike canon begins with *The Carpentered Hen*.

Yet the melancholy associated with athletes dying young or old is not the predominate tone of this book of poetry. Many of the poems are exercises of wit, lyrics which show the acrobatics of language and the delight of pun and rhyme. One point in these poems is celebration of language itself. A true author revitalizes his materials. As the epigraph suggests, Philosophy disdains to comfort when the pleasures of a light–hearted muse remain by the bedside. "Player Piano," for example, illustrates the fun of internal rhymes and the appropriateness of a jiggling anapestic trimeter rhythm reminiscent of automated pianos. The first three lines alone rhyme stick/click/snicker, chuckling/knuckle, and steel/feelers. In the next poem "Shipbored," Updike uses the monotony of a regular iambic tetrameter beat, end–stopped lines, and perfect rhymes to illustrate the pun in the title. The changing colors of the sea and sky do not fascinate him with the possibilities of altered perspective as they do Wallace Stevens in "Sea Surface Full of Clouds." (Stevens is the subject of "An Imaginable Conference" and a kindred spirit lurking in the background of many of these poems.) Stevens' observer sees the intricate workings of imagination and reality as he comments on the minute variations of green and blue, but Updike's is mostly bored:

> Sometimes a drifting coconut
> Or albatross adds color, but
> The blue above is mostly blue.
> The blue below and I are, too.

Repetitions of nature can dull inspirations of art.

So can editorialists who call for the Great American Novel. In "An Ode: Fired into Being by *Life's* 48-Star Editorial, 'Wanted: An American Novel,'" Updike satirizes the fuzzy thinking of those who want fiction to reflect the surface prosperity of the 1950s. He quotes sections of the editorial to show the contradictions of the opinion which holds that in a "decade of unparalleled prosperity," authors should forget the "atomic fear" to write about the "incredible accomplishments of our day" as "surely the raw stuff of sagas." "A Pollyanna literature" can be avoided while healthy men reach beyond memory to "the primeval rivers" to express "a yea-saying to the goodness and joy of life." "What?", asks the reader; so does Updike. His "Ode" is a parody of inspiration. Written in formal eight line stanzas of alternating tetrameter and trimeter lines with ABABCDCD rhymes, the "Ode" illustrates the folly of trying to cram all of the editorialist's instructions into a work of art as if the artist were completing a recipe:

> I shan't play Pollyanna, no,
>   I'll stare facts in the eye:
> Folks come and go, experience woe,
>   And, when they're tired, die.
> Unflinchingly, I plan to write
>   A book to comprehend
> Rape, fury, spite, and, burning bright,
>   A sunset at The End.

Designation of strophe, antistrophe, and epode does not make an ode; neither do prescriptions make a novel. To follow the advice of the writer for *Life*, the artist would have to become a player piano. Art gives way to automation.

The best way to use language is to find joy within its own workings. The result may not be the "raw stuff of sagas," but variations of vocabulary may be employed to encourage a smile. In "Even Egrets Err," Updike writes a quatrain of alliteration which illustrates his delight in rhythm and diction. He even supplies two footnotes of definition.

> Egregious was the egret's error, very.
>   Egressing from a swamp, the bird eschewed
> No egriot (a sour kind of cherry)
>   It saw, and reaped extremest egritude.

As in reading Wallace Stevens, one pulls out the dictionary. Individual words have their own texture and may stimulate the imagination as much as weighty prose. Although the effect here is witty as it often is in Stevens' poetry, one is reminded of the verbal displays in "Wife-wooing" (*Pigeon Feathers*) and its homage to James Joyce's delight in the variations of vocabulary in *Ulysses*. A similar pleasure is evident in "Tune, in American Type," a two-stanza poem in which Updike takes the colophon of an English book as an occasion to celebrate the craft of British bookmaking. The poem may be merely clever, but one admires the apparent ease with which he uses every name and nearly every word in the colophon to write a song in which even the typesetting itself calls attention to the craft. Similar verbal facility, more often in the service of meaning and content, sparkles in the short stories to the satisfaction of many readers and the frustration of some. The debate about the value of Updike's style should begin with *The Carpentered Hen* where he has so much fun with just language.

This sense of delight is especially evident in the contrast between "Sunflower" and "Poetess." The former questions the incongruity of the long-stemmed flower which sports a wrinkled "old lion face" in front but a "girl's/bonnet behind." Each line is rhymed, but the dimeter rhythm and unusual descriptions keep the poem from degenerating into a traditional nature poem in praise of a conventional flower. The lady scribbler of "Poetess" fails to avoid the clichés. Although her poetic feet are "neatly numbered," she oft divines rather than guesses, softly weeps rather than cries. Thus like the "fragrant, pliant" flowers of her verses, she never dies but withers. One wonders if the editorial writer for *Life* would appreciate her attempts at meaningful verse more than Updike's playful poems of puns and interesting rhymes.

The Carpentered Hen is full of these witty but serious efforts to keep language alive. In "Capacity," the occasion of which is a sign in a bus noting that capacity is twenty-six passengers, Updike imagines the bus filled with words representing the alphabet. Typically, however, he includes himself indirectly with the "my" although he omits the "u" for Updike:

> seductive, tart, vert-
> iginous, willowy,
> xanthic (or yellow),

young, zebuesque are my
passengers fellow.

Many of the words are unusual, not part of the vocabulary one
normally expects to hear on a bus. Yet Updike manages to write
a ditty in rhymes which suggests that we might better check through
source materials like the dictionary to find our place in the confusing mass of mankind for which the bus crammed to capacity is
a metaphor. To ignore the bus-load of passengers is to make the
mistake of the man in "Mr. High-mind" who would like to disdain
his place in the multiplicity of the world, in what Updike calls
"a massy tribe." All men, including Mr. High-mind, are alike in their
inability to solve the "issues and alternatives" which have plagued
and yet enticed humanity since "first plotted by the Greeks."
How much more refreshing than the poetess' "soft weeping" is
Updike's oblique call to shore up the language. "Philological" calls
to mind in five and a half lines the lovely descriptive words which
children assign to describe the sounds of animals. American children, for example, say that cows "moo," while British children
speak of "lowing." The contrast between the naturalness of children's observations and the sterile speech of adult specialists is commented on in "The One-Year-Old." Noting that the occasion of
this little poem in couplets is the book *Infant and Child in the
Culture of Today* by Arnold Gesell and Frances Ilg, Updike suggests
that the obfuscations of jargon have as deadening effect upon children as upon the language they will be taught to use. Parents are
warned in the child-rearing book to "shun excess acculturation."
Babies that like to crawl demonstrate that "gross motor drives are
strong." No wonder Updike ends the poem with the telling line
that baby "jargons, jargons all day long." His exposure of nonsense
here looks toward the sociologist's ridiculous comment in "The
Hillies" (*Museums and Women*). Trying to account for the youth
rebellion of the late 1960s, the sociologist advises that the rebels
are seeking to "reëmploy human-ness as a non-relative category."
Specialists in education and sociology are about to undermine communication.
So are the ad men who write the copy for the Rolls Royce ad-
vertisements satirized in "Duet, with Muffled Brake Drums" as well
as the editorial writer for *Life*. In "Superman" Updike shows how
the language is in danger of degenerating to the point where exag-

gerations take the place of sane description. The threat is real, for the varieties of subtle shading are lost when everything is described and hawked in superlatives. Most items are not the brightest or the best or the quickest, but the colloquial language of today suggests otherwise:

> I drive my car to supermarket,
>   The way I take is superhigh,
> A superlot is where I park it,
>   And Super Suds are what I buy.

Other poems such as "Publius Vergilius Maro, The Madison Avenue Hick" ("It takes a heap o' pluggin' t' make a classic sell") and "Little Poems" ("Afraid that 'as' of yours is quasi-/Classy. We like 'like.' O.K.?") decry the fate of language in the hands of advertisers and media men.

Understandably, then, Updike concludes *The Carpentered Hen* with "A Cheerful Alphabet," a twelve-page poem which is a kind of updated *McGuffey's Reader* designed to educate his son in the wonders of vocabulary.[13] For each letter of the alphabet, he writes a poem of fresh perspective and imaginative verve. The reader who groans when he sees that A is for Apple grins when he reads Updike's post-Puritan preachings:

> Apple
> Since Time began, such alphabets begin
> With Apple, source of Knowledge and of Sin.
> My child, take heart: the fruit that undid Man
> Brought out as well the best in Paul Cézanne.

With instructions such as these, he need not elaborate on the once-accepted notion of the proximity of art to sin or on past analyses of the relationship such as *The Scarlet Letter*. Later sections of "A Cheerful Alphabet" are just as new. L, for example, is for "Letter Slot," T for "Trivet," and X for "Xyster" of all things. Even Updike goes to the dictionary for that one:

> Xyster
> "An instrument for scraping bones"
>   Describes the knife.
> The word is rarely used—but why?
>   What else is life?

As the title notes, alphabets are cheerful, and language is fun.

Those who want evidence of Updike's own joy should read "A Modest Mound of Bones" where he describes the mysterious relationship between skin and bones:

> How it sags!—what bunting
> is flesh to be hung from such ele-
> gant balconies?

Equally impressive is "Cloud Shadows" which recalls Stevens' "Sea Surface Full of Clouds." Changing light changes perspective. The descriptive faculty is engaged:

> Beyond Laconia the hills,
> islanded by shadows, take
>
> in cooling middle distance
> a motion from above, and lo!
> grave mountains belly dance.

The Carpentered Hen ends as it begins—with a comment on philosophy. Philosophy which denigrates poetry in the epigraph is in turn dismissed in the conclusion. Z is for Zeppelin, a product of Germany, as was Hegel:

> It fell, as do Philosophy's
> Symmetric, portly darlings,
> Fell from skies where one still sees
> Religion's narrow Starlings.

The last line foreshadows the resolution of "Dentistry and Doubt" (*The Same Door*) as the minister survives a minor crisis of faith by watching the starlings and wrens feed together. Much of Updike's work after *The Carpentered Hen* touches upon questions of faith and distrust of reason. Why, he implies, look for solace from philosophy when poetry is so near at hand? Boethius may seek what consolation he will, but art is eternal. The art in Updike's first book is not great. It will not spark esthetic movements, nor will it change the course of poetry. Yet it is much more than updated versions of Ogden Nash. Although his later books of poetry are progressively more somber in tone, he never abandons the delight in language and the fascination with little things first illustrated in *The Carpentered Hen*.

Notes to *The Carpentered Hen*

1. John Updike, *The Carpentered Hen and Other Tame Creatures* (New York: Harper and Brothers, 1958). Further references are to this edition.
2. John Updike, "Foreword," *Assorted Prose* (New York: Knopf, 1965), p. ix.
3. Updike, "Rhyming Max," *Assorted Prose*, p. 259.
4. Updike, "Rhyming Max," p. 260.
5. Charles Thomas Samuels, "John Updike: The Art of Fiction XLIII," *Paris Review*, 12 (Winter 1968), 88.
6. Updike, "Rhyming Max," pp. 258-259.
7. John Updike, *Pigeon Feathers* (New York: Knopf, 1962), p. 106.
8. John Updike, "Auden Fecit," *Picked-Up Pieces* (New York: Knopf, 1975), p. 254.
9. John Updike, "One Big Interview," *Picked-Up Pieces*, pp. 514-515.
10. Louise Bogan, "Books: Verse," *New Yorker*, 18 April 1959, p. 170.
11. Rachael C. Burchard, *John Updike: Yea Sayings* (Carbondale and Edwardsville: Southern Illinois University Press, 1971), pp. 10-29.
12. Elizabeth Matson, "A Chinese Paradox, but Not Much of One: John Updike in his Poetry," *Minnesota Review*, 7 (1967), 157.
13. The lesson apparently worked, for David Updike, to whom "A Cheerful Alphabet" is dedicated, is now publishing his own short fiction. *See* "Apples," *New Yorker*, 18 September 1978, pp. 34-35; and "Out on the Marsh," *New Yorker*, 7 August 1978, pp. 24-25.

Telephone Poles

"How promiscuous is/the
world of appearances!"

—"Suburban Madrigal"

Updike's second book of poems, *Telephone Poles*, was published in 1963.[1] Although he does not include his usual epigraph as an entry to the collection, he does provide a kind of gloss in the foreword to *Olinger Stories*. In this short essay, he reminisces about how as a boy in Shillington, Pennsylvania, he had the impression of being surrounded by "an incoherent generosity":

... a quiet but tireless goodness that things at rest, like a brick wall or a small stone, seem to affirm. A wordless reassurance these things are pressing to give. An hallucination? To transcribe middleness with all its grits, bumps, and ano-nymities, in its fullness of satisfaction and mystery: is it possible or, in view of the suffering that violently colors the periphery and that at all moments threa-tens to move into the center, worth doing? Possibly not; but the horse-chestnut trees, the telephone poles, the porches, the green hedges recede to a calm point that in my subjective geography is still the center of the world.[2]

The stability of the past, suggested by the permanence of telephone poles and porches, remains, because of memory, the still point of his present world. The dust jacket blurb for *Telephone Poles*, which Updike may have written, affirms his concern for "the paradox of the mundane... the elusive surface of created things." Middleness has its own charm in the Updike canon.

He explains elsewhere: "There is a great deal to be said about almost anything. Everything can be as interesting as every other thing. An old milk carton is worth a rose; a trolley car has as much right to be there, in terms of aesthetics, as a tree."[3] *Telephone Poles* is Updike's homage to the world in which small things are infinitely fine and the daily cycle is forever. The religious implications are clear: "I describe things not because their muteness mocks our subjectivity but because they seem to be masks for God."[4]

Telephone Poles is thus a more "serious" collection than *The Carpentered Hen*. Although the theory of rhyme explained in "Rhyming Max" and especially appropriate to the first volume of poems applies to most of Updike's poetry, the sheer delight in puns and rhymes, the reveling in language, is not a primary feature in many of the lyrics of *Telephone Poles*. The second collection is not a mirror of the first. Several critics nevertheless treat *Telephone Poles* as if it were, suggesting that his poetry is merely a throwaway effort, something to fill the time between the composition of his novels. X.J. Kennedy, for example, pays Updike a guarded compliment by designating him as "our leading pyrotechnist" among younger writers, an author who "on occasion" writes poems of "rare depth and competence."[5] But to evaluate *Telephone Poles* by the achievement of, say, Robert Frost or T.S. Eliot is a disservice, for Updike aims for scrutiny rather than "rare depth." His poetry is the art of the miniaturist. Yet Kennedy decides that Updike has committed his genius to fiction and that he only "kids" with his muse when he turns to poems.

Peter Stitt agrees but from a different perspective. The point, he argues, is not that Updike generally writes light verse but that the style in *Telephone Poles* is artificial and mediocre whereas in *The Carpentered Hen* it is pointed and precise. The first collection is witty and thus a success; the second is mannered and thus a disappointment. Admitting that Updike is a master of the arresting rhyme, Stitt insists that he rarely shows his wit in *Telephone Poles* and thereby is forced to fall back on the externals of word play to finish a poem. Verbal pyrotechnics are acceptable in light verse except when they are the only source of wit.[6]

The response to this criticism is, of course, that many of the poems in *Telephone Poles* are not light verse. The collection will be remembered in the Updike canon not for "Recital," the ditty which bothers Mr. Stitt, but for poems like "Telephone Poles" and "Seven Stanzas at Easter." As Edmund Fuller recognizes, the latter alone is worth the price of the book. Even the word play in the minor poems, says Fuller, has a "refreshing, crackling quality."[7] Too many readers demand too much seriousness from Updike's early poetry or else dismiss it altogether as too light. Patrick Callahan does neither. Celebrating Updike as a poet "who feels obliged neither to avant-garde his readers to death nor to choke them in metaphysics," he points to his ability to find value in the "unglamorous" and to write amusing poems which have the touch of wisdom.[8] Even the lightest verse takes on with reflection the weight of religious query when Updike rejoices in the imperfect quality which all things share and which thus links all things.[9]

An examination of the critical reception of *Telephone Poles* suggests that when a fiction writer is both good and successful, his poems may be unappreciated. Timing has something to do with the response to the second collection of poetry, for *Telephone Poles* was published in the same year as *The Centaur*, the National Book Award winner for 1963, and just one year and three years respectively after the highly acclaimed *Pigeon Feathers* and *Rabbit, Run*. In 1963, *The Carpentered Hen* was largely unknown, Updike was praised nearly everywhere for his contributions to American fiction, and many readers were unprepared for a volume of poems which did not seem to share the serious intent of the short stories and novels. Perhaps the natural response was to laugh at the word play or to lament the defection from fiction. Only careful readers saw that gimmickry was not the point of *Telephone Poles*.

— Of the sixty poems in this collection, the title poem occupies the center. A lyric in praise of the mythology of man-made objects, "Telephone Poles" celebrates the ingenuity of man's ability to fulfill his needs by placing his mark on the natural world. Conscious contributions to the planet strengthen his position. While trees remind him of the annual cycle of death with the yearly sloughing off of leaves, telephone poles, for all of the paucity of their shade, remain constant and utilitarian. The heart of the poem is in the following lines:

> The Nature of our construction is in every way
> A better fit than the Nature it displaces.

The beauty of telephone poles, suggests Updike, is that they serve our desire for both myth and necessary construction. They have been on the street a long time, and they will outlast the elms which fall to disease. For a modern populace unable to believe in the giants of "mere mythology," the tops of telephone poles are "fearsome crowns," Gorgon heads which, if touched, can literally "stun us to stone." Lest the reader think that the poet is becoming too elaborate with his analogies, Updike concludes with a witty turn which illustrates man's need to counter mutability:

> True, their thin shade is negligible,
> But then again there is not that tragic autumnal
> Casting-off of leaves to outface annually.
> These giants are more constant than evergreens
> By being never green.

Telephone poles are part of that calm point of things which in Updike's "subjective geography" is the center of the world. As readers of his fiction know, the origin of this personal world is Shillington, a small town in Pennsylvania translated as Olinger in the short stories and novels. The poem "Shillington," written on the occasion of the semicentennial of the borough's incorporation in 1908, defines Updike's still point in the flux of time which changes all things, eventually even telephone poles.[10] The inevitability of time and the necessity for memory have been primary concerns in his writing since the beginning. One returns to his past to find the vacant lots occupied and the woods diminished. How can snapshots capture what no longer is? Without the subjects of the photographs still available, the reliability of the camera eye cannot be corroborated. Better, suggests Updike, to visit the always departing past through the eternity of art. Yet paradoxically the calm point remains, constantly reestablished by the young who always see the town anew:

> Yet sights that limited our truth were strange
> To older eyes; the town that we have lost
> Is being found by hands that still arrange
> Horse chestnut heaps and fingerpaint on frost.

Time "shades" the alleys of Shillington, but nothing is ever totally lost. Even the pavement cracks are mapped somewhere, perhaps in someone's memory:

> We have one home, the first, and leave that one.
> The having and leaving go on together.

"Shillington" has nothing to do with verbal pyrotechnics or the gaudy surfaces of light verse. It is serious in intent and execution, and it typifies the poems in the second half of *Telephone Poles*. More important, "Shillington" provides an entry to the short stories about Olinger, for Updike here creates the balanced tone of nostalgia for that "good remembered town" and acceptance of the present which generates the emotional impact in much of his fiction. The diction is also exact. The vacant lots of childhood fill up while the woods diminish because of the inevitable homage to commercial need, all suggested by "solvent," "marketable," and the allusion in the title to a coin. Description in the first stanza becomes reflection in the second, as Updike realizes that such changes are unavoidable, "Perhaps a condition of being alive." Given the demands of mutability, or, to use Updike's metaphor, the necessary changes of clothes, one holds on with memory to the pavement cracks and realizes that the children who reenact the highlights of his own youth will one day face similar alterations as adults. Because of the exactness of art and the persistence of memory, the "having and leaving go on together."

The stability of cracked sidewalks, telephone poles, lightning rods, and wash on the line is worthy of celebration. All illustrate Updike's ability to see significance in the unglamorous. The concreteness of things neutralizes the lure of appearances. In "Suburban Madrigal," he writes, "How promiscuous is/the world of appearances!" The man inside his own living room who thinks the "window is filled with his/things" does not realize that when viewed from the outside the window reflects the "gorgeous green sunset" of a blue-green parked car. Snapshots are often inexact. Distance brings proportion. Perhaps the truth of appearances comes only in the realm of dreams. In "Fever," Updike writes of the "good" message gathered from the "land of 102°": "God Exists." But lest some readers think that such confidence is too easily won, he ends this short poem on the same note of doubt with which it begins:

It is hard, now, to convey
how emblematically appearances sat
upon the membranes of my consciousness;
but it is a truth long known,
that some secrets are hidden from health.

Reason fails in the face of eternal questions, but revelations glimpsed from the world of appearances may not suffice either.

"Fever" suggests the contemporary man's dilemma of disbelieving reason and distrusting faith. Telephone poles are at least solid and useful, but they do not supply answers. In "Seven Stanzas at Easter," perhaps the best poem in the collection, Updike faces the mystery of revelation and its challenge by the mind:

Make no mistake: if He rose at all
it was as His body;
if the cells' dissolution did not reverse, the molecules
    reknit, the amino acids rekindle,
the Church will fall.

The paradox is nicely stated in these five lines. The Church itself rests upon the foundation of the resurrection, but the resurrection is described in the scientific language of amino acids and molecules. The speaker calls for literal acceptance of this cornerstone of Christianity. Deploring efforts to account for miracles, he dismisses any effort to explain the resurrection by symbol or science:

Let us not mock God with metaphor,
analogy, sidestepping, transcendence;
making of the event a parable, a sign painted in the
    faded credulity of earlier ages;
let us walk through the door.

Those who deny the rolled-back stone, "the vast rock of materiality," or who "seek to make it less monstrous" may one day awaken at the final call "embarrassed by the miracle." Yet those who read this poem as a testament of confident faith read too quickly. "Seven Stanzas at Easter" turns on the "if" in the first line. *If* Christ was resurrected, His literal body rose. Committed Christians must accept not a symbol but the actual fact. But Updike's poet figure is too much the contemporary man to acknowledge the resurrection without dissent. *If* Christ rose, it will not do to make a parable of the miracle. Metaphors mock God. But the poet figure is never sure. Wanting to walk through the door of faith, yet unsure of the way, he remains the uncertain modern man.

Clearly, Updike the poet is much more than the astonishing trickster he is reputed to be. Reading *Telephone Poles*, especially the serious lyrics in the second half, one understands his delight in the things of this world. The "nature of our construction" is always a better fit than the world of appearances. In "Wash," he uses an amusing simile when he describes a June storm which lasts a week as "turning around like a dog trying to settle himself on a rug;/We were the fleas that complained in his hair." But storms are part of nature; they subside. On the eighth day the neighbors rise before the poet so that when he awakens he sees clothes on the line which "lifted up their arms in praise." The comic allusions to the Biblical flood (as well as, perhaps, to Richard Wilbur's "Love Calls Us to the Things of This World") are part of Updike's celebration. God sent the flood, but man built the ark. Let us give thanks, therefore, for washed underpants and diapers:

> Underpants, striped towels, diapers, child's overalls,
> Bibs and black bras thronging the sunshine
> With hosannas of cotton and halleluiahs of wool.

With eyes "washed clean of belief," man finds a new mythology in the "fearsome crowns" of telephone poles. He appropriates old myths to contemporary needs. In "Mosquito," for example, he lies awake in bed while an insect Succubus buzzes the feast of his flesh. He is, in turn, a strong Gargantua guarding his body as well as his slumber against the bite of an invisible antagonist. They are, the poet notes, "Fair-matched opponents." The poem is a conceit about the sting of passion.

In Updike's celebration of constructed things, the spire to be revered is not only the steeple on the church but also the lightning rod on the house. The three crosses of the Crucifixion become the "sturdy curlicues of wrought/iron," and the magical rod, a kind of wand, is the crown of all:

> a star
> of five radiating thorns...

("Old-Fashioned Lightning Rod")

Given the immortality of the mundane, "polycentric orbits" which once inspired notions of heavenly bodies are better used as tools for man's art. In "Mobile of Birds," Updike points to the analogy between the "birds on their perches of fine wire" and Ptolemaic heavens, the Byzantine Trinity, and Plato's Ideals. Man may be small, but each presence balances another in the "planetary weave." Just as one philosophical system gives way to the next, so each artful bird twirls as if free: Both philosophy and mobile are illusions. The birds turn alone in their "suspenseful world" just as the earth rotates unaccompanied in its lonely sphere. Updike praises not the illusory philosophical system but man and his metaphorical mobile. Little wonder that one of his new saints, in "Les Saints Nouveaux," is Cézanne. Once again Updike implies that proper theology is earth-weighted, that myth must mirror man. Looking about him and seeing the world in orange and green, Cézanne

> ... weighted his strokes
> with days of decision,
> and founded on apples
> theologies of vision.

These lines echo his celebration of Cézanne in the final poem of *The Carpentered Hen*.

All of Updike's homage to the things of this world comes together in "Movie House." Knowing that "Monumentality" [pun intended] "wears one face in all ages," he honors the huge buildings in which we search for stars. As our movie stars are illusions, so are the myths about real stars created by past cultures. These beliefs are long discredited, but the edifices built to glorify the legends still stand. The other monuments of twentieth-century America—the bank, town hall, and supermarket—will be dwarfed by the movie house, "this temple of shades." Theaters may not equal in grandeur the creations of ancient civilizations, but in the twentieth century they tell man's story best. The poem ends with a gently ironic thrust toward the future:

> ... stand, stand by your macadam lake
> and tell the aeons of our extinction
> that we too could house our gods,
> could secrete a pyramid
> to sight the stars by.

Most of the poems discussed thus far are from the second half of *Telephone Poles* headed by the title poem. Readers who recall Updike's delight in pun, rhyme, and language in *The Carpentered Hen* and who wonder what happened to all that wit should turn to the first half of the collection. Many of these poems continue his unofficial, unannounced campaign begun in the first collection to save language from cliché and jargon by illustrating how delightfully it can be used. If he shows his skill as a serious poet in the second half of *Telephone Poles*, he reiterates his mastery of the light verse, the occasional poem, and the startling turn of phrase in the first. Indeed, one of the central poems in the volume is "The Menagerie at Versailles in 1775," Updike's bow to the great dictionary maker and language preserver Dr. Samuel Johnson. The statement of occasion notes that the poem is taken verbatim from Dr. Johnson's notebook, and the footnote reveals where the passage may be found in prose albeit punctuated a bit differently. The importance of the poem is not what it means but what it illustrates about the vivacity of language well used after careful observation. Dr. Johnson used it well. Thus a rhinoceros has skin like folds of loose cloth; the dromedary has "two bunches"; and the pelican's feet are "well webbed."

Updike honors other keepers of the language throughout the book. Some are not named, yet "Recital" echoes the verbal antics of Ogden Nash. The occasion is a headline in the New York *Times*: "Roger Bobo Gives Recital on Tuba." One can imagine what Nash would do with such a statement; Updike does just as well. As usual in a verse of this sort, the rhymes teeter between genius and ridiculousness. Thus "indubitably" is hyphenated after "bi" to rhyme Indubi-/Pooh-Bah. Most of all, Updike understands the tongue-twisting possibilities of such delightfully inviting words. "Tuba," "solo," and "Bobo" would cause any reader to stumble if read fast enough. This nonsense verse in praise of sound and rhyme ends in nonsense with tongue firmly in cheek:

> "there is simply nobo-
>
> Dy who oompahs on the tubo,
> Solo, quite like Roger Bubo!"

Peter Stitt complains about the conscious misspellings, but to do so is to take the poem too seriously. Nash's name is not called, but he receives a bow.

Other authors are specifically named. In "I Missed His Book, But I Read His Name," Updike salutes not *The Silver Pilgrimage* but the name of its Indian author, M. Anantanarayanan. The title of the book is common enough, but no lover of language can miss what Updike calls "that sumptuous span/Of 'a's' and 'n's.'" Not even Coleridge in "Kubla Khan" concocts such a glorious sound. In the simply named "Agatha Christie and Beatrix Potter," Updike honors two women writers who write well because they know their material, having sniffed the cabbage, "heard the prim post-mistress snicker," and spied murder in the vicar:

> Many-volumed authoresses
> In capacious country dresses,
> Full of cheerful art and nearly
> Perfect craft, we love you dearly.

Finally, in "Meditation on a News Item," Ernest Hemingway is mentioned, in connection with a fishing tournament in Havana which Fidel Castro won, as a writer who may not finish any of those "many rumored books," but who now seems great enough to create his world. The photograph of the two men in *Life* and the quoted dialogue between the bearded giants is too perfect, says Updike, too reminiscent of Nick Adams talking. The creation absorbs its creator, and Hemingway and Castro seem as magical as Alice and the Queen in Wonderland. The tournament becomes Hemingway fiction.

Not all writers, of course, succeed in preserving the life of language. Updike turns his wit on authors who dodge originality for safety. Hedging does nothing but dull edges and stultify perception. In "The Moderate," for example, his target is Patrick Heron's comment in *Arts*: "Frost's space is deeper than Poliakoff's and not as deep as that of Soulages." What can any reader make of such nonsense? Updike laughs his way through a sonnet based on "deep" space, "shallow" space, and "the nicest space you ever saw," and he concludes that he is "delighted to be relative." In the eight and a half line "Kenneths," he chides Kenneth Rexroth, Kenneth Patchen, and Kenneth Fearing for writing literary criticism of T.S. Eliot which all sounds as pedantic as if it were composed by a three-headed Kenneth with six arms and thirty fingers. And finally, in "Tome-Thoughts, from the Times," Updike takes the occasion of a literary review by Orville Prescott to point out in two funny stanzas how ridiculous criticism can be which praises novels not "overly ambitious nor overly long." Recalling "Poetess" (*The Carpentered Hen*), he makes fun of critics who give good notices to novels with "heroines with small frustrations,/Dressed in transparent motivations." Language degenerates when fiction is supported merely for being neither "Overly this nor that."

Instead of such drivel, Updike offers comic verse which has the serious purpose of reminding us how versatile the English language can be. Rhyme, puns, and nonsense twists are often the germs of these poems, but occasionally the dictionary alone will do. In "Reel," he takes the fascinating definition of "Whorl"—"something that whirls or seems to whirl as a whorl, or wharve...",—, and he constructs a tongue twister of words beginning with the letter *W* which convinces us to remember the interesting word with its witty definition. More important, however, is the comment on ambiguity, for the man who attempts to define "manners, habits, morals" will be sent reeling. The pun on "reel" is the key, for while man never knows the meaning of manners and morals, the stars affirm that "whatever whirls is real":

> We whirl, or seem to whirl
> Or seem to seem to; whorls
> Within more whorls unfurl
> In manners, habits, morals.

No wonder the poet reels. The tongue-twisting round of echoing sounds becomes a metaphor for humanity's confusion as the world reels within "solar rings" whose meaning is never revealed. Things always "seem to seem to"; all we know for sure is that they exist.

All is not pride in vocabulary and wit, however. The Updike who can describe the "Winter Ocean" as "Many-maned scud-thumper, tub/of male whales" can also assume the mask of a man driving home from a party wondering if he has been witty enough ("Thoughts While Driving Home"). The speaker who worries about such things is more concerned with personal image than language. Impressing the girl with white shoulders by mouthing opinions on Eliot and Kierkegaard will not rescue speech from jargon and clichés. Updike knows this truth. The cocktail parties in Tarbox seem just around the corner.

Notes to *Telephone Poles*

1. John Updike, *Telephone Poles* (New York: Knopf, 1963). Further references will be to this edition.
2. John Updike, *Olinger Stories* (New York: Vintage, 1964), p. vii.
3. John Updike, "One Big Interview," *Picked-Up Pieces* (New York: Knopf, 1975), p. 518.
4. Charles Thomas Samuels, "John Updike: The Art of Fiction XLIII," *Paris Review*, 12 (Winter 1968), 116.
5. X.J. Kennedy, "A Light Look at Today," New York *Times Book Review*, 22 September 1963, p. 10.
6. Peter A. Stitt, "Let Bobo be Bubo," *Minnesota Review*, 10 (Winter 1964), 268-271.
7. Edmund Fuller, "The Versatile Updike," *Wall Street Journal*, 31 October 1963, p. 16.
8. Patrick Callahan, "The Poetry of Imperfection," *Prairie Schooner*, 39 (Winter, 1965-66), 364.
9. British critics seem much happier with *Telephone Poles*. The *Times Literary Supplement*, for example, notes that Updike must be "enormously pleased with his own aplomb," and it praises the very poem which Peter Stitt dislikes by calling "Recital" "terrific fun." Finally, Peter Porter argues that many of the poems which are "dressed casually as light verse" remain in the reader's imagination. The best illustrate a special angle toward experience, and even the "gimmicks" give pleasure. *See* "Rustic and Urbane," London *Times Literary Supplement*, 20 August 1964, p. 748; and Peter Porter, "Experts," *London Magazine*, 12 (June-July 1972), 148.
10. For a good discussion of "Shillington," *see* Edward R. Ducharme, "Close Reading and Teaching," *English Journal*, 59 (October 1970), 938-942.

Midpoint

"Nothing has had to be, but is by Grace."

—"Midpoint"

In 1969, when Updike published *Midpoint*, his third collection of poems, he was thirty-seven years old.[1] Apparently, few read the book. He comments: "When asked about what my philosophy was I tried to write it down in *Midpoint* in handy couplets and discovered that of all my books it is the least read, and it was hardly reviewed at all. I concluded that nobody really cared what my philosophy was. That's all right."[2] He is correct about the paucity of reviews. Not many critics were impressed. The British reaction, for example, is reflected in the anonymous opinion in the *Times Literary Supplement*. Comparing the title poem to the collages Ezra Pound put together in the *Cantos*, the reviewer writes, "if you found it piercingly boring to come across a page of music in the *Cantos* wait until you take a hinge at Mr. Updike's pix." He concludes that the light verse at the end of the volume is "easily the best."[3] The American reaction was not quite so harsh but still generally doubtful. William Heyen recognizes that the vision in the title poem is comic and that many sections are "technically impressive," but he finds the achievement dubious. The shorter lyrics are more memorable.[4]

Some critics made an effort to unravel the complexities of the difficult title poem. In a short but sensitive notice, Anne Gates realizes that "Midpoint" is an intellectual inventory of Updike's first thirty-five years designed to specify his bearings for the next three and a half decades. "Poised on a pinnacle of meditation," the poet gives up his search for solidity in life and accepts experience as pointillism, "a dance of dots."[5] Alice B. Hamilton, a critic who nearly always finds religious complexities in Updike's work, apparently dismisses his claim that the title poem has a comic spirit, and she argues that in "Midpoint" science supports his "Christian perspective."[6]

Noting these comments, the reader who is familiar with *The Carpentered Hen* and *Telephone Poles* but who has not yet read *Midpoint* realizes that the collection is not typical of Updike's poetry. This is not to say that Updike has discarded his sense of fun. The dust-jacket blurb, for example, which he apparently wrote, explains that the cantos of the title poem "form both a joke on the antique genre of the long poem and an attempt to write one," but it also notes that "Midpoint" is "an earnest meditation on the mysteries of the ego, lost time, and the mundane."[7] The implications are clear. "Midpoint" should not be taken too seriously; it is not an epic. But neither should it be considered too lightly; it is not a capricious joke.

The long title poem, covering forty-one pages, is the author's statement at the midpoint of not his career but his life: Implying the validity of the Biblical injunction that a lifespan measures three score and ten years, Updike traces his intellectual growth from childhood. He concludes "Midpoint" with a comic wink at Modernism and a thrust toward the future. Most readers have been taught to beware of the tendency to identify the author with his narrator or poet figure, but in "Midpoint" the connection is indisputable. Those who insist on defining the speaker as a mask for Updike should consult Canto Two which is a gallery of photographs depicting his parents as children, himself as baby and youth, and his first child. "Midpoint" is a portrait in both words and pictures of the artist as a young man.

The collection is divided into four parts: "Midpoint," "Poems," "Love Poems," and "Light Verse." Although the volume is more ambitious than *The Carpentered Hen* and *Telephone Poles*, the poems on the whole are not so distinguished. The light verse poems are a delight to read as usual, for they show to good effect Updike's skill with comic rhyme and occasional lyrics based on short quotations from newspapers and journals. The love poems are especially interesting primarily to those who have read the short stories, for they express in a different genre many of the concerns which form the core of his domestic tales: Adultery and guilt, sex, love, and divorce. But these two sections are placed at the end of the volume. By the time the reader reaches them, he has struggled with "Midpoint" and read "Poems," sections which many may believe do not reward the effort demanded. For all of the impressive erudition of the title poem, it is likely to appeal to those who are committed to the entire Updike canon and who wish to know not only more about the author but also how he sees himself.

Without insisting upon a close relationship, I suggest that "Midpoint" recalls Wallace Stevens' "The Comedian as the Letter C." Both long poems trace in largely witty terms the development of the would-be artist. Updike is clearly more successful than Crispin, for he does not stop short of his major opus to contemplate a plum. Still, both accept what Updike calls in Canto Five "intelligent hedonistic advice," and both finally feel at ease with the quotidian which urges, again in Updike's words, "avoidance of extremes." The primary difference is, of course, that Updike continues to write, to quest, as it were, after a masterpiece, while Crispin accepts immortality in the guise of four daughters with curls.

One key to the poem, as suggested by the title, is the word "point." The interspersed photographs are not conventional pictures but arrangements of black and white points which indicate his final awareness of the connection of all things and of the necessity to determine the appropriate distance to establish the desired perspective. Clear understanding of one moment in time elucidates surrounding points. Recall the line from "Tao in the Yankee Stadium Bleachers" (*The Carpentered Hen*): "Distance brings proportion." At midpoint in his life, Updike has a correct angle—a point from which to look both backward and forward. A primary theme is thus the relationship between perspective and vision.

An eye/I pun, established in the first Canto, illustrates the normal perspective of youth. The young artist defines himself as the dominant point in the center of a radius of dots all subservient to him as specks of memories about parents, childhood, maturation, and identity. At any given moment, a person views experience from a single point. Yet such solipsism must be tempered, as the pointillistic photographs suggest. Becoming clearer when held at arm's length, the pictures illustrate Updike's understanding that distance both aids proportion and tones down solipsism. The primacy of appropriate points is then reaffirmed in an allegorical canto about the nature of solids, themselves so many particles and dots controlled by the correct relationship of time and space. Finally, the poet understands the connections among self-love, familial love, and erotic love, and how identity and self-knowledge depend upon the ability to step toward a metaphorical point which, with the aid of distance, will sharpen the vision of the eye/I.

The most complete reading of this difficult poem at this writing is Alice and Kenneth Hamilton's "Theme and Technique in John Updike's *Midpoint*."[8] Although long and impressively detailed, their essay revolves around its own dominating focal point of Christian faith. Despite this slant, they do a good job discussing his technique and allusions. The jacket blurb of the book explains that in "Midpoint" Updike uses the meters of Dante, Spenser, Pope, Whitman, and Pound, so the Hamiltons track down his borrowings from these "source" poets. For example, they not only call attention to each one of the twenty-seven quotations from Whitman in Canto Four, but they also correlate each stanza of Canto Three with the various essays in the September 1967 issue of *Scientific American* on which the Canto is based. The Hamiltons correctly note that Updike expects educated and alert readers because, for one reason, he creates his allusions as bonuses for the sensitive observer. For the intelligent reader who does not have time to follow up each hint, the Hamiltons' essay will serve as a resource article, pointing out such bits of information as the facts that Dante wrote *The Divine Comedy* at age thirty-five by beginning with the line "Midway his way of life we're bound upon," and that Whitman stresses his age of thirty-seven in "Song of Myself."

Although the Hamiltons' spade work corroborates the intellectual underpinnings of "Midpoint," the poem may be read with pleasure and profit even if some of the allusions are not noted. Many readers may miss the homage to Dante in the terza rima form of the first Canto, but few will fail to note the parody of the opening of "Song of Myself" when Updike begins his poem with these lines:

> Of nothing but me, me
> —all wrong, all wrong—

The first line refers to Updike's attitude while a child and adolescent; the second is the response of maturity. Whitman is a dot in the formal pointillism of the author's life, but unlike the nineteenth-century poet who believed that honest celebration of the self could reveal the universe, Updike shows that such subjectivity is unreliable, that only distance provides proportion. The technique is comic, but the point is serious. Faced with the realization that his universe is no longer explainable in Dante's religious terms or Whitman's Romantic intuition, he begins with unreliable subjective experience as the first step toward what will become in the poem an affirmation of order in disorder.

Uncomfortable with his current maturity at age thirty-five, with what he calls "fame with its bucket of unanswerable letters,/wealth with its worrisome market report," he recognizes intimations of mortality. Others may tell him that the "livelong day is long," but at his age he feels the "nip of night." How, he implies, can he know where he is going if he loses contact with where he has been? Since this poem is autobiography rather than fiction, he turns not to Olinger and Tarbox but to Shillington. His memories of childhood there reveal that he lived the experience with as much dread as wonder. The crucial question, *"Why am I me?"*, is still difficult to answer. Like Crispin accepting the permanence of the daily cycle, Updike as a boy

> tried to cling
>
> to the thought of the indissoluble:
> a point infinitely hard
> was luminous in me, and cried *I will.*

Canto One captures the ego and fear of the sensitive child. The world revolves around him when a boy so that he imagines himself point 0, "the crux of radii" which gives Heaven and Earth their "slant and spin." This kind of self-centeredness dissipates with growth. Updike comically tells how maturity, even "uncomfortable maturity," overcomes the unreasonable demands of a child's "giant solipsism" so that the problems of love, death, food, ignorance, traffic, competition, and remorse become more immediate than those "crux of radii." Now on the downward side of the "Hill of Life" at only age thirty-five, he looks at his "rewards" for living actively this long: a drafty house, a voluptuous wife, four children (shades of Crispin with his "prismy blonde" and four daughters), and a picture on the cover of *Time* which illustrates the workings of mortality. Still, hope and life are the keys. Grateful that the luminous indissoluble point still shines within him, he urges other boys to "get things done."

The first Canto may seem opaque to those who have not yet read the entire poem, but the metaphorical dots eventually take their places in the pattern of the artist's life. Although Updike realizes that solipsism is not enough, he concludes the section with his "faith in the eye/I pun" intact. The allusion to the *Time* cover portrait carries over to Canto Two of "Midpoint" with its gallery of grainy photographs. Combining photographs, unusual typography, and poetry, Updike writes a poem which he defines elsewhere as "concrete poetry": "I'm interested in concrete poetry, in some attempt to return to the manuscript page, to *use* the page space, and the technical possibilities. My new book, a long poem called *Midpoint*, tries to do something of this. Since we write for the eye, why not really write for it—give it a treat? Letters are originally little pictures, so let's combine graphic imagery, photographic imagery, with words. I mean *mesh* them."[9] His statement about writing for the eye is questionable, since many authors would insist that poetry appeals to the ear. Yet the use of photographs in "Midpoint" to illustrate the theme of pointillism is interesting. Updike suggests the proximity of mortality and immortality with this cycle of pictures which captures his parents as children eventually giving way to maturity, parenthood, and finally to the birth of their own child's children. Lost time, writes Updike, "sifts through these immutable old screens," and "distance improves vision." Literally, the black and white dots which comprise the photographs are clearer when held at arm's length, and metaphorically one understands the past better with the perspective of time.

The point may be, however, his emphasis on the immutability of the photographs. Time seems captured there. The pictures may be grainy, suggesting the haziness of memory, but they provide a clue to where he has been and to the "radii" connected to his eye/I. Solipsism shrinks when other links are recognized. The ability of the photographs to solidify a moment in time is one manifestation of the indissoluble point that Updike longs for as a child in Canto One. Thus the pictures paradoxically confirm both the passage of time and the immutability of the moment. The paradox of solidity is the subject of Canto Three as Updike discusses in Spenserian "stanzas associated with allegory" the atomic structure of solids.

Originally published in the January 1969 issue of *Scientific American*, and based on the September 1967 issue, "The Dance of the Solids" is short but complex. This section dissects the indissoluble point in eleven stanzas which trace the history of the scientific investigation of solids, but the connection with the middle-aged poet inquiring into the substance of his own life may seem strained to some readers. Updike's knowledge of science and control of unusual rhymes are nevertheless dazzling.

Solidity, he notes, is "an imperfect state." Probe a rock, and one will find atoms; investigate a life, and one will discover a past. The second half of the previous sentence is not stated, but the relevance of the idea to the entire Canto is implied. "The Dance of the Solids" is another answer to the "me" of Canto One, for in studying science the poet learns that no one thing is isolated or dependent on only itself. Atoms and their components make up the apparently solid state of matter just as moments long gone comprise the substance of the present. The key lines in the Canto are:

> *X-ray diffraction pierced* the Crystal Planes
> That roofed the giddy Dance, the taut Quadrille.

Updike's comment on the mistaken notion of the indivisibility of the atom is an allegory for the false Romantic notion that the universe may be understood by contemplating the self as the poet does when a child. Since all things are connected in a dance of being, a "song of myself" is inadequate today. The meditation on atomic structure is also an allegory for the permanence of order in the face of apparent disorder. The dance may be "giddy," but it follows the formal design of a "taut Quadrille." Change is constant, but random motion is not possible. The poet has come a long way from the opening cry of "Of nothing but me, me."

For all of the ideas expressed in this short Canto, the reader admires primarily not the knowledge but the way Updike transforms the vocabulary of science into Spenserian stanzas without resorting to forced rhymes. The final stanza illustrates both theme and technique:

> *Magnetic* Atoms, such as Iron, keep
>   Unpaired Electrons in their middle shell,
>   Each one a spinning Magnet that would leap
>   The *Bloch* Walls whereat antiparallel
>   Domains converge. Diffuse Material
>   Becomes *Magnetic* when another Field

Aligns domains like Seaweed in a swell.
How nicely microscopic forces yield,
In Units growing visible, the World we wield!

Microscopic matter contributing to the makeup of larger particles comprises the world. Updike at the midpoint of his life is one such imperfect solid state.

In "The Play of Memory," Canto Four, he reenters his past to remember those he loves. The typography alone of this section illustrates its eclectic nature. Quotations from Walt Whitman's "Song of Myself" mingle with numbers, boldface type, arrows, rows of dots, photographs from Canto Two, and a sonnet to his father. Recalling the dust at the bottom of a playground slide and alluding to Longfellow's "footprints in the sands of time," Updike transfers the pointillism of the grainy photographs to myriad points of sound. He listens "last night" to the rain, and he remembers the various women of his life.

The persistent contrast in this section, as it is generally throughout the entire poem, is that of youth and his "uncomfortable" maturity. Pictures of Updike as a child and references to playground games surround memories of sexual desire and consummation. At one point he comments on his "wifeless home" and her loose bathing suit which he lends to a campaigner for Eugene McCarthy. The time is 1967-68, and Shillington has given way to Ipswich, Massachusetts. For all of the many mistresses and explicit sexual descriptions, however, the dominant woman of the section is his mother. She who nurses him, feeds him tomatoes to make him grow, and entices him with dreams of escape from the small town to the big city of Manhatten also tells him that his writing, including presumably this poem, is a "waste" about "terrible people." (One cannot help but think of *Of the Farm*.) Such abrupt transitions approach the layman's definition of surrealism, for a picture of Updike and his mother alternates with a description of a sexual encounter on the beach which in turn leads to reveries on physical love. Thus Updike approximates the workings of memory, the non-linear, scatter-shot appearance of images and words which anyone lying on his bed listening to the rain might experience. If "The Dance of the Solids" is a tour de force, "The Play of Memory" is an interior monologue. The hero turns out to be not the poet but his father. Mother criticizes his art as a waste, but Father is more direct: "Your poetry began to go to pot/when you took up fucking housewives." The suburbia of Ipswich/Tarbox challenges the dreamer of Shillington/Olinger. Accepting the criticism, Updike pronounces his father a saint and explains that he lacks his father's fortitude and faith. This moving sonnet to his father is the high point of the poem. He salutes an unknown great man and wonders why, at midpoint, he cannot release the hidden spring that might propel his life toward resolution.

Like the grainy photographs which reveal proportion when held at a distance, so the welter of images from memory illustrates what Updike terms his "pointillism theme." Feet at the playground slide scratch out a depression which holds raindrops just as this poem is a trough to catch the scattered dots of memory. Since his father is correct, Whitman is wrong: Sex cannot explain knowledge. But the father is mistaken if he believes that the poet's sexuality diminished his poetic genius, for the sonnet to the father testifies to a renewed and lively muse. "Dreadful nights of dust" connect with the playground dust raised by carefree children, and the specter of mortality is once again glimpsed. In the face of death, Updike reaffirms love. Memory cannot supply all the answers to the pointillism of his life, but love is eternal. He closes Canto Four with a celebration of his wife who presents him with a point of immortality in the personification of their child.

The only conclusion he can foresee is described in the final Canto. Once again demonstrating his skill with poetic form and rhyme, he turns from the eclectic structure of the preceding Canto to write a conclusion in heroic couplets reminiscent of Alexander Pope's poetic technique and concern with the proper role of man in society. The last section of "Midpoint" catalogues Updike's heroes (Karl Barth, Kierkegaard, Henry Green among them), men who passed before to make up some of the atomic substance of the point now known as John Updike. The most important statement in Canto Five is the "intelligent hedonistic advice" which he gives himself and apparently, although reluctantly, accepts. The current plague of "easy Humanism" is not enough. Man cannot force his meaning upon the world, but he may work:

> Cherish your work; take profit in the task:
> Doing's the one reward a Man dare ask.[10]

In the absence of final answers, and because of the unreliability of the solipsistic self, Updike advises acceptance of the moment in an effort to live for joy within the "giddy" dance of experience.

Wallace Stevens' Crispin may again be lingering in the wings. Compare, for example, these lines and Crispin's final acceptance of a "nice shady home" with plums:

> The meanwhile, let us live as islanders
> Who pluck what fruit the lowered branch proffers.
> Each passing moment masks a tender face;
> Nothing has had to be, but is by Grace.

Crispin concocts "doctrine from the rout," while Updike works, but both decide to stop worrying and live. Adulthood has its own comforts, and besides, Updike has grown to appreciate his life at midpoint. The fears of mutability momentarily stilled, he can admit that the earth will eventually "have" him. But not yet. Conscious of his role as writer, and aware of the immortality which art can bring, he resolves to create even if it means ironically impersonating the seriousness of contemporary literature as a mask for his own laughter.

"Midpoint" is a complex poem with homage to Dante, Spenser, Pope, Whitman, and Pound, but its portrait of the artist as a growing man supplies a greater interest than the technique. Reading it, one learns how a writer tries to step outside himself to examine where he has been. Although some of the poems in the rest of the book are more pleasurable to read, none carries the importance of this autobiographical investigation. Two of the lyrics in part two, titled "Poems," illustrate interesting variations on the traditional form of the sonnet. "Topsfield Fair," for example, comments on man's affinity with the mortality of animals in two quatrains and a sestet. "The Origin of Laughter" has the unusual form of quatrain, sestet, quatrain; it is a blank verse sonnet. Both lyrics look back to "Midpoint" with the observation on mortality and the proximity of laughter and fear. Similarly, the list of heroes catalogued in Canto Five of "Midpoint" is expanded in "The Angels" where Updike celebrates composers, artists, and writers like Mozart, Matisse, and Shakespeare whose work continues to influence everything from post cards to memory. On the whole, however, the poems in part two of *Midpoint* are not as distinguished or even as clever as those in *The Carpentered Hen* and *Telephone Poles*. Three lyrics, "Pompeii," "Roman Portrait Busts," and "The Average Egyptian Faces Death," recall the references to museums in "Midpoint" and look forward to the importance of art galleries in the story "Museums and Women," but none of the poems has the quality of the later tale.

The last two sections titled "Love Poems" and "Light Verse" are another matter. Both are lively and a delight to read. The reader familiar with Updike's fiction about suburban adultery and the mixture of guilt and desire will have a special interest in some of the love poems. Of note is "My Children at the Dump." As if he were Richard Maple (of the Maple stories dating in Updike's canon from 1956), the poet figure recognizes and regrets the parallel between the "wonderland of discard" with its armless dolls and bent tractors and his children who will soon be thrown away, as it were, in a divorce. The waste and the "Sheer hills of television tubes" entice him for a moment just as the junk enthralls his children, but although he feels the surge of his instinct to preserve, he knows he cannot rescue anything from the dump:

> These things
> were considered, and dismissed
> for a reason.

Watching the children wander among these leftovers, he realizes that his own life has been reduced to the junkheap:

> I came to add
> my fragments to this universe of loss,
> purging my house, ridding a life
> no longer shared of remnants.

There is no promise of renewal here as there is in Wallace Stevens' "The Man on the Dump," no cleansing of worn-out images so that the imagination may once again create. The bleakness of life is continual loss. For the sad man of this poem, the universe itself is a junkpile where he can love his children but cannot take them home. No reader of Updike's short stories can fail to sense the special poignancy of "My Children at the Dump." The glowing days when "everyone was pregnant" are long gone.

Not all of the lyrics in "Love Poems" are about defeat, for the title of this section has several meanings. The combination of the Eden myth and the dust of mortality in "Nuda Natens" looks forward to the reverie of "Fellatio," but Updike also writes a love poem to the nation's capital in "Washington" and to America in "Minority Report." The latter two are less compelling than the more conventionally oriented love poems because Updike is at his best observing and commenting on the complications of family love and loss. The strengths of his greatest short stories are often those of his better poems: Lyricism, an acute awareness of passing time, an eye for detail, and a celebration of ordinariness. When he moves too far from the inspiration of memory and guilt and from the consciousness of longing and despair, he often loses the emotional impact which gives substance to his consistently brilliant uses of language.

A strong sense of emotion is obviously not a factor in "Light Verse," but these poems invite attention to rhyme and language. Many of them recall similar verses and occasional poems in the first two collections. Points made in the earlier discussions of these volumes need not be repeated here. Yet it is interesting to note that once again Updike uses his wit to suggest rejuvenation of language through unusual rhymes and jaunty rhythm. His celebration of "Some Frenchmen" is an exercise in history and an invitation to laughter, and his satire of "The Amish" is both clever and on target. Suggesting that the "surly" Amish "wink at sex" and disdain strong drink, he points out the interesting contrast between their taboos and the names of the towns in their part of Pennsylvania. Note the allusions to religion, liquor, masturbation, and sex:

> Believing motors undivine,
> They bob behind a buggied horse
> From Paradise to Brandywine,
> From Bird-in-Hand to Intercourse.

This section of light verse is largely a scrapbook of Updike's travels, as if the writer at the midpoint of his life sets off from Olinger and Tarbox after the complexities of marital discord and noticeable aging. Journeys to and funny poems about Antibes, Russia, Antigua, and the Azores are solace for both the disappointments of domestic crises and the struggles with a demanding art. Reading of a colonel's wife on Antigua, one can only wonder if Richard Maple has survived "twin beds in Rome" and can now smile both at women and his own witty phrases:

> His wife, in modest half-undress,
>> Swings thighs pinched red between the sea
>> And sky, and smiles, serenely free
> Of subcutaneous distress.

The possibilities for eroticism contrast comically with the realities of this matron, and the poet figure sails on to comment on nearly everything from his gnarled toes to the "manacle" of wristwatches to miniature dinosaurs in cereal boxes:

> And lo! beyond the Sugar Pops,
> An acetate *Triceratops*.
> And here! across the Shredded Wheat,
> The spoor of *Brontosaurus* feet.

Such nonsense is not important, of course, but taken together Updike's light verse provides an interesting balance to his short stories about memory and defeat. The author who can compose the lovely cadences of "Wife-wooing" (*Pigeon Feathers*) can also delight in cereal boxes and ear-catching rhymes. *Midpoint* is not Updike's best collection of poetry, but the title poem is of paramount importance to those who would know his achievement. Some of the love lyrics and light verses are impressive examples of his shorter poems. Perhaps the poet figure in "Thoughts While Driving Home" (*Telephone Poles*) was more intelligent at the cocktail party than he thought.

Notes to *Midpoint*

1. John Updike, *Midpoint* (New York: Knopf, 1969). Further references will be to this edition.
2. John Updike, "One Big Interview," *Picked-Up Pieces* (New York: Knopf, 1975), p. 509.

3. "Answers to Questions Unasked," London *Times Literary Supplement*, 29 June 1970, p. 104.
4. William Heyen, "Sensibilities," *Poetry*, 115 (March 1970), 428.
5. Anne Gates, "John Updike—Wearing His Poet's Hat," *Christian Science Monitor*, 15 April 1969, p. 9.
6. Alice B. Hamilton, "Book Reviews," *Dalhousie Review*, 50 (Autumn 1970), 403.
7. On the Dick Cavett Show for 15 December 1978, Updike commented that he often wrote the blurbs for the dust jackets of his books.
8. Alice and Kenneth Hamilton, "Theme and Technique in John Updike's *Midpoint*," *Mosaic*, 4 (Fall 1970), 79-106.
9. Charles Thomas Samuels, "John Updike: The Art of Fiction XLIII," *Paris Review*, 12 (Winter 1968), 88.
10. This couplet recalls Robert Frost's line in "Mowing": "The fact is the sweetest dream that labor knows."

Tossing and Turning

"Prosperity has stolen stupor from me."

—"Sleepless in Scarsdale"

Tossing and Turning (1977), Updike's fourth volume of poetry, is his most impressive.[1] The transition from *Midpoint* is made explicit on the jacket blurb which describes the contents as the "shades of bliss and variety of phenomena accessible to a man past the midpoint of his life, trying to pace himself as he heads toward Nandi." Once again one suspects that Updike had a hand in the jacket commentary, for his wit seems to sparkle in the description of this book which takes its title from a short poem about insomnia and which is "poetry with its eyes wide open, restlessly alert for the oddities of reality and the *double entendres* of imagination."

Updike is justly proud of *Tossing and Turning*: "Did you notice, the Brancusi head on the jacket of 'Tossing and Turning' is shaped like an egg? And my first book, a book of poems, was called 'The Carpentered Hen.' That was my first book, this is my 20th, and none in between has seemed more worth—how shall I say?—crowing about."[2] Although no critic agrees that the collection is the best of all his books, most admit that it is impressive. The unsigned review in *American Book News*, for example, complains that Updike's "fascination with sex grows tiresome," but it applauds the variety of subject, the "directness of style," and the "temperament of regretful bitterness" which make *Tossing and Turning* distinctive. "Leaving Church Early" is singled out for its rendering of "emotional trauma."[3] Victor Howes celebrates Updike's ability to convince the reader that he shares the world which the poet describes:

"Though Updike's poems take no daring leaps toward either despair or affirmation, vault no logical or rhetorical fences, they are good, literate vehicles of thought and feeling. Exposing no intimate private world, they image instead our shared contiguous environment...."[4]

Tossing and Turning is by no means confessional poetry, but Updike's private experience is quietly revealed. Readers familiar with most of his achievement will find touchstones to earlier books: A few light verses of verbal fun and games, the landscapes of Shillington and Olinger, the love affair with sports, and the sexual candor which comments as much on contemporary standards of beauty as on adultery. But tone and perspective have changed from the other volumes of poetry. The author of *Tossing and Turning* is no longer the young adult from the farm made good but a man past midpoint graying toward middle age. The successes at Harvard are still a highlight of the escape from Shillington/Olinger, but Updike is further away than ever from the lives and landscapes that sparked so many of his earlier poems and short stories. As the successful, award-winning author now associated with New England, he returns to the high school, family, and farm not as a son but as a stranger. He remembers how it was in Olinger, but not how it is. Thus the sense of loss which informs the tone and perspective of his earlier work is now complicated by the effort to find his bearings amid success and advancing years. Many of the poems in *Tossing and Turning* suggest that his two decades of adulthood have absorbed most of the position once occupied by Shillington/Olinger as the source of his art.

This change is especially noticeable for the first time in *Midpoint* in which the title poem acts as a summation of the early half of Updike's life. In one sense, this long poem is a bow to his past, a musing on the elements which helped get him where he is. The point about *Tossing and Turning* is not that he abandons Olinger to embrace Tarbox but that the newer challenges of success, suburbia, and aging make different demands upon him. How does one have time to long for the moment "when everyone was pregnant" if he finds his current life slipping away? Updike himself may not experience all of the crises expressed in *Tossing and Turning*, but his poet-figure does. Crossing midpoint to head toward Nandi, he knows that he has changed. So has his art.

The restlessness following midpoint is expressed in "Sleepless in Scarsdale," a poem of seven unrhymed quatrains which makes its point in the first line: "Prosperity has stolen stupor from me." Wide awake in well-to-do suburbia with his terraced lawn and matching furniture, the poet rejoices in the trappings of success and security. Marital crises are not a problem at the moment, and the children are happy and well. Yet the opening line tells the tale. Material success steals spiritual sustenance. Updike does not resort to the cliché about the evils of accumulated wealth, but he does point out the negative side of domestic calm. This poem is about the tension between family security and the individual artist's need for crisis. Indeed, the word "stupor" in the first line suggests a double meaning. On the one hand he cannot experience the stupor needed for sleep because he is too prosperous, but on the other hand prosperity lulls him into the kind of stupor which dulls his reaction to things, the sharp edge of the artist. The books on the shelves look too arranged. The bathroom shows off the wealth of too many towels. As he says, "Life can be too clean." His success is so loud that it "pollutes the tunnel of silence." Suspecting that art is impossible in such an atmosphere, he awaits one hour in the long night with which he can make a deal.

"Sleepless in Scarsdale" is clearly a poem about the other side of midpoint. Although it may seem obvious to say so, the poem could not have been written at the time of *Pigeon Feathers* or *Telephone Poles*. The problem posed by books too carefully shelved—life too neatly arranged—is not the same as the demand on a younger man to woo the world while holding on to the past. The acuteness of the poet-figure's dilemma is made clear in the title poem "Tossing and Turning." Sleeplessness cramps not the body but the spirit. The turnings and tossings of insomnia may pinch the circulation of an arm or a leg, but Updike asks the reader to "unclench" his philosophy as much as his ankles. Like the unfortunately open-eyed artist in the too-comfortable home in Scarsdale, he knows that to sleep is to explore the invisible landscapes of the spirit:

> know we go
> to sleep less to rest than to participate
> in the orthic twists of another world.
> This churning is our jouney.
> > It ends,
> can only end, around a corner
> we do not know
> > we are turning.

Two of the longer poems in this collection touch on places from Updike's past which serve as landmarks along the way to success and sleeplessness. The pre–midpoint world seems bound by Shillington and Harvard, the respective locales of "Leaving Church Early" and "Apologies to Harvard." Reading the former, one is reminded of "Pigeon Feathers" and *Of the Farm*, narratives which suggest both the religious aura and the family tension of those years on the Shillington/Olinger farm. Yet the poem also describes the background of the insomniac nights in Scarsdale, for the furniture in the farmhouse is not perfectly matched but a "living dismal history" of "pretension, compromise, and wear." Similarly, the books which are too perfectly arranged years later when the poet is famous are here incapable of transporting the adolescent boy out of loneliness. One point to note in "Leaving Church Early" is that the past does not always loom in Updike's imagination as the realm of grace and peace.

Told from the perspective of a middle-aged man looking back and addressing his mother, "Leaving Church Early" insists on the aloneness which dogged his life as a boy. He asks a difficult question: Why do they leave church early if all they rush home to is isolation and despair? Recalling life in the small farmhouse with parents and grandparents, he knows now what was wrong then. Each member of the family lived his own life, "kept home by poverty,/with nowhere else to go." Their misery was their entertainment. In concise lines of blank verse, Updike communicates the absence of communication on those Sundays when he suggests their progressive lapse into silence. Note how the conversation tails off:

> "Jesus," my father cried, "I hate the world!"
> "Mother," my mother called, "you're in the way!"
> "Be grateful for your blessings," Grandpa advised,
> shifting his feet and showing a hairless shin.
> "*Ach*," Grandma brought out in self–defense,
> the syllable a gem of German indignation,
> its guttural edge unchipped, while I,
> still in the sabbath shirt and necktie, bent
> my hopes into the latest Nero Wolfe....

Reminiscent of the story "Flight" *(Pigeon Feathers)* and of Joey's need to escape in *Of the Farm*, his plan in this poem is a plot of "How to Get Out of Here." Now having fled to suburbia and success, he wonders why they were in such a hurry on Sunday, why a family "diseased, unneighborly, five times alone" would rush home to act out the mother's myths as if they were more important than church. But this is the lesson as Updike remembers: Their myth *was* better than the minister's Bible fables. Thus at the end of the poem, Updike addresses his mother as the only other survivor of those long Sunday afternoons. They had trouble forgiving each other then; they cannot forgive each other now. Forgiveness may be necessary, but time pushes them apart.

Updike's description of Sunday is a kind of written photograph which recalls the literal snapshots in "Midpoint." The honesty of his family picture is impressive because he peers back at his past through a lens different from the one used in many of the short stories about Olinger. The emotion associated with some of those tales is here tempered by an awareness of the friction and pain which mingled with the love. As Updike notes in *Picked-Up Pieces,* he writes of the sense that in "time as well as space we leave people as if by volition and thereby incur guilt and thereby owe them, the dead, the forsaken, at least the homage of rendering them."[5] By including an "Envoi" to "Leaving Church Early" in which he directly addresses his mother, he suggests the alteration of the family snapshot to a formal portrait which today sits in the museum of his imagination and continues to influence his art. Only now, from the perspective of distance and age, can he confront these strange corners of the past which "wouldn't bear describing."

Updike escapes from the farmhouse to Harvard where in 1973 he read the Phi Beta Kappa Poem "Apologies to Harvard." This poem is not as good as "Leaving Church Early" if only because he often excels when writing about home and family. "Apologies to Harvard" owes its existence more to the occasion than to the muse, and it should be read in its spirit of commemoration rather than inspiration. The Phi Beta Kappa Poem joins "The Christian Roommates" (*The Music School*) as two of Updike's more significant accounts based upon his university years. In the poem, Harvard is remembered, often sentimentally, as a refuge from riots and causes, a kind of incubator which hatches its sons and certifies them as gentlemen of learning. Although Updike reveals that he feels little gratitude to Harvard, he does admit that the University provided the escape he needed by introducing him to a world of living knowledge supplied by deceased men:

My parents' house had been a hothouse world
of complicating inward-feeding jokes.
Here, wit belonged to the dead....

Detailing his four years at Harvard in the 1950s, he is aware of a past tranquillity which seems foreign to the current class of seniors. More important perhaps, the students of the 1950s never even thought of themselves as a generation. The special unity assigned to the university classes of the late 1960s and early 1970s was alien to them as they read Pound and Yeats, graduated into the "System," and watched the depreciation of railroad stocks, hair, and confidence.

The third long poem in the collection, "Cunts," shows how far the small-town Harvard graduate has come from the time when, as he explains in the Phi Beta Kappa Poem, "Sex came wrapped in rubber/and veiled in supernatural scruples—call/Them chivalry." The title alone suggests the elimination of chivalric trappings, as does the epigraph to *Tossing and Turning* from *Ulysses*. More important to the poem than the Joyce quotation, however, is the epigraph to "Cunts" itself: "(Upon Receiving The Swingers Life Club Membership Solicitation)." For in this poem, Updike celebrates the demystification of sex, rejecting the time when he felt "supernatural scruples" in order to praise the beauty of sex in explicit terms. The ethereal gives way to the physical: "We must assimilate cunts to our creed of beauty." Yet the poem is as much a criticism of the new sexual freedom as it is a celebration. Dismissing the tawdry exploitation by The Swingers Club, Updike comments on the sad contrast between the commercialization of "groovy parties" and the loveliness of female sex organs. One attitude reflects lust while the other approaches religion: "the beauties we must learn to worship now all/have spread legs." Although it may be difficult to accept for those who misread *Couples* as Updike's praise of the adulterous society, "Cunts" invites us not to overthrow conventional morality but to exchange the idealization of demure females like Venus de Milo for the admiration of sensuous women like Botticelli's Venus.

A primary consideration in "Cunts" is Updike's insistence on mimesis. He accepts as one of the author's obligations the need to be factually correct. Good art illustrates reality. Although he develops his thoughts about mimesis more completely in the essays collected in *Assorted Prose* and *Picked-Up Pieces*, a comment in his *Paris Review* interview indicates his general ideas: "About sex in general, by all means let's have it in fiction, as detailed as needs be, but real, real in its social and psychological connections. Let's take coitus out of the closet and off the altar and put it on the continuum of human behavior.... In the microcosm of the individual consciousness, sexual events are huge but not all-eclipsing; let's try to give them their size."[6] "Cunts" takes sex away from the prude and the pornographer and places it in the realm of the ordinary where it belongs.

Updike's notion of laughter, not someone else's idea of taste, is also at work in the poem. "Cunts" should be read with a sense of play: "The poem...is meant to be among other things funny.... I think 'taste' is a social concept and not an artistic one. I'm willing to show good taste, if I can, in somebody else's living room, but our reading life is too short for a writer to be in any way polite. Since his words enter into another's brain in silence and maturity, he should be as honest and explicit as we are with ourselves."[7] To encourage our laughter, he writes one blank verse stanza in "Cunts" from the perspective of the vagina, describing its yearning for sex "like a shark gone senile yawns for its meal." Significantly, suggests Updike, this exchange of the ethereal for the physical encourages the assertiveness of woman in an act of love and grace. "Something vital" may depart with the loss of mystery, but recognition of beauty in all its physical properties more than fills the gap. He has come a long way from the days of leaving church early.

Although the remainder of the poems in *Tossing and Turning* are not as long as the three just discussed, many of the shorter lyrics are as serious. Indeed, the most successful poems are those which explore the proximity of sleeplessness and death, perhaps because Updike does not lapse into statement as he often does in his long poems. "You Who Swim," "The House Growing," and "Bath After Sailing" are among his more thoughtful lyrics. A tone of regret often combines with recognition of eternal loss to make many of the shorter poems more than nostalgic reveries about the past.

The sleeplessness of tossing and turning is at the core of "You Who Swim." A sixteen-line celebration of his lover, this poem suggests the androgynous nature of a woman who looks like a male in her bathing cap, who is at ease on both land and water, who seems as much animal as human, and who, though very much alive, is an expert at the dead man's float. She plays at death while air slices her "throat with shards of glare." Even at night, awake in her bed of love, her relationship with the water is noticeable: Her face is "wet with the dark"; her lips are spaced "to hold the bubble love." Yet this hymn of praise is not a song to the eternity of love, for death leers in the background. The last sentence of the poem—"We swim our dead men's lives"—points to the way we play at life. In the final moment, our androgynous nature does us no good. His lover rises beside him in the bed as if she were surfacing from the deep, a drowned corpse.

The hovering presence of death also directs the irony of "The House Growing." A cross reference to the "Envoi" of "Leaving Church Early," the poem is a short elegy to Updike's grandparents and father. Each death ironically makes the house grow through the addition of another room of silence. The house itself is personified, carnivorous in its vastness, taking bites of the sky, fattening itself on the vanished. Just as we "swim our dead men's lives," so we live in houses which devour our presences. The emotion associated with the portrait of the father in *The Centaur* and "In Football Season" (*Olinger Stories*) is not a factor here. All is now silent.

Updike's confrontation with the immensity of non-human otherness is most impressive in "Bath After Sailing." Surviving another foray into the deep, the poet, now snug in his bath, is aware of the relationship between tub and ocean. His day of sailing is no idyllic interlude of sunshine, salt air, and sea. He describes the waves as hostile, heartless, mirthless, and black, and he realizes that although the sloop whacks the waves, the passengers are helpless as they heel through the lurching mass. Unlike the people on the beach in "Lifeguard" (*Pigeon Feathers*), the poet has taken the risk of deep water, perhaps a metaphor for an act of faith. Being face-to-face with divinity causes fear. His prayer to the "God of trees and air" is partly ironic, for God has a face of "tar-green" like the "toppling" tons of sea-water which threaten him with the final darkness. Updike knows that a dead man's float and an androgynous nature will do no good in the vastness of such indifferent power. If once he falls over, "inhaling bubbling lead," he would sink "opaque as stone." Death's face shows itself in the "timeless weight" of ocean. God and the ocean are eternity while man is caught in time. Acknowledging the strength of the sea, he recognizes the force of a supreme being.

What gives "Bath After Sailing" its impact is the poet's awareness that his transfer from hostile ocean to safe tub is ironic. The sea may threaten and the bath may soothe, but he understands the relationship of tub to coffin. The sway of the sloop still haunts the bath as he notices his "fingertips shrivelled as if dead," his "rippling legs," and his penis now "small/and pallid in reprieve." Although he is as white as a swimming pool cork while stretched out in the bath, he senses the black sea waiting beneath him even now. His rest may be a respite from fear, but the meeting with non-human otherness has jolted him into the recognition that sleep prefigures death. Still, he is grateful for the momentary release:

> how much I prefer
> this microcosmic version
> of flirting with immersion.

The very next poem, "On An Island," is another description of his terror when facing a tranquil ocean which is nevertheless "enormous in its noise." If airplanes and islands eventually sink, how can he ward off this force of water which is "sleepless, inanimate, bottomless, prayer-denying"? The sea which is a place of recreation in many of Updike's short stories and poems is here merely one more manifestation of the huge, anonymous universe which wipes out all before it and communes with only itself. The darkness of the poems in *Tossing and Turning* is astonishing when compared with those in *The Carpentered Hen*. Mortality matters most when one passes midpoint. Loneliness looms ahead, beckoning him beyond Olinger and Tarbox toward the foreign land of Nandi.

A series of poems in Part III of *Tossing and Turning* describes Updike's various responses to loneliness and all of its attendant threats. The isolation experienced in "The House Growing," for instance, has found its way to his current home in "The Melancholy of Storm Windows." Ostensibly a description of a household chore endured twice annually at the two turns of winter, the poem shows how this task is a metaphor for the way we try to shore up our deteriorating selves, the "mortal shell,/they used to call the body." Each year our protections fit less well. A seam leaks here; the light gets in there. We paint and wash and wipe, but when stacked the storm windows still "savor of the crypt." The immense power of otherness which swells so forcefully in Updike's poems about the ocean threatens the house as well:

In place, they merely mitigate
death's whisper at the margins,
the knifing chill that hisses how
the Great Outer cares not a pin for our skins
and the airtight hearts that tremble therein.

Alone in our own homes, we are even more isolated when considered in the sweep of the indifferent universe. The cold wind of winter foreshadows not the rebirth of spring and the removal of storm windows but the last chill of death and enclosure in the tomb. Our place in life remains ambiguous until we die. Only then are we eternally screwed into position where we can say, "*At last*."

The stark awareness of mortality which permeates many of the lyrics in *Tossing and Turning* should go a long way toward refuting the mistaken notion that Updike is merely a marvelous stylist who hovers between memories long past and domestic crises now present. The impact of advancing age hits like an onslaught. Even the religious aura which one senses in the earlier poems and tales takes on the trappings of loneliness approaching despair. In "The Grief of Cafeterias," the customers eat alone with their sorrows and their overcoats on. What joy is present is merely the ironic happiness of vacancy mopped, painted, and cleaned. The food is neatly cased, and the Hopper light shines, but the servers present to help the faithful "attend to each other, forever." Sustenance is not possible in such sterility. Significantly, "Rats," the next poem, describes the illusion of cleanliness. In sixteen lines of irregularly rhymed iambic pentameter, Updike tells of the vermin which invade his house just as wind and rain seep through the storm windows. The metaphorical connection between house and human is well established in this collection of poems, and "Rats" is no exception. The building, like the inhabitants, has rotten places where dead air grows and where "rubble deepens crumb by crumb." Whether godly or human, the repairman is difficult to find. One cannot help but visualize the all-devouring worm when Updike describes the rats whose avenues "run parallel to chambers of our own/where we pretend we're clean and all alone." Mortality festers within man though he daily scrubs his exteriors. Some lines from "Phenomena" are especially appropriate here. In this poem, the repairman is indeed found, but in fixing the furnace he exposes the poet to the ease with which the vital flame is extinguished. The crumbling house is a metaphor for the decaying body. Sleep brings little relief:

> the frost of death
> has found a chink in me, is all.
> I breathe easier and, breathing, sleep.
> The tide sighs and rises in my sleep.
> The flame is furious in its cell below.
> Under the moon the cold stones wait.

One is reminded of "Plumbing" (*Museums and Women*) as man is everywhere "outlasted."

The threat of isolation pursues the poet. In "Night Flight, Over Ocean" and "Heading for Nandi," Updike suggests that escape from the house does little good. Travel merely exchanges locales for crises already entrenched. The Maples learn this lesson in "Twin Beds in Rome" (*The Music School*), and the poet understands it in the sonnet "Night Flight, Over Ocean." Nationless, nowhere, encased in "the innocence of sleep," each passenger can only dream the ocean below and the firmament around as he plunges through the dark. The cross references to "You Who Swim" and "Bath After Sailing" are unobtrusive but persuasive when Updike describes the travelers as "dim swimmers borne toward the touchdown spank." In this poem fear is caused not by the specter of annihilation but by the illusion of abandonment. How can one know who he is if he cannot determine where he is? In "Night Flight," each isolated passenger seems to find his way the best he can. The final poem in *Tossing and Turning*, "Heading for Nandi," suggests that the destination is indeed finality. Alone, as the poet figure usually is in the poems in this collection, the traveler observes the passengers of various nationalities who make up the microcosm of the world as they join together for another night flight across yet another ocean. His isolation is particularly noticeable, for he is surrounded by couples and groups who laugh and love. Not only does he lack a woman to touch him, but he must ask the locale of his destination. Although he is informed that Nandi is in Fiji, we know that his journey may take him even farther west to death itself:

Nandi? I'll see it
or die in these hours
that face me like panels
in a chapel by Rothko.

The light verse and witty vocabulary which make Updike's other collections of poetry such fun to read are present in *Tossing and Turning*, but his arrangement of the humorous lyrics suggests his intention to downplay their importance. Serious poems comprise Parts I and III and thus flank the light verse of Part II. Even golf, the sport of such metaphysical speculation and delight in earlier tales and essays, takes a beating in the sonnet "Golfers" as Updike exposes the shrunken men behind the swaggering week-end athletes with their tans, colorful dress, and bourbon. Not all of the verbal play is reserved for the light verses. In "You Who Swim," for example, Updike shows his skill with near rhyme as he composes four quatrains with couplets rhyming one/stone, shorn/drown, moth/death, and so on. For the most part, however, direct concern with a vital language is not a primary issue in this collection. "The Cars in Caracas" is offered in both English and Spanish, and it compares favorably with the best nonsense verse of *The Carpentered Hen*. Similarly, the spoofs of waterbeds in "Insomnia the Gem of the Ocean" and "To a Waterbed" tone down some of the seriousness of the connection between annihilation and the sea which is such a major theme in this book. One does not brood about eternity when making fun of "Columbia, the Gem of the Ocean" and "To a Water-fowl." The most impressive light poem is "Mime," placed in Part III perhaps because it contains a reference to an airplane plummeting while passengers shriek. The proximity of illusion and reality is explored in this poem of verbal dexterity which points out the relationship between mimesis and mime: Both imitate reality. Surely the poem is also about the author himself. A magician with words, the writer is an artist to whom the "real world" is "what his/head told his hands to delimit."

Head and hands work together astonishingly well in *Tossing and Turning*, a volume of poems in which Updike takes a look at his place in life following his transition to the other side of midpoint. Crossing the border into middle age undoubtedly has been one of the major steps of his career. The title poem of the collection *Midpoint* is a significant expression of his life to that crucial year, but he does not fulfill his potential as a poet until eight years later in *Tossing and Turning*. "You Who Swim" and "Bath After Sailing" are among the more impressive poems he has yet written. The antic mood associated with *The Carpentered Hen* and the verbal facility which encourages comparisons with Ogden Nash and Phyllis McGinley are not abandoned, but neither dominates *Tossing and Turning* despite the public's misconception of Updike as a poet of light verse. Nor have the life rhythms of Olinger or the memories of early marriage been left entirely behind. Yet it seems fair to say of this collection that while John Updike takes an occasional glance over his shoulder, his primary motion is a firm step toward a future of unknown destination and advancing age. Departing the farm by way of Harvard and Tarbox, he crosses the ocean toward Nandi. Uncertainty is his companion.

Notes to *Tossing and Turning*

1. John Updike, *Tossing and Turning* (New York: Knopf, 1977). Further references will be to this edition.
2. Helen Vendler, "John Updike on Poetry," New York *Times Book Review*, 10 April 1977, p. 28.
3. "Review of *Tossing and Turning*," *American Book News*, 1 (Summer 1977), 13.
4. Victor Howes, "Updike Verses Tally Some Mixed Blessings," *Christian Science Monitor*, 29 June 1977, p. 19. *See also* William Cole, "Too Explicit," *Saturday Review*, 16 April 1977, p. 50; Cole praises the light verse.
5. John Updike, "One Big Interview," *Picked-Up Pieces* (New York: Knopf, 1975), p. 498.
6. Charles Thomas Samuels, "John Updike: The Art of Fiction XLIII," *Paris Review*, 12 (Winter 1968), 102-103.
7. Vendler, "John Updike on Poetry," p. 28.

SHORT STORIES:
The Same Door (1959)
Pigeon Feathers (1962)
Olinger Stories (1964)
The Music School (1966)
Museums and Women (1972)

The Same Door

"... the irremediable grief in just living"

—*Picked-Up Pieces*

Although *The Same Door* (1959) is Updike's first collection of short stories, it is his third book, published one year after the poems in *The Carpentered Hen* and in the same year as the novel *The Poorhouse Fair*. The sixteen stories were written in a five-year period beginning in 1954 during which Updike published all of them separately in the *New Yorker*. As early as 1959, his success was astonishing, for he was only five years out of Harvard. Indeed, the *New Yorker* bought his first story, "Friends from Philadelphia," the year he graduated. In 1954-55, Updike studied as a Knox Fellow at the Ruskin School of Drawing and Fine Arts in Oxford, England, and from 1955-57 he worked on the staff of the *New Yorker* before moving to Ipswich, Massachusetts, to earn his living by writing. The pattern seems classic: The poor boy from the small town makes his mark in the big city before his thirtieth birthday.

Updike's tales are more than just impressive by-products of a career which many might think is concerned primarily with the novel. Although his National Book Award is for a novel, *The Centaur* (1963), and his biggest best-seller is a novel, *Couples* (1968), some readers consider the short stories his supreme achievement. Alice and Kenneth Hamilton, for example, write, "What Updike has to say he says first in his short stories. His novels are, in a sense, second tries."[1] Rachael Burchard agrees: "Updike reaches his highest range of achievement in this medium."[2] For those who think highly of his longer fiction, especially of *Rabbit, Run* (1960), *Of the Farm*

61

(1965), and *Bech: A Book* (1970), these opinions may seem extreme. Yet few would deny Updike's distinguished work with the short story.

Updike's stories are unusual. At first glance, readers may even judge them slight, beautifully written sketches which all but dissolve when the book is closed. His tales have little external action in the sense of maintaining interest through plot, little rise and fall of extreme emotion, and no sudden endings or unexpected psychological revelations designed to jolt the reader. In place of action, Updike understated epiphany. In place of emotional intensity, he offers mundane experiences. In place of sudden endings, he offers quiet insights often dealing with the small losses which diminish life daily. A high-school basketball star graduates with no place to go except to his memories of the Friday night applause and the Saturday morning headline; today they cannot even remember his nickname. A man returns to his hometown with his faculties intact but his eyesight deficient as he tries to remake a married woman into the adolescent he once loved. An implicit invitation to adultery is turned down; a teen-ager quits his job at the A & P; a non-believer takes his daughter to a music school in the basement of a church. One can often explain what happens in an Updike tale in a sentence or two. The point is not the plot but the nuance, the feeling, the details so lovingly described. As he explains in *Picked-Up Pieces*, there is "irremediable grief in just living." His characters are rarely concerned with violence, poverty, politics, hatred, or painful death; but they often worry about marriage, salvation, family, middle age, and, most of all, the past. In a phrase, he gives us insights instead of events.

These qualities are now expected in an Updike short story, but such was not the case in 1959 when *The Same Door* was published. The negative reactions to his canon had not yet set in, and there was little cry of "writes like an angel but has nothing to say." Instead, the reviews which greeted *The Same Door* expressed admiration for Updike's brilliant handling of delicate moments as if his tales shared a kinship with poems or still-lifes. Rather than lament the expense of exquisite prose wasted upon description of minute details, a charge that would dog Updike's short fiction and especially his novels after 1962, many reviewers of *The Same Door* celebrate his genius for showing the magic of the ordinary in a form which seemed so different from the usual short story as to be excitingly new. Praising both insight and style, for example, A.C. Spectorsky suggests that the tales in *The Same Door* should be called stories only by lack of a term to describe them: "A more accurate and clumsy designation might be 'fictional essays.' They are vignettes, slices of life, anecdotes ...a viable new form has been created."[3] Spectorsky correctly describes Updike's relationship with his characters and scenes as "a caring non-participant." Emotion is always implied because the controlling factor is not the heart but the eye. Delicate observation joins elegant style to make *The Same Door* a new experience.

Most of the reviews praise Updike's ability to communicate the wonder of the commonplace. Thomas Cassidy writes, "There is a point in each story, when the ordinary becomes literary make-believe of a quietly exciting kind...his people do make their disappointments and their dreariness shine just a little bit, no matter how."[4] The muted tone charged with emotion distinguishes Updike's first collection from other tales published in the *New Yorker*. The style is more poetic than slick. The author seems more interested in showing his concern than his urbanity. The images which reveal character are more organic than decorative. These effective stories, skillfully rendering the usual, are refreshing because they are quiet.

Yet some critics wonder if Updike's strengths mask limitations which are exposed in the later volumes. William Peden lauds *The Same Door* as a collection which avoids sentimentality, cynicism, and melodrama.[5] Yet five years later he suggests that Updike's style and observation have become repetitive. Ordinary events have a drama worth telling. Unsatisfactory jobs, disappointing spouses, loss of adolescent glory, and questions of belief are problems which harrow many people burdened with a sensitivity that no one notices. Large catastrophes happen to the other guy as reported in the newspaper, but few see the unspectacular ups and downs, often no more than insomnia or memory, which make or break a day or a life. Updike notices. But, asks Peden, does he notice too much from the same angle of vision and record it all in the same style? Read singly, the stories are a triumph. Taken as a collection, they may satiate the reader. Thus Peden becomes bored with what he calls the "triviality" of the family sketches. The "palpable achievement and exciting talent" shown in *The Same Door* become only beautifully written nonsense in *Pigeon Feathers*:

Even more disappointing than the mannerisms and repetition of these stories is the inclusion of 'Archangel,' a florid two-page prose poem which tends to make me wonder when Mr. Updike is going to start publishing his laundry lists.[6]

This comparison of *The Same Door* and *Pigeon Feathers* illustrates a complaint which becomes more insistent as the Updike canon grows.[7]

These criticisms are forcefully stated, but they do not undermine the achievement of *The Same Door*. Even the negative critics admit that the tales are a delight if read singly. Yet Updike has a collection in mind. The book may not be organized around a dominant theme, but the general tone is consistent. The key to the door is found in the epigraphs:

And yet, how many of our present pleasures, were we to examine them closely, would shrink into nothing more than memories of past ones! What would there be left of many of our emotions, were we to reduce them to the exact quantum of pure feeling they contain by subtracting from them all that is merely reminiscence?

—Henri Bergson, *Laughter*

But there's no vocabulary
For love within a family, love that's lived in
But not looked at, love within the light of which
All else is seen, the love within which
All other love finds speech.
This love is silent.

—T.S. Eliot, *The Elder Statesman*

Both epigraphs set the tone, point the direction, as it were, toward the correct entrance through *The Same Door*. Memories of the past determine pleasure in the present. Thus we should enter and leave a house by the same door. Where we have been is who we are. Since most of us come from families, our reminiscences begin there. But how can the author be worthy to the demands of the past? If he enters that door, will he be able to express what he knew, what he felt? Thus Updike's second epigraph suggests the futility of his effort even while the first insists upon its necessity. Silence may be best, for no vocabulary can adequately express familial love or even memories of it. The danger is that silence may facilitate forgetfulness. Given that dilemma, Updike offers a vocabulary, this collection of fictions based on memory.

When read with the epigraphs in mind, the title of the volume suggests the impossibility of discovering the gateway to eternity. Sensing that the door to immortality is closed, Updike's characters step through the more accessible doors of mundane experience which often lead to indulgence and personal pleasure. The search for confirmation of the soul gives way to the need to satisfy the body. Yet the eternal is rarely entirely abandoned. The details of the commonplace hint of immortality if only the character will look at a telephone pole or a tree. When he does, says Updike, he finds that he is "*rewarded unexpectedly.* The muddled and inconsequent surface of things now and then parts to yield us a gift."[8]

The unexpected gift in "Friends from Philadelphia," the first story in *The Same Door* and the first one Updike sold to the *New Yorker*, is a bottle of wine. The tale does not depend upon familiarity with the fine points of American life styles, despite the protests of some British reviewers, but it is clearly a story of the early 1950s. The lesson learned from the unexpected reward, how to act generously, may be timeless, but the details which define John's relative innocence reflect a specific decade. Milk is still delivered in bottles instead of waxed cardboard containers. Television sets are not commonplace items in every household. Automatic transmissions in automobiles are new.

Updike stages the story with unobtrusive irony. John is a friend in the Lutz house just as the friends from Philadelphia will be guests in his. Mr. Lutz even treats John like a guest: He shakes his hand, asks after his parents, offers to drive him to the liquor store so that John may buy wine for the guests, shows him how to drive a new car with automatic transmission, and goes into the store while John remains behind with Lutz's daughter Thelma. More important, perhaps, considering John and Thelma's efforts to make their conversation sophisticated, the teen-aged girl touches his neck in a "hostesslike" motion. John is treated kindly, but he is not at home in their house.

The unexpected gesture develops when he gives Mr. Lutz two dollars and his mother's instructions to buy a bottle of wine that is "inexpensive but nice." Mr. Lutz returns with the bottle, drives John home, and gives him a dollar and twenty-six cents when the boy asks for the change. Only then does John look at the bottle and read Chateau Mouton-Rothschild 1937. The label means nothing to him, but it will probably impress the friends from Philadelphia.

This story, Updike's first professional tale, is a prototype for the dozens that will follow. Dialogue is more extensively used, and thus the prose lacks the lyrical descriptions normally present in his best stories, but action gives way to nuance and ambiguity. Nothing much happens, but how do we evaluate what does? "Friends from Philadelphia" is about the ambiguity of kindness and the inexperience of youth. John clearly does not recognize the extent of the unlooked-for gift. For him, Mr. Lutz's generosity has already been shown by providing transportation to and from the liquor store and by letting him drive the new car. Our reaction depends upon not appreciation of John's innocence but evaluation of Lutz's gesture.

If Lutz makes too much of the difference between his income and John's father's, then he may be condescending:

"Now isn't it funny, John? Here is your father, an educated man, with an old Plymouth, yet at the same time I, who never read more than twenty, thirty books in my life... it doesn't seem as if there's justice."[9]

John gets the point. He is ashamed that their family car is old. He also knows that he is a bit of an outsider in Thelma's crowd, for he is not notified when the other teen-agers congregate at the Lutz house earlier in the afternoon. Perhaps Mr. Lutz acts generously to boost his own self-esteem. To accuse him of condescending, however, is to ignore not only his refusal to embarrass John in front of Thelma by explaining that there is no change but also his tone when he mentions the lack of proportion between education and income: "'I never went to college... yet I buy a new car whenever I want.' His tone wasn't nasty, but soft and full of wonder"(8). He talks about college and education enough to suggest that he may feel as inadequate in the adult world, despite the security of his position, as John does in Thelma's. John will not recognize the quality or cost of the wine, but the friends from Philadelphia might. Two points are significant. He must mature before he can understand the many guises of kindness, and Mr. Lutz acts generously from ambiguous motives.

The character known as John will reappear as other characters named Alan, Clyde, and David. As an adult, he may even be Richard Maple. If as a boy he is intelligent, sensitive, and polite, he is also awkward, a bit egotistical, and an outsider. He is not crushed by his forays into adult company and feelings, but he is often puzzled. Unsure about relationships with parents, girls, and the mysteries of life and religion, he looks for answers which point toward the future even while he clings through memory to the highlights of his past.

Not all of these variations are present in "Friends from Philadelphia," of course, but from the vantage point of hindsight one can recognize the beginnings. As Updike writes in the Foreword to *Olinger Stories*: "He wears different names and his circumstances vary, but he is at bottom the same boy, a local boy—this selection could be called *A Local Boy*."[10]

The boy has grown up but has not made good in "Ace in the Hole." The germ of the later novel *Rabbit,Run*, this story also captures the details of the 1950s. "Blueberry Hill" is a hit tune, and "ducktails" are the male hairstyle of the day. Fred "Ace" Anderson foreshadows Harry "Rabbit" Angstrom, the small-town basketball hero who finds himself on the sidelines several years after graduation from high school. The future is nowhere in sight. All that exist are past memories and present motion. Only the rhythm of graceful movement sustains Ace. Worried about his situation, he picks a cigarette from the pack, moves it to his mouth, stikes a match, lights it, inhales, and blows out the flame all in time to "Blueberry Hill." But he is a one-time athlete now out of shape. One half-a-block sprint and two flights of stairs make him pant.

Unlike *Rabbit, Run*, the story does not give Updike the room to develop the potentially complex reader attitude divided between disapproval of Ace's longing to be a teen-aged star again and understanding of his instinct to enjoy life, to lash out at a dull domestic routine which cramps his easy motion and natural grace. Still, the story works well. Because it relies more on the nuances of mood than on the counterpoint of dialogue, "Ace in the Hole" is a better illustration of the developing Updike style than "Friends from Philadelphia." Ace can put a ball through the hoop, but he cannot park a used car in a lot. This time the crisis is real, something his usual show of indifference cannot shrug off. He is fired. His gradual loss of stature and hence identity is shown when the daily newspaper reviews his past scoring records but calls him Fred instead of Ace. He does not protest when Evy stuffs the sports page into the trashcan. In a few years he will reach the point that so terrifies Rabbit: "They've not forgotten him; worse, they never heard of him."[11]

What makes Ace sympathetic is his refusal to give up. After a muted argument with his wife about being fired, he recovers a bit of his rhythm by jitterbugging with her. He daydreams about both past and future, about when he was a star and when his as yet unconceived son will inherit his athletic skills. He is one of Updike's earliest characters to experience what becomes a general dilemma: How to reconcile the need for freedom and applause with the demands of stability and family. Compromise seems impossible, for it suggests a fatal loss of momentum. Grabbing his wife for the dance, Ace does not so much jitterbug away his problem as keep himself in motion. The crisis will remain after the music stops, but for the moment he must dance within the freedom of the improvised pattern, keeping time with the only rhythm he is willing to acknowledge. Perhaps his son will inherit his sense of grace and coordination, and thus keep him alive, but behind that hope rests the dimly sensed fear that once his marriage becomes routine the dance band will call it a night:

> ...he spun her out carefully, keeping the beat with his shoulders....he could feel her toes dig into the carpet. He flipped his own hair back from his eyes. The music ate through his skin and mixed with the nerves and small veins; he seemed to be great again, and all the other kids were around them, in a ring, clapping time. (26)

Ace does not grow up because the realities of adult life which normally jolt people out of adolescence only make him retreat to the flickering spotlight of past glories and the dim echoes of applause. "Ace in the Hole" is not a typical initiation story because Ace neither learns nor is disillusioned. Despair may set in later as the result of early fame too easily won, but for the moment directionless momentum is all. Perhaps his mother is too indulgent and his wife too prosaic. Perhaps his job is dull and his capabilities limited. But none of this is to the point. Updike shows astonishing skill for one just beginning his career as a fiction writer. He convinces the reader to understand, sympathize with, and most of all regret the already wasted life of a young man in motion whose joy at fluid movement will join his inability to cope and lead him eventually into a cul-de-sac.

Ace could have graduated from the high school where Mark Prosser teaches English in "Tomorrow and Tomorrow and So Forth."[12] Although ducktail hairstyles are not mentioned, the boys observe the dress code of the 1950s and wear key chains and turned-back shirt cuffs. Like Ace, they cultivate glide, "the quality of glide. To slip along, always in rhythm, always cool, the little wheels humming under you, going nowhere special" (39). Prosser's class is going nowhere special either as illustrated by the title which shows Shakespeare's poetry degenerating to slang under the impact of uninterested students. The approaching storm which they all see through the window suggests the lack of communication in the classroom and the force which awaits them after graduation.

"Tomorrow and Tomorrow and So Forth" is the first of Updike's several stories about teachers based largely upon his father and developed to novel length in *The Centaur*. Prosser is a teacher who likes to teach. He cares: "... his students still impressed him; they were such sensitive animals. They reacted so infallibly to merely barometric pressure" (27). Yet the comment about sensitivity could be ironic, for Prosser's students do not respond. To his credit, he realizes that he overreacts to the point of playing a role for the class's benefit. Not only is he susceptible to the sexual appeal of Gloria Angstrom's pink sweater with the brief sleeves; he cannot help himself when he responds sarcastically to another student's comment. If he understands that despite the facade of cool arrogance, most of his students suspect the uncertainty of life after school, he also realizes that they laugh at him in a non-malicious way. The boy, for example, who asks a question about *Macbeth* out of what Mark assumes to be "adolescent premonitions of the terrible truth" doodles while he gives an answer that strays from the subject.

The point is that Prosser understands his own mistakes when dealing with them. Staring at Gloria embarrasses her. Letting Sejak doze may not be true kindness but a kindly pose. This self-honesty impresses the very students who take advantage of him. Like Caldwell in *The Centaur*, Mark is a teacher feeling his way with half-rebellious adolescents who respect him. They do not know how to react to Shakespeare just as he is unsure how to handle them. His doubt is shown in his immediate awareness whenever he suspects that he has made a tactical mistake: "His answer was weak; everyone knew it.... Mark winced, pierced by the awful clarity with which his students saw him" (35).

The juxtaposition between the lines from *Macbeth* and their own situations, the relevance of Shakespeare that Mark wants them to see even while he shrinks from frightening them with such despair, is suggested by the initial description of the impending storm. Cloud movement, says Prosser, illustrates the slow rhythm of Shakespeare's gray line. In a hazy sort of way, some of the students are beginning to accept the darkness of Shakespeare's truth, but Macbeth's soliloquy still seems "stupid" to them. The incongruity of teaching classics to bored students who play everything for laughs is resolved when Mark intercepts Gloria's note.

Recognizing the tension between the storm which strikes just as he grabs the note and Gloria's "love" for him, he wonders if he will ever get through to his pupils. The end of the story hints that he communicates with just one. Detaining Gloria, he lectures her about the pitfalls of using words like love too lightly. All masks are off as he talks. The lecture is no longer teacher to student but person to person. When she leaves his classroom on the verge of tears, Prosser is convinced he has made a breakthrough. But Updike does not leave the matter so clear. Maybe Gloria has solicited his earnest speech as one more joke. When he hears the gossip that she has written identical "love" notes about other teachers, he is defeated and even angry. Yet cynicism is not his style. Upset at perhaps being the butt of another student prank, but also flattered by what may be Gloria's sincere attention to him, he chooses a generous interpretation of the incident: "The girl had been almost crying; he was sure of that" (40). Shakespeare's "petty pace from day to day," surely an indirect comment upon Prosser's years as a teacher, is enlivened by significant communication. Fellow-instructor Strunk treats the note as a laugh, but not Prosser. He is the better man and thus the better teacher. He may be self-deluded about his talk with Gloria, but he cares.

Prosser the innocent teacher becomes Burton the troubled minister in "Dentistry and Doubt." Beginning as a comic account of the American abroad, the story develops into a mental debate upon the value of pain and the presence of God. Burton, the Pennsylvania minister in Oxford, is funny in his effort to anticipate the English reactions to his clerical collar, in his pride in his native state, in his tendency to find the devil in a toothbrush, and, most of all, in his private theological musings as he ponders the English dentist's polite question about novocaine:

Burton hesitated. He believed that one of the lazier modern assumptions was the identification of pain with evil. Indeed, insofar as pain warned us of corruption, it was good. On the other hand, relieving the pain of others was an obvious virtue—perhaps the *most* obvious virtue. And to court pain was as morbid as to chase pleasure. Yet to flee from pain was clearly cowardice. (44)

The allusions to Robert Burton's *The Anatomy of Melancholy* are unmistakable, but the minister's convoluted thinking here veers toward the ridiculous.

Yet for all of the comic hairsplitting, Burton's reservations are serious. He has begun the morning convinced of the devil and doubtful of God. Cavities in the teeth reflect slits in the spirit, and he needs several kinds of help. Although he accepts the dentist's offer of novocaine to neutralize the physical pain, he cannot resist debating with himself about the meaning of creation. He defines his own confusion after watching blackbirds fall out of the sky with only a few ascending: "There were things Burton could comprehend.... And then there were things he could not" (47). Later he sees that blackbirds can live beside wrens; peace is possible. Perhaps his vision needs healing, for the dentist decides first to mend the eyetooth. Thus Burton accepts the new filling as if it were the communion host. The dentist's kindness when dealing with pain reminds Burton of a God trying to show benevolence.

By now we know that the minister's dilemma is a crisis of faith. Doubts are debated but countered; pain threatens but is neutralized; blackbirds steal from wrens, yet all share the feeding station. The dentist, a doctor of physical ailments, heals the minister, a caretaker of the spirit. Throughout the story, Updike emphasizes the sharp contrast, gulf even, between the dentist's confidence and obvious success with his healing and Burton's sincere but perhaps pedantic doubts about his own efforts. The physical world yields more easily to answers than the spiritual, and yet contrasts are somehow mysteriously necessary: Pain and novocaine, dentists and priests, starlings and wrens. Only after being healed physically, only after the cavity in the eyetooth is filled, does Burton recall a line from Richard Hooker, the sixteenth-century divine who tried but failed to reconcile another set of extremes, Christian theology and Tudor reality: "I grant we are apt, prone, and ready, to forsake God; but is God as ready to forsake us? Our minds are changeable; is His so likewise?" (50). Burton will fail to assuage all doubts, but his experience with the dentist and his memory of Hooker allow him a view of life's emotional health. His eyetooth now mended, he sees the starlings and wrens mixed together, and he interprets their motions as seeming "essentially playful." God rules. Man's confusion is only a momentary violation of eternal order.

If "Dentistry and Doubt" is Updike's first professional story about faith, "The Kid's Whistling" is his initial tale about art. Both the formal art of Roy's meticulously hand-painted signs and the informal spontaneity of Jack's whistling have their place. The department store attic where they work is hot, dark, and all but deserted in the after-hours. The workroom itself suggests acceptable disorder, the kind of place which offers calm because the artist is surrounded by a comfortable conglomeration of empty jars and paint brushes forever stiff from neglect. Updike's description of the room borders on the extreme of verisimilitude, for he specifies inches, half-inches, broken drawing boards, obsolete displays, and the contents of several shelves. One assumes that descriptions such as these are what Richard Mayne has in mind when he complains of *The Same Door*: "Short of ideas? Stuck for a plot? Words won't come? Just slit the thermofoil package, dissolve the contents into a martini shaker, and out comes a story just like Salinger used to write."[13] Updike's long paragraph describing the contents of the workroom does indeed bear an unhappy resemblance to J.D. Salinger's extended account of the Glass's medicine chest, but it is not as typical of the entire collection of stories as Mayne implies.

Updike's point is that the supplies in the room are not as well arranged as Roy's poster paints. Art is order. In the midst of the confusion, Roy's careful work satisfies him and by extension helps control his situation. His primary mistake is the assumption that Jack's whistling represents an intrusion. He understands that the kid modifies his whistling to the demands of each tune, alternating from a cool, restrained rendering of "Summertime," to a brassy "After You've Gone," but he fails to see the connection between the improvised whistling and his own instinctive choice of colors and strokes: "He was not sure that the yellow would stand out enough against the white, but it did, especially after the Silverdust was added" (53). Improvisation eases the potential rigidity of arrangement. One point of the story is that together the two men create order. Jack prints while Roy paints. Jack supplies peanuts while Roy buys the cokes. The parallels are clear. Despite his irritation at the whistling, Roy's workbench with its brushes and jars matches Jack's table with its cigarettes and type.

Roy's comfort amid the apparent chaos, his ability to control his lettering while surrounded by overstuffed boxes and piled-up shelves, is challenged when his wife Janet interrupts him. First questioning his rendition of a Gothic Y, then criticizing his choice of colors, she inspects the room as the outsider she is, seeing only junk and disorder: "Why don't you clean this mess out?" (57). Through all of Janet's questions and the kid's whistling, Roy holds on to his artistic control. Each sure stroke of the brush, each correct spacing of a letter gives him pleasure. Nothing rattles him. He even selects a color for the last letter that matches the first in order to create unity.

But following Janet's departure, something is askew. For the first time his hand slips. The kid has stopped whistling. Jack's contribution to the order necessary for creativity is more important than Janet's uninterested disruption of his concentration. Her presence resembles an outsider entering a team locker room. Roy and Jack are at ease again only when she leaves. Supplying different tones and rhythms while he whistles different tunes, the kid humanizes the workroom. Art is not created in a vacuum. Jack adds a personal touch, and he delights in his whistling as much as Roy does in his lettering. No one else will hear Jack's variation on the tune just as no one but Roy will understand that his sign is not merely decorative but a personal creation which pleases him. The two work together, though apart, a truth Roy senses immediately after the kid's silence leads to a botched letter that only he will notice.

The stories discussed thus far are excellent examples of Updike's early work. Lacking both the nostalgic tone and the distinctively rhythmical prose of his later volumes of tales, these stories show his skill at developing nuances out of quiet situations which turn on the slightest act. A bottle of wine, a jitterbug dance, and a mingling of birds all make a difference. Moreover, these stories are not specifically associated with Olinger or Tarbox, Updike's fictional locales based on fact which signify different phases in his own life and different attitudes toward experience. With "Snowing in Greenwich Village," however, he introduces the Maples, a couple who will show up in Tarbox and whom he will follow through the periodic crises of marital tension.

In this story, Joan and Richard have been married less than two years. She is proper and straight-laced, sitting to full height in a Hitchcock chair despite the discomfort of a headcold. He seems dreamy to the point of immaturity, given to striking dramatic poses before guests. When Rebecca Cune arrives, he is thrilled to remove her coat and place it on the bed. He uncorks the expensive sherry so that the women may share the drama. He purchases cashew nuts with the intent of impressing both the store proprietor and his guest. Indeed, most of his actions are a show for Rebecca who clearly excites him to posing. The narrator makes fun of him despite his genuine concern for Joan's comfort.

One does not read far before realizing that Rebecca Cune is a threat. Her last name echoes the slang term "cunt." She is a temptress, a uniter of sex and death, as her tale of the meat salesman, the "Purveyor of Elegant Foods" who keeps a woman, suggests. Rebecca is an amusing guest because she tells funny stories about others which always make her appear sane against their oddity. When Joan affectionately hugs Richard in her delight at seeing the first snow of the year, he realizes that Rebecca will make fun of the gesture on some other evening in some other apartment.

Still, her presence excites him. When he offers to walk her home, even though she lives only three quarters of a block away, we have the first troubling hint of the Maples' future domestic particulars which Updike details in later stories. Richard's instinctive yearning is for Joan, for when they hug while watching the snow, Rebecca is left the alluring but definite bystander: "Rebecca, where another guest might have turned away, or smiled too broadly, too encouragingly, retained without modification her sweet, absent look and studied, through the embracing couple, the scene outdoors" (75). Their love has already lasted two years, while her invitation is for the moment. Perhaps the policemen riding by when they first see the snow suggest Richard's need to guard against such intruders.

When Rebecca invites him in, he easily connects illicit sex with a visit to her apartment. Significantly, she does not respond when he points out a church dwarfed by secular steeples. Her room, which is dominated by an incongruously large bed, is hot, and he feels uneasy when she stands unnecessarily close. More important, Richard does not understand Rebecca's refusal to remove her coat despite her comment, perhaps too pointed on Updike's part, that the apartment is hot as hell. Updike tells us twice on the next-to-last page that the coat has not yet been removed. Rebecca has made the first gesture by standing so close; Richard must make the second by taking off her coat the way he has done in his own apartment, putting it on his bed with romantic yearning. He escapes with his virtue intact but his desire aroused. His final thought, "Oh but they were close," is ironic, for it reveals only the truth of their positions at Rebecca's door. Richard's weakness spells trouble for his marriage to Joan, and one is left wondering how long Joan with her cold can keep Richard away from Rebecca with her allure.

"Snowing in Greenwich Village" is well done, perhaps the most polished story in *The Same Door*. Updike skillfully draws the scene as a struggle between Joan's "Modiglianiesque" features and Rebecca's da Vinci charms. Richard is the prize which Joan can hold onto only by her appeal to his sympathy for her discomfort and her intuitive gesture of love. Much more aggressive and thus exciting in a new way to Richard, Rebecca cleverly sets up a trap which entangles him from the start: He can betray his wife or he can refuse and become the subject of her next joke at another party. That he realizes the gravity of the predicament is shown when he tries to laugh himself out of her apartment only to stumble over the punch line. In just a few pages, Updike shows the insecure line between desire and fulfillment, lust and love, temporal and eternal. Some readers may interpret Richard's retreat to Joan as a victory, but Updike suggests its fragility when Richard's final thought is not of his wife but of his closeness to Rebecca.

"Snowing in Greenwich Village" is Updike's first published fiction about the tenuousness of marriage. Marital tension is a major theme in his writing after 1959, for he uses the threats to marriage to mirror the cracks in culture and society. Mercantile buildings dominate church steeples, and apartments rented by morally questionable young women are hot as hell. Individual responsibility may not be possible when disloyalty in marriage is widespread, but Updike also writes about the equally difficult predicament facing people who feel threatened by the demands of spouse and children. From Richard Maple to Rabbit Angstrom is not such a long step.

Manhattan and the Village menace the quieter avenues of Olinger. Updike's stories of New York usually detail loss and disappointment just as many of the Olinger tales do, but there is little nostalgia associated with the memories of Manhattan. New York is harder, faster, more impersonal than Pennsylvania. Another story of the city, "Who Made Yellow Roses Yellow?" recalls "Ace in the Hole." Although separated by education, wealth, culture, and athletic ability, Ace and Fred Platt (German for "low") are two sides of the same burnt-out case. Both are young men adrift in adulthood with only the memories of past successes in high school or college to serve as ballast. Ace still lives in the past, resentful that the sports writers now ignore his nickname. Fred Platt has more self-awareness and thus views himself with irony: "I keep forgetting to look up 'wastrel' in the dictionary" (85). He is associated with wealth, Henry James, and the Oxford University Press, while Ace has only used cars and a county basketball record, but both are failures.

Fred Platt is Updike's most unlikable character. The narrator's attitude is suggested in the description of the Platt living room which recalls Huckleberry Finn's awe of the Grangerford style. The difference is, of course, that although Platt's decoration may show taste, taste unfortunately dominates life. Updike's narrator uses the description to illustrate sterility, while Huckleberry is genuinely impressed, but in the end both rooms suggest emptiness despite the furniture and the doodads.

Fred has trouble reconciling his views of adulthood with the hard world of business represented by his college friend, one-time poor boy Clayton Thomas Clayton. He may not be entirely culpable for his aimlessness, for the narrator tells us that he is three generations removed from the making of the family fortune. But he is nevertheless a snob who cannot stop showing off to waiters or wasting his intellect forming amusing but useless puns. Desiring a job which he considers "foolishly natural" for Clayton to offer since he had helped the poor boy in college, Fred is unprepared for Clayton's embarrassing hesitation at his effort to draw upon past friendship. As an acquaintance tells Fred, the once pimply, naive, uncultured Clayton is now a killer in the advertising business.

The chasm between them is best illustrated by their approaches to art. Although a dilettante, Fred respects and recognizes the real thing. Clayton uses drawings to advertise chemicals. Fred is linked to Henry James, but Clayton is associated with the Carson Chemical Hour on television. Fred travels and knows a smattering of French; Clayton chooses Ballantine over Lowenbrau. Yet in the business of making money, Clayton now has the upper hand.

Vaguely believing in comradeship and the obligations fostered by memory, Fred is surprised by his friend's inability to respond to him today as if they were meeting again for a beer following vacation from college. All he can do is helplessly condescend in a futile effort to impress Clayton with his superiority. In a marvelously succinct scene, Updike sketches the distance between them although they are only a lunch table apart. Still impressed by Fred's facade of worldliness and grace, Clayton does not believe that Fred needs a job. All Fred can do is confuse Clayton with subtle insults. He orders a lamb chop which is not on the menu while Clayton settles for chopped sirloin. He rattles off French phrases which Clayton cannot understand. He so impresses the waiter that Clayton is clearly omitted from deliberations about the relative values of beers and desserts: "The waiter bowed and indeed whispered, making an awkward third party of Clayton" (92).

Although Clayton is the better person is some ways, the two young men are similar. Clayton no longer draws, but he makes money. Fred no longer writes, but he has wealth. Neither has changed appreciably from college days. One is an idler who does not know how to ask for a job; the other is a company man who is confused by condescending social amenities. There is no answer to the question about yellow roses, one of Fred's pointless but witty turns of phrase. Communication has been stifled. The magic of nostalgia, so potent a force in the Olinger stories, is not even a possibility in the impersonality of New York.

Although "Who Made Yellow Roses Yellow?" is well done, a skillful ordering of dialogue and scene, it does not draw the reader into nuances of tone and mood. The story is as impersonal as Manhattan, as if Updike enlists the reader in a conspiracy to scorn two generally unpleasant fellows. There is a sense of us versus them. In his tales of marital or religious doubt, however, Updike draws upon experiences to which many readers may respond. He encourages us to identify rather than merely observe.

The married couple in "Sunday Teasing," for example, could be Richard and Joan Maple suffering through a muted argument only a week or two after entertaining Rebecca Cune. Arthur's cruel teasing reflects a hesitancy about his marriage which makes Macy insecure. The story is also specifically religious, as if Updike decided to flesh out the suggestions scattered thus far through the collection. All of "Dentistry and Doubt" details a religious crisis, but Updike offers other scenes: Fred ironically blesses Clayton ("Who Made Yellow Roses Yellow?"); Rafe helps a woman "ascend" the bus steps, and he sees God in a huge Spry sign ("Toward Evening"); Mark has ideas about heaven ("Tomorrow and Tomorrow and So Forth"). Arthur's Sunday reading of First Corinthians eleven, verse three, looks forward to the minister's sermon on relationships among man, woman, and God in *Of the Farm*: "But I would have you know, that the head of every man is Christ; and the head of the woman is the man; and the head of Christ is God" (102). In *Of the Farm*, the minister attempts to reconcile the Biblical implication that woman may be secondary. In the story, Macy mistakenly thinks that Arthur teases her when he reads the verse aloud and explains how his grandfather used to infuriate his mother by quoting it.

When they entertain their Jewish friend for luncheon, the conversation turns to a discussion of demonstrable affection in a family and to the individuality of Protestantism as contrasted with the togetherness of Catholics and Jews. Arthur shows his meanness when he uses the conversation indirectly to hurt Macy. Although their friend participates in the discussion on the abstract level, Arthur distorts the notion of Protestant individuality to rationalize the denial of affectionate gestures. The conversation is subtly drawn, for at first Macy, like the reader, has difficulty determining the point of what may be only bantering. Arthur's disavowal of the need to show love clearly upsets Macy, displeases their guest, and threatens the domestic peace of the traditional day of rest.

Updike's control is shown when he coordinates Arthur and Macy's reading with their attitudes toward love and loneliness. "Man *should* be lonely," he insists, and she shrinks from his cruelty. He is unable to observe the line between teasing and hurting. He reads Unamuno's *The Tragic Sense of Life* while she reads a French short story, and his inability to respond to her emotional needs when she becomes upset with the story about an unhappy marriage exposes his own insecurity. Rather than solace Macy after she apparently reads the story in light of her own marriage, Arthur interprets the tale as a defense of the careless husband. His explanation unwittingly reveals his assessment of their life: "this perceptive man caged in his own weak character" (109). He apparently accepts St. Paul's derogation of women. Perhaps his comment is a confession. Perhaps he truly does not know how to love. But Macy is hurt: "It's awful when you have an ache and don't know if it's your head or your ear or your tooth" (109).

Arthur does not understand Unamuno, the Bible, Macy, or himself. Unfortunately, his attempts to reorder the shattered day are limited to physical rearrangements of the appropriately messy apartment. He picks up the glasses, straightens the newspaper, and puts away the records. Worse, he persuades Macy to quote the famous Garbo line from *Camille*, "You're fooling me," as if the inability to care were merely an act. Only at the end, while washing his hands, does he realize the truth: "*You don't know anything*," he says to himself

(111). Too afraid to tell the truth to his wife, he attacks her indirectly with teasing. His head is far from Christ's. Although caged and weak, he is not as perceptive as he thinks.

Updike's stories of domestic particulars in Manhattan normally turn on marital tension. The religious implications found in "Sunday Teasing" are not always present, but the unspectacular unhappiness of strained relationships indicates his opinion of a troubled urban culture. It is almost as if Manhattan itself were at fault. In "His Finest Hour," George Chandler is explicit about New York. He hates it: "The walls were thin, the ceiling flaked, the furniture smelled lewd, the electricity periodically failed. The rooms were tiny, the rent was monstrous, the view was dull" (112). Updike's renowned control of the small detail is evident in "His Finest Hour." What people eat, read, wear, sit on, and talk about are all carefully rendered. More important, some of the prose shows the joy with language that is a hallmark of his later short story collections. The following description of a glass broken in the next-door apartment suggests how far he has come since "Friends from Philadelphia": "It was a distinct noise, tripartite: the crack of the initial concussion, the plump, vegetal *pop* of the disintegration, and the gossip of settling fragments" (112).

With just a few strokes, Updike sketches George and Rosalind Chandler. George studies Arabic every evening while she washes dishes. He despises New York while she does not seem to mind. He teases her when she becomes upset at the unexplained screaming next door. Many of Updike's married couples face similar crises under different names. George considers himself superior to his wife. He is "fearless and lucid" while he accuses her of "gaps in judgment," eccentric dressing, and embarrassing mispronunciations. Updike hints at the quirks in their marriage by interrupting the story of the fight in the next apartment to relate George's retelling of it years later in words and tones meant to tease Rosalind for causing his skinned elbow, torn shirt, and lost blanket.

Yet for all the grimness of the knife attack next door, one wonders if Updike is parodying the detective thriller. Apparently, no other critic considers the possibility, but I find the story comic. George's last name is Chandler (cf. Raymond Chandler), Rosalind thinks one of the two policemen who answer their call resembles movie star John Ireland, and the cops themselves seem to mimic the investigations of Raymond Chandler's policemen: "'It's nine-oh-five now,' the other cop said, looking at his wristwatch.... The other cop wrote scrunchily in a little pad. 'Six minutes or so,' he muttered" (119). Aren't we supposed to laugh when we read Mrs. Irva's pleasantry following the Chandlers' rescue of her from Mr. Irva's knife attack: "My husband.... Yes, he doesn't blame you and your wife in the slightest" (124)? Rosalind, after all, chain-reads paperback thrillers. She all but expects something like this to happen in New York. Their inability to solve the mystery of the next-door neighbors illustrates George's failure to understand either Manhattan or Arabia. The puzzle is only intensified when the Irvas send them a carload of flowers. Yet this unexpected gesture of kindness stays with them when they leave the country for Basra, for whenever they are homesick for America, they think of "those massed idiot beauties." George's finest hour is not the rescue of Mrs. Irva but the receipt of the flowers. Kindness is possible, even in New York.

In "Incest," the young, urban, married couple has a child. The emotional honeymoon is clearly over, for the tale begins and ends with the husband Lee dreaming of another woman. The title, of course, suggests that the forbidden temptress is another version of his wife, eighteen-month old daughter, or even his mother-in-law. Perhaps it is better to dream away desire than to walk Rebecca Cune home. As Lee explains to Jane, "Well for God's sake, I can't be held accountable for the people I meet in dreams. I don't invite them." Yet he knows that the dream of a sexually exciting woman indicates an unspoken frustration: "He was safe, of course, as long as they stayed away from the real issue, which was why he had told her the dream at all" (146).

Updike does not tell "the real issue," but he supplies enough details to indicate the problem. Hovering behind the dreams in "incest" is the domestic tension involving the tired, bored wife who works all day in the apartment and who partially resents the return of her equally tired husband who, she imagines, has had an exciting day at the office. As usual, Updike is especially good describing the small crises which are the unavoidable trials of married life. The baby daughter spills the sugar. The pork chops get cold. The hour is too late to make love. These details worm into a marriage to fester like ground glass. Again and again one is impressed by Updike's adherence to verisimilitude. In "Incest" and the other stories of young marriage, he raises an interesting question: Is the pain caused by these domestic details as unavoidable as the details themselves; is a fulfilling permanent marriage possible? Lee and Jane tell their daughter the same bedtime story about the owl and mouse flying away, but, significantly, neither "had ever worked out what happened on the moon" (157).

The male point of view directs this story, and thus the wife seems on the defensive. For all the sympathy encouraged for Jane, the narrator's tone when describing her is often sarcastic. When she reads *New Republic*, he says that she is working at "being liberal." When he smiles at her after the baby is finally asleep, she mistakes the cause. When he compliments her on her beauty, she misinterprets the remark, "mistakenly judging it to be a piece of an obscure, ill-tempered substance" (160). Little wonder that the story begins and ends with his dreams of another woman who may be his vision of the daughter grown up, beautiful, blond, and available.

Yet it is partially his fault that he and Jane do not make love that evening, since he spends too much time reading the poetry of Jones Very. He is also well into Proust's *Sodom and Gomorrah*, an appropriate title considering his dream. If anything, the dream for all of its Freudian implications suggests his acceptance of his domestic situation. Married, in effect, to wife, daughter, and mother-in-law, he feels no more sensation from the imaginary blond than "he would get when physically near girls he admired in high school." Dreaming that he is dousing the docile blond with water from a garden hose, he understands that "the task, like rinsing an automobile, was more absorbing than pleasant or unpleasant" (162). Blame and temptation are not yet issues. But "Incest" shows Updike's skill at detailing the dissatisfaction and the daily frustrations which lead to a gradual breakdown in domestic harmony. The marital crises of *Couples* and *Marry Me* are not that far away.

Another jaundiced picture of New York is in "A Gift from the City." Apparently this story is considered one of the best in *The Same Door*, for it is consistently praised in reviews and essays. Yet for all of its simplicity of action, interpretations vary considerably. Jack De Bellis, for example, says that "the city's gift to the hero is confirmed cynicism and suspicion."[14] But Thomas Cassidy argues that the "total effect of the story is pleasant—the effect of love."[15] Rachael Burchard says that Jim feels "great concern for his fellow man," but Robert Detweiler suggests that he is "immersed in a world of things."[16] It seems to me that while Jim loves his wife and daughter, he does not love humanity in the sense of giving his worldly goods to the poor as a means of discovering the road to salvation. Surely a crucial point in this story is that Jim and Liz are forever strangers in New York. Updike's first sentence is the clue: "Like most happy people, they came from well inland" (163).

The implication is clear: Most happy people do not live in Manhattan. The other side of the coin is also evident: Happy people may lose their tranquillity in the city. Jim and Liz live in New York not because they want to but because they desire the well-paying jobs. Thus Jim resembles many of the other husbands in *The Same Door*, for he has abandoned the dream of becoming a painter for the security of industrial design. Like Fred in "Who Made Yellow Roses Yellow?," he is closer to Ace ("Ace in the Hole") with his dreams of past glory than to Roy ("The Kid's Whistling") with his commitment to well-painted signs.

But "A Gift from the City" is not about frustrated aspirations. It is about fear: "As the months passed harmlessly, James's suspicion increased that the city itself, with its steep Babylonian surfaces, its black noon shadows, its godless millions, was poised to strike" (167). His fear may be exaggerated, but he is nevertheless afraid. Only love, he believes, can protect his loved ones, but love is immaterial: "If only there were such a thing as enchantment, and he could draw, with a stick, a circle of safety around them" (163). Jim holds off the anonymous millions and the unseen threats the only way he knows, by giving to beggars. The crisis occurs when the charity work unexpectedly becomes personal. Following Liz's description of the black man who mysteriously shows up to ask for work or money, Jim fears that the strangeness of New York is finally about to breach the enchanted circle of love. He feels betrayed by "a whole tribe of charity seekers" (168).

Updike sketches Jim with some irony. Besides suggesting that his fears are exaggerated, he undercuts Jim's sense of doing good deeds for the charity tribe when he shows that Jim gives only money and that he offers it in the manner of buying off the faceless city. What he fears from the black man is not the loss of ten dollars which Liz gives, or even the additional twenty-one dollars he himself will hand over, but the man's insistence on meeting him face-to-face in order to thank him. Charity is fine, but personal contact is abhorrent. Updike, however, is too good a writer merely to set up a straw man in order to blow him down. Despite the irony, he encourages sympathy for Jim. His fear is frightening. His bafflement is genuine. He is frustrated that his toddler daughter, a native of New York, is fearless in the park, and he resents the advice of his New York baby-sitter: "You really can't be so softhearted" (171).

His frustration seems eased when he finally shakes hands with the poor man, gives him additional money, and ushers him out the door. There is no question that the person in need is a flim-flam man. In the interview with Jim for example, he tries to make himself cry by pinching the bridge of his nose. Somehow the man senses Jim's need to give away money in order to ward off his fear of the city. But Jim is also at fault, for he refuses to acknowledge the humanity of the masses who seem to threaten him. Not only has he given up painting for industrial design; he also compares the flim-flam man's face to the successful shaver he has created for his firm. The Episcopal Church is only four buildings down from his apartment, but the true spirit of charity does not get through the door. He even sees the dinner party with his poorer academic friends as a kind of giveaway.

The experience so upsets Jim that dissension begins to invade the marriage. Perhaps, he muses, a man should have certain hours when he is not married, when the wife draws her own magic circles. Ironically, the festering anger and frustration are eased when Lee and Jim discover that the man is a con artist after all. They would rather be known as victims of a lawbreaker than as sentimental dupes for every sob story in New York. In this way they may find relief in their own victimization. Being a victim, Jim decides, is better than being a sucker. The story ends with, "and their happiness returned," but we can only wonder how long it will last. The total effect of this story is not pleasant.

The same is true of "Intercession." Ostensibly a comic account of a struggling golfer's entanglement with the unyielding spaces of a round of golf, the story is primarily a modern account of Paul's trek down the road to Damascus. The religious implications of "Intercession" look forward to Updike's later pieces on the spiritual dimension of this most demanding sport, especially Rabbit's golf round with Rev. Eccles in *Rabbit, Run*, "The Pro" in *Museums and Women*, and "Is There Life After Golf?" in *Picked-Up Pieces*. The point of this story is that paradise is never reached, the conversion is not successful, and the golf round is never completed.

"Intercession" begins with illusions. A drought has fallen on Connecticut so that the grass looks orange, the road dust seems rose, and the putting greens, the havens for every golfer, are hallucinatory. On his way to the golf course, Paul defies the workers trying to improve the road, parks his car, and heads for the pro shop. Religious trappings are everywhere. He feels guilty for leaving his family at home; the proprietress of the shop sits like a brooding prophetess; Paul worries about teeing off in public for the initial time, for the experience is like first communion. Everyone stares. Although he hopes to hit his drive as well as the man in front of him whose soul "flies with the ball," he slices his tee shot among the fallen fruit of an apple tree. He belongs there. On the modern road to Damascus, he fails to help a lonely, arrogant teen-ager who needs companionship even though he cheats at golf.

The irony is that Paul has a "primitive faith." He truly believes that if he commits himself he will be "rescued" from the hell of a bad score. But like Jim in "A Gift from the City," he lacks charity. When distressed or angry, both pull out their wallets. Upset with his young companion's bragging and casual disregard of the rule which stipulates that only one ball per shot may be hit, Paul, believing in miracles, asks that his drive on the fourth hole be "brilliant." His prayer is not heard:

If miracles, in this age of faint faith, could enter anywhere, it would be here, where the causal fabric was thinnest, in the quick collisions and abrupt deflections of a game. Paul drove high but crookedly over the treetops. It was dismaying for a creature of spirit to realize that the angle of a surface striking a sphere counted for more with God than the most ardent hope. (206)

But it does count for more. Paul's call of "Jesus look out!" when his drive is about to hit the boy is heeded because, he thinks, heaven protects fools. Yet Jesus will not look out for him because his faith is primitive and his charity non-existent. Although he realizes that the teen-ager longs for companionship, he cannot respond. Paul is no Good Samaritan. Frustrated, he challenges the boy to a wager which is refused.

Finally, guilt and anger cause him to leave the course following a hooked tee shot on the fifth hole, thus forcing him to miss seeing the hidden fifth green for the second time. The point is significant, for he has inadvertently pictured that green as "paradisiacal—broad-leaved trees, birds, the cry of water," in short, an oasis on the drought-stricken road to salvation. Crossing the road to his car, abandoning the boy and the fifth green, he walks among road–building machines which resemble pre-historical beasts. He is isolated, alone with his guilt, a pilgrim who has failed the test: "In all the landscape no human being was visible, and a fatiguing curse seemed laid on everything" (209). Unfortunately, he does not recognize the sign of his failure which occurs when he imagines heaven reaching down to grab what he thinks is a good tee shot. The ball is lost, and so is Paul.

This impressive but generally ignored story illustrates Updike's development from "Friends from Philadelphia," especially in showing his extraordinary use of correspondence and metaphor. The young golfer has "ambitious, rather familiar" ears (199). Another golfer has a swing "as lucid and calm as the perfect circle that Giotto in one brush stroke drew to win Pope Benedict's commission" (195). The same golfer replaces a head cover "so gently he might have been hooding a falcon" (195).[17] The dialogue is natural, the descriptions persuasive, the religious theme unobtrusive. "Intercession" is a story written by a maturing author.

The final tale, "The Happiest I've Been," encourages the reader to leave by the same door through which he has entered the book. John Nordholm, the naive main character in "Friends from Philadelphia," is the narrator of "The Happiest I've Been" as Updike returns from the anonymity of New York to the warmth of Olinger. During the intervening years between fifteen and nineteen, John has matured, and he knows it. Awkward with Thelma in "Friends from Philadelphia," he has now met the girl he will marry. Unfamiliar with automatic transmissions in the first tale, he is eager to drive seventeen hours to Chicago in the last. The title is not at all ironic. At age nineteen, John is ready to walk toward manhood, but just before he takes the final step, he glances back over his shoulder to look once more at the small town where he will always be happy. Thus is the past frozen in memory. Nostalgia is all.

Updike makes the same glance in his stories of boyhood and youth. Those who question why he devotes so much of his energy to recalling the ever-waning past should read this story, for it balances the uninitiated boy on the line between regret over leaving the town of happiness and eagerness to enter the city of responsibility. Chicago is a long way from Olinger. No wonder John Nordholm—and Updike himself—pauses to set down for all time the story of his moments of joy before abandoning the dirt road by the farm to plunge onto the turnpike. Once he leaves, he can never return except in memory.

John does just that. The story has a double perspective. Although the teen-ager's view is the primary angle of vision, the maturity of adulthood frames the tale. Without this sense of John the man looking back at John the boy, the story would lose the tone of nostalgia which makes it effective. Updike stresses the significance of John's move when he emphasizes that the boy lives with both parents and grandparents. Leaving Olinger is more than departing a home town; it means stepping away from heritage. The grandmother may be nearly crippled with arthritis, and the grandfather may offer useless advice, but they represent John's ties with a time he cannot know personally. His secure link with the past encourages a confident feeling for the future. John and his friend Neil know who they are:

But it seemed to me the most important thing…was that he and I lived with grandparents. This improved both our backward and forward vistas; we knew about the bedside commodes and midnight coughing fits that awaited most men, and we had a sense of childhoods before 1900, when the farmer ruled the land and America faced west. (223)

The tension between ties with home and the break toward the future is suggested by the road they have to travel before reaching the turnpike. One turn will take them to Olinger and the familiar; the other will lead them to the highway and beyond. Significantly, they turn toward Olinger and a last party with their friends. The time is New Year's, and they need to linger a final moment in their youth before the long drive to the city and a new dawn.

The New Year's party allows John to relive segments of his past. His mother senses the importance of the trip, for she speaks of him as if he were helpless: "'Well, good-bye boys….I think you're both very brave.' In regard to me she meant the girl as much as the roads" (222). Although no sexual experience literally occurs, John's few hours at the party look both backward and forward in his association with women. His memory guides the story toward meaning instead of sentimentality if only because his journey is universal. Stepping into the Schuman's house for the New Year's get-together, he recalls a Hallowe'en party years before which he attended dressed in a Donald Duck costume. Today they may continue to play silly party games, but the situation has changed. Rather than look at funny costumes, John notices the "white arc" of bras beneath the necklines of semi-formal gowns and the stockinged feet of girls who kick off shoes in order to run around the ping-pong table.

Aware of a "warm keen dishevelment" within himself, John is conscious of the change which sexual maturity brings:

But the girls who had stepped out of these shoes were with few exceptions the ones who had attended my life's party. The alterations were so small: a haircut, an engagement ring, a franker plumpness. While they wheeled above me I sometimes caught from their faces an unfamiliar glint, off of a hardness I did not remember, as if beneath their skins these girls were growing more dense. (228–229)

At the chime of midnight, the boys all want to kiss the only married girl at the party. She seems to them extraordinary.

Hovering in the background of this initiation rite is the specter of the Korean War and the implication of violent death. Updike's imagery is appropriate. At six in the morning, Olinger is "deathly still"; John imagines that with a rifle he can easily shoot out his parents' bedroom window from the road; he has a scare when the car hits a patch of ice at eighty-one miles per hour. Yet through it all, through the awkwardness and the emotion and the fear, John is happy. He kisses a girl, touches her breast, and feels contented while she falls asleep on his shoulder. Her trust of him in the early dawn tempers the final night of irresponsibility. And after Neil and John say good-bye to the girls and begin the long ride toward the future, Neil asks John to drive and then goes to sleep. Again he welcomes the adult burden of trust:

We were on our way. I had seen a dawn.... There was the quality of the 10 A.M. sunlight as it existed in the air ahead of the windshield, filtered by the thin overcast, blessing irresponsibility—you felt you could slice forever through such a cool pure element—and springing, by implying how high these hills had become, a widespreading pride: Pennsylvania, your state—as if you had made your life. And there was knowing that twice since midnight a person had trusted me enough to fall asleep beside me. (241–242)

The initiation rite is over. The party is held in a friend's house, but the parents are out for the evening. The unexpected trust is joyously accepted as an entry into the adult world. But while driving toward the skyscrapers of Chicago, John takes in the hills of Pennsylvania. Home will forever hold the background of his memory.

The local boy with his various names returns to Olinger in *Pigeon Feathers*, the next volume of short stories. *Pigeon Feathers* is Updike's most popular collection of tales, but its renown does not undermine the success of *The Same Door*. Stepping boldly toward his eventual mastery of the mood of nostalgia and the tone of regret, Updike reveals in *The Same Door* a narrative skill which will help him change the American short story.

Notes to *The Same Door*

1. Alice and Kenneth Hamilton, *John Updike: A Critical Essay* (Grand Rapids: William B. Eerdmans, 1967), p. 22.
2. Rachael C. Burchard, *John Updike: Yea Sayings* (Carbondale: Southern Illinois University Press, 1971), p. 133.
3. A.C. Spectorsky, "Spirit Under Surgery," *Saturday Review*, 22 August 1959, p. 31.
4. Thomas E. Cassidy, "The Enchantment of the Ordinary," *Commonweal*, 11 September 1959, p. 499.
5. William Peden, "Minor Ills That Plague the Human Heart," New York *Times Book Review*, 16 August 1959, p. 5.
6. William Peden, *The American Short Story: Front Line in the National Defense of Literature* (Boston: Houghton Mifflin, 1964), p. 71.
7. The British reviews of *The Same Door* point to a second possible flaw: Updike's genius with the small detail narrows his appeal to those familiar with daily living in America after 1950. Thus the stories may be limited. The emotions are universal, but the minute descriptions which frame and often trigger the feelings are so closely associated with a special way of life that an outsider will inadvertently miss the subtleties on which the stories depend for substance. David Lodge, for example, seems familiar enough with the *New Yorker* to note Updike's love of America despite the absurdities and ironies he points out, but the anonymous reviewer for the *Times Literary Supplement* insists that "the success of these stories seems to depend on a catching of the exact nuances of American scene and dialogue ... an English reader may be at a disadvantage when judging them." Similarly, Richard Mayne argues that a culture gap affects the British reception of *The Same Door* because the stories are too good technically. They are so well written, so emotionally sure, so right in their "needling verisimilitude" that they lack the touch of the accidental or unmeasured necessary to vary the formula. *See* David Lodge, "Instant Novel," *The Spectator*, 11 May 1962, p. 628; "Fragments of America," London *Times Literary Supplement*, 27 April 1962, p. 277; and Richard Mayne, "Instant Literature," *New Statesman*, 27 April 1962, pp. 606–607.
8. John Updike, "Foreword," *Olinger Stories* (New York: Vintage, 1964), p. vii.
9. John Updike, *The Same Door* (New York: Knopf, 1959), p. 8. Further references will be to this edition.

10. Updike, "Foreword," *Olinger Stories*, p. v.
11. John Updike, *Rabbit, Run* (New York: Knopf, 1960), p. 5.
12. Apparently this story is a favorite in high-school English classes. *See* Ruben Friedman, "An Interpretation of John Updike's 'Tomorrow and Tomorrow and So Forth,'" *English Journal*, 61 (November 1972), 1159-1162; and R. Jeff Banks, "The Uses of Weather in 'Tomorrow and Tomorrow and So Forth,'" *Notes on Contemporary Literature*, 3 (November 1973), 8-9.
13. Mayne, p. 606.
14. Jack De Bellis, "The Group and John Updike," *Sewanee Review*, 72 (July-September 1964), p. 534.
15. Cassidy, p. 499.
16. Burchard, p. 136; Robert Detweiller, *John Updike* (New York: Twayne, 1972), p. 23.
17. For another meditation on golf, *see* John Updike, "Golf Dreams," *New Yorker*, 19 February 1979, p. 35.

Pigeon Feathers

"What is the past, after all, but
a vast sheet of darkness in which
a few moments, pricked apparently
at random, shine?"

—"The Astronomer"

Updike's moving, nostalgic final story in *The Same Door* looks forward to many of the tales in *Pigeon Feathers* (1962). As the boy in "The Happiest I've Been" takes the last turn in the road toward the burdens of adulthood, he looks back around the bend to Olinger. Experience and memory fuse, and the past becomes the stuff of fiction. Many of the stories in *Pigeon Feathers* build on the tone of nostalgia and the sense of regret. The narrator returns home to certain moments remembered or imagined, but he finds that the past forever fixed in memory does not coincide with the present forever changing. The "pricked" moments may randomly shine, but the "vast sheet of darkness" seems to stretch on toward infinity. Only in art does the past become immortal.

Updike does not merely record the past. He invents it from the materials of his own life: "Once I've coined a name, by the way, I feel utterly hidden behind the mask and what I remember and what I imagine become indistinguishable. I feel no obligation to the remembered past; what I create on paper must, and for me does, soar free of whatever the facts were."[1] This statement suggests Updike's sensitivity to the complaint that he does little more in his stories than relive his own youth, an opinion which makes no sense whatever but which is widespread among his disparagers. Rather than try

90

to wedge himself through the ever-narrowing passageway to the past, he creates characters who are fleeing from or lamenting the loss of earlier times. The characters are frustrated when inner needs based on past experiences are not fulfilled by current conditions. Updike explains: "My books feed, I suppose, on some kind of perverse relish in the fact that there are insolvable problems. There is no reconciliation between the inner, intimate appetites and the external consolations of life."[2]

Updike is concerned in *The Same Door* and *Pigeon Feathers* not with his life in Shillington, Pennsylvania, specifically but with the ambiguities of small-town living generally. When he describes his subject matter, he is clear: "My subject is the American Protestant small-town middle class. I like middles. It is in middles that extremes clash, where ambiguity restlessly rules. Something quite intricate and fierce occurs in homes, and it seems to me without doubt worthwhile to examine what it is."[3] Readers who argue that Updike writes exquisitely but has nothing to say perhaps miss the ambiguity of domestic fierceness in stories which purposely avoid the more obvious dramatics of social commentary or cultural myth. Updike's definition of his subject refers to the stories before *The Music School* (1966). His description reflects the continuing saga of the Maples, but it is much closer to *Pigeon Feathers* than to *Museums and Women* (1972), a volume in which he is more interested in current pressures than past memories.

Still, to say that Updike does not write exclusively about his own early years in the first two collections of short stories is not to suggest that he scraps his heritage when he picks up his pen. Like most authors, he writes about what he knows, and what he knows in *The Same Door* and *Pigeon Feathers* is youth, adolescence, and emerging maturity in an American small town. He admits, "I'm still running on energy laid down in childhood. Writing is a way of keeping up with that childhood."[4] But while this comment was expressed in 1966, the year of *The Music School*, it looks back to *Pigeon Feathers* and to what he calls "an intensity, perhaps, of ordinariness" which provides the incentive for the Olinger tales.[5] To write about the middle is to take chances. The ordinary surface of his subject matter and stories apparently puzzles some readers who urge him to write about big issues, but Updike is aware of the gamble both for himself and his reputation: "It took courage initially to be able to write frankly about my own boyhood, which, funnily enough, was a very innocent boyhood. Nevertheless it seemed to be a step forward to write some of the short stories that have been collected here and there.'"[6] The motion forward became a giant step in 1962 with the publication of *Pigeon Feathers*. Many of the stories in *The Same Door* are good, but most in *Pigeon Feathers* are excellent.

Not everyone agrees. R.B. Larson could write in 1973 that despite the critical controversy over Updike's novels, Updike is indisputably a master of the short-story form, but an analysis of the commentary about *Pigeon Feathers* suggests that a challenge to the designation of master surfaced in the early 1960s.[7] Part of the problem in discussing the short stories involves the variations Updike brings to the form. Many of his short fictions are not stories in the standard sense. Often uniting the occasional essay and the trappings of poetry with the traditional tale of rising and falling action or character development, he catches off guard those readers who have a type of short story in mind when they pick up *Pigeon Feathers*. Unhappiness in an Updike story moves the character not to large-scale significant action but to quiet frustration, and thus some readers respond by saying that nothing happens. Plot and characterization often give way to layers of meaning usually dependent upon an image or a gesture so that dramatization becomes meditation. The question to ask, it seems to me, is not what happens but what is felt or exposed.

Those who praise *Pigeon Feathers* do so in glowing terms. Major reviews, for example, by critics the stature of Granville Hicks and Arthur Mizener set the tone for many who responded favorably. Arguing that the stories in *Pigeon Feathers* far outdistance those in *The Same Door*, Hicks points to Updike's "astonishing" gift for figurative language when writing about the ambiguities of the commonplace. Updike may pursue the past, but he grasps for it not out of simple nostalgia but because those moments define and thus give meaning to life. Hicks concludes: "I think that some of these stories, and especially the two at the end, hold out an even larger hope for the future. We hear talk now and then of a breakthrough in fiction, the achievement of a new attitude and hence a new method; something like that seems close at hand in 'Pigeon Feathers.'"[8] Arthur Mizener agrees. Observing that the collection shows Updike's celebration of the blessed moment, he begins with an eye-catching announcement: "John Updike is the most talented writer of his age in America...and perhaps the most serious...'Pigeon Feathers' is not just a book of very brilliant short stories; it is a demonstration of how the most gifted writer of his generation is coming to maturity; it shows us that Mr. Updike's fine verbal talent is no longer pirouetting, however gracefully, out of a simple delight in motion, but is beginning to serve his deepest insight."[9] Note how Mizener alludes to the question of whether Updike's prose is all dazzle with no thought. Clearly, he does not accept this criticism which will gather more supporters as the Updike canon grows, but he does realize the challenge Updike faces to blend verbal brilliance with substance.[10]

Confirming Mizener's opinion that Updike is the most gifted young writer in America, Stanley Edgar Hyman nevertheless expresses reservations which look toward the critics who disapprove of *Pigeon Feathers*. He likes Updike's way of ending a story with a pointed, summarizing, and often quotable sentence because these endings "not only resolve but deepen," but he wonders if Updike illustrates the weakness of facility by publishing too much too quickly. He falls, says Hyman, into cuteness when he has nothing to say: "Walter Briggs," "Dear Alexandros," "You'll Never Know, Dear, How Much I Love You," and "A & P." "The stories at times suggest Babel and Kafka, if at other times they seem to have been most influenced by the machine that makes cotton candy at the fair. If this young man can bring himself to slow down, to stay backstage, to choose larger subjects and shape them more fully, he cannot help becoming a major writer."[11] One can already hear in these comments echoes of what will become the outcry that Updike is too subjective and that he writes like an angel who has no insight.

I do not accept Hyman's opinion of, say, "A & P," but many do. Suggesting that *Pigeon Feathers* is an uneven collection despite Updike's extraordinary gifts as a writer, Hyman praises the best stories and laments the artifice. Yet it is often difficult to agree upon what should be dismissed. Hyman says that "Walter Briggs" is silly, but J. M. Edelstein notes that it is "brilliantly done." Still, Edelstein disapproves of *Pigeon Feathers*, for he dislikes the general cleverness and mannerism which he finds throughout. Arguing that the volume is weaker than *The Same Door*, he writes, "And yet, reading Updike, rewarding as it is, can also be terribly frustrating, as if either something were missing or there was too much of a good thing. Although the best of Updike is overwhelming, I wonder if it is still good enough."[12] The problem is that Edelstein's negative opinion of *Pigeon Feathers* seems prompted by the mistaken notion that Updike hopes to dismiss the unpleasantness of the present by recalling the sweetness of the past. Reading such a statement, one can only point to the sense of defeat in stories like "A Sense of Shelter," "The Persistance of Desire," or "A & P," and then reply that such is not the case.

Still, Edelstein's judgment that *Pigeon Feathers* is a lesser achievement than *The Same Door* has supporters. In a balanced, quiet, and finally negative evaluation, Stanley J. Rowland, Jr., discusses *Pigeon Feathers* as a work by an author who suffers from the "limits of littleness." Writers may develop, says Rowland, but judging by this collection, Updike has not grown. Read individually the stories are effective, but taken together they expose the narrowness of his artistic vision and the smallness of his emotional response. The problem, argues Rowland, is that Updike consistently makes people smaller than they are: "We are given, most persistently, the motif of the belittled man. The motif and its themes are certainly legitimate. The trouble is, Updike does not make us feel that this human shrinkage is tragic or even important."[13] Apparently writing from the perspective of orthodox Christian faith, Rowland believes that Updike fails because he lacks the vision to point to an ironic contrast between the little man and something much larger. Rowland wants a sense of transcendence which Updike does not supply.[14] None of these negative evaluations of *Pigeon Feathers* is, however, as hysterical as Alfred Chester's essay in *Commentary*.

Few today much care what reviewers for *Commentary* think about John Updike because they are usually virulently negative when they write about his fiction. Chester's blast loses its intended impact because one expects *Commentary* to criticize Updike. Titling his essay "Twitches and Embarrassments," he "hastens" to tell us that nothing is said in *Pigeon Feathers* because no character is ever bitter or violent or ribald or outrageous or despairing. Mr. Chester does not review; he harangues. And he aims his harangues as much at the *New Yorker* as at Updike: "But the *New Yorker* and John Updike are both deeply immersed in the image of men as trivia.... Updike has no sense of invention, no imagination—he seems incapable of making anything up to save his life—no ability to create living people, conflict, or drama."[15] For all of the hysteria, Chester touches upon a consistent complaint in the adverse reactions to this collection, that Updike dwells too much on little things and little people.

This criticism is, of course, related to the more general opinion that an author must create large characters engaged in overwhelming issues if he wants to have something to say. Those critics, like Hicks and Mizener, who appreciate Updike's genius in showing the mysteries of the commonplace laud the delicacy, detail, and nuance of his short fictions. Others, like Hyman and Rowland, who want expanded canvas and dramatic conflict, dislike what they consider to be the elevation of style over content. Interestingly, the best negative evaluation of *Pigeon Feathers* in particular and Updike's short stories in general urges him not to see more but to judge more. Thomas Molyneux's "The Affirming Balance of Voice" is the most clearly stated, most reasonably considered analysis of what many believe to be shortcomings in Updike's short fiction. His analysis boils down to the following: "There is in them too much sensibility spread too thin. I keep yearning for something to strike me deeply, something to amaze me, some fancy not of language but of vision.... Perception *is* all in these stories and that is not enough. Fiction is essentially a dramatic form."[16] Reading these remarks in the context of the entire essay, we understand that Molyneux is a traditionalist, that he has the standard definition of the dramatic short story in mind when he finds fiction like "A Sense of Shelter" deficient. He criticizes the ending of this tale for not being dramatic, for having a tacked-on quality as if it could stand alone. But this disapproval seems unfair since Updike usually does not try to write the standard dramatic short story. When he elevates perception over judgment, the very act Molyneux dislikes, he does so to vary the traditional form of the story and thus to make his short fiction more lyrical meditation and essay than dramatic conflict and resolution. He concentrates on the ordinary because he hopes to make us see. Those who demand judgment want a different form of tale from the kind Updike offers in such abundance.[17]

One obvious point is that critical opinion of the short stories is extremely divided. Yet while expected about an author so widely read and reviewed, the divergence reveals an irony apparent only to those with an overview of the various analyses of *Pigeon Feathers*. Except for Alfred Chester, every commentator names a story or two as "exquisite" or "beautiful" or "moving" even if he dismisses the collection as a whole. The irony is that with so many different nominations, as it were, for the best story in the book, the overall volume is likely to be impressive indeed. It is. "Flight" and "A Sense of Shelter" draw a lion's share of the attention, but over one half of the stories are listed as some critic's favorite.

In many cases, a reviewer's praise of or reservation about *Pigeon Feathers* depends upon his attitude toward Updike's talent for locating a moment in time and then describing the details which make it special. As we have seen, some readers believe that his lingering over the details of life, the ambiguities of the daily routine, and the nuances of the smallest gesture indicates a narrow vision which brands him as unworthy of the designation "major author." I disagree. As the epigraph to this discussion of *Pigeon Feathers* suggests, Updike knows that we understand the past only as we seize upon the few shining moments of memory in the vast blankness of forgetfulness. We may misunderstand the "pricked" moment, or we may misinterpret its affinity with the present, but the effort to see it must be made. So many of the stories in the first two collections detail the threats to the security one gains in a precise evaluation of the moment that Updike will probably always have to endure the criticism that he is a minor author because he writes about little things. To insist upon this argument is, however, to suggest that loss of family stability, the insecurity of maturity and age, the conflict between marriage and imagination, and the pressures of memory are not dilemmas of immense proportions. Updike may praise in "Archangel" "Certain moments, remembered or imagined, of childhood," but he is concerned with more than that.[18]

The epigraph to *Pigeon Feathers* from Kafka's "A Report to An Academy" sets the tone:

In revenge, however, my memory of the past has closed the door against me more and more. I could have returned at first, had human beings allowed it, through an archway as wide as the span of heaven over the earth, but as I spurred myself on in my forced career, the opening narrowed and shrank behind me; I felt more comfortable in the world of men and fitted it better; the strong wind that blew after me out of my past began to slacken; today it is only a gentle puff of air that plays around my heels; and the opening in the distance, through which it comes and through which I once came myself, has grown so small that, even if my strength and my will power sufficed to get me back to it, I should have to scrape the very skin from my body to crawl through.

Updike scrapes the skin—willingly. As if hurrying backward, stretching toward moments already experienced but not yet obliterated, he protests against the slamming of the door. Like Kafka's narrator, he finds that his archway is no longer as wide as the span of heaven.

He cannot, for example, tell the complete story of his Grandmother's thimble or of Fanning Island: "For I thought that this story, fully told, would become without my willing it a happy story, a story full of joy; had my powers been greater, we would know. As it is, you, like me, must take it on faith" (245). He has pursued his career, so the opening to the past has narrowed and shrunk. But it has not closed. *Pigeon Feathers* is Updike's race with time, his homage to the ghosts of the past. He *will* remember and create. Yet the collection also looks forward, for it is his offering to the gods of immortality, part of an achievement on which he will stake his future. This tension informs many of the stories in *Pigeon Feathers*. Yearning toward the future necessitates grappling with the past.

Jack and Clare face this challenge in the first story, "Walter Briggs."[19] Generally ignored except to be dismissed as a piece of fluff, "Walter Briggs" is an excellent beginning to a collection largely concerned with the nagging demands of memory. Updike carefully sets the time with references to Archbishop Cushing, Khrushchev, and Nasser—this is a tale of the 1950s. Yet the specific decade is not as important to the story as the difficulty involved in remembering the past. Updike structures the story along the lines of a rough parallel: The two-year old daughter fantasizes a make-believe "Miss Duni" just as Jack and Clare probe their memories in an effort to recall a name from a past that might as well be fantasy.

Neither the child Jo nor the mother Clare cares about identifying Miss Duni. They merely enjoy the memory game. But Jack needs a "minimal element of competition" to excite him. To declare, as Robert Detweiler does, that Jack's ability finally to say "Walter Briggs" affirms his "joy about and satisfaction from their mutual past" is to overlook the sense of competition he feels with Clare.[20] His determination to remember Walter Briggs contrasts with the easy tone of playfulness expressed by his wife and daughter. Usually their name game is fun, a bit of nonsense he and Clare play when "whiling away enforced time together." But this time the game breaks down because while they can describe guests at a party they are apparently returning from, they cannot call names. When they stumble while trying to name adults at the camp where they spend their honeymoon, we know that the highlights of their past together are beginning to shade away into that gray area no longer significant to the valuable persistence of memory: "Walter Buh, buh—isn't that maddening?" (7).

They remember everything else about the man. He was fat, played bridge every night, was good at shuffleboard, fished near the men's tents, stayed behind after the closing of camp to help dismantle the metal pier, spent winters in Florida, and wore droopy hats. But they cannot recall his last name just as Jo cannot identify Miss Duni.

The point of the story is not the recovery of a name but Jack's compulsion to defeat Clare: "'I can remember their professions but not their names,' he said, anxious to put in something for himself, for he felt his wife was getting ahead of him at this game" (7–8). Frustrated nearly to the point of childishness, Jack gets hung up on this trifling blockage in the narrow passageway to his past. Inability to call the name from his memory affects his mood and attitude toward the present. But Clare keeps the game in perspective, side-stepping the stumbling block called "Briggs" to dance ahead: "It made him jealous, her store of explicit memories... but she moved among her treasures so quickly and gave them so generously he had to laugh at each new face and scene offered him, because these were memories they had collected together" (9–10).

Although he is jealous, he tries to enjoy her easy access to their happy past. But his unfortunate sense of competition with Clare will not let him laugh as freely as he might. Upset not only at his "unsatisfactory showing" in the game but also at his realization that "their past was so much more vivid to her presumably because it was more precious," he enters his reluctant memory after Clare falls asleep:

All around the cabin had stood white pines stretched to a cruel height by long competition, and the cabin itself had no windows, but broken screens. Pausing before the threshold, on earth littered with needles and twigs, he unexpectedly found what he wanted; he lifted himself on his elbow and called "Clare" softly, knowing he wouldn't wake her, and said, "Briggs. Walter Briggs." (11)

Shared experiences turn commonplace moments into the kind of private highlights a couple may build a lifetime upon, and thus scraping the skin on the door of memory may be a blessed act. But the ending of this story is ambiguous. Is Jack's quiet comment a triumph for them, an affirmation of his past with Clare, or is it a way for him to assert himself against her? Because of the description of the pines around their honeymoon cabin "stretched to a cruel height by long competition," the latter interpretation seems more likely. Jack's victory is ironic because Clare is innocently unaware of the intensity of his competition with her. The future of their marriage is as fragile as his memory of their past.

The transition from Jack's story to Clyde Behn's in "The Persistence of Desire" is smooth, for Clyde goes beyond Jack to plunge into his past. As he tells Janet, he is "always coming back." The marvelous first sentence, stressing the linoleum checkerboard pattern, pinpoints Clyde's sense of living in areas of intensity alternating between his present identity in Massachusetts and his "disconsolate youth" in Pennsylvania. Clyde, unfortunately, has faulty eyes, so he returns to his hometown to visit his childhood ophthalmologist and to stand once again between the "two infinities of past and future" (13). The metaphor of eyes in need of corrective lenses exposes his distorted view of the past and thus his uneasiness in the present.

Updike's gift for the minute detail which contributes to the sense of reality allows him to describe Dr. Pennypacker's waiting room and simultaneously to point to Clyde's dilemma. The checkerboard floor suggests Behn's sense of intersection. The new clock on the table shows the time in Arabic numbers and thus with each digit change drops another moment of the present into "the brimming void." Upset by this stark revelation of lost time, Clyde looks to the familiar grandfather clock for comfort. Its hands are stopped. Unfortunately, his life has not. His comfort in this suggestion of frozen time where the past is only a checkerboard away is reflected in the accidental meeting with his old flame Janet. Hoping to recapture a sense of past love, he tries to ignore the flow of each moment to the void. He fails to understand, for example, when he reads that the human body replaces its cells *in toto* every seven years. Clyde prefers the old cells, the old self. Memory, he hopes, stops time. Updike's allusion in the title to the limp timepieces in Salvador Dali's 1931 surrealistic painting "The Persistence of Memory" is unobtrusive and effective. Understating both the allusions and Clyde's urge to validate his past, Updike suggests the distorted nature of Clyde's desire and yet the poignancy of his need.

Both are contrasting colors on the checkerboard. Clyde is lonely in the waiting room and thus is grateful when the door opens to reveal his boyhood love. He is like a child again trying to hold on to some moment of pleasure long since terminated in the flow that turns experience to memory. His persistence of desire is misguided because it fails to help him validate his past in order to reaffirm his present. He prefers, instead, to neutralize the present in order to relive the past. Unhappily, he is unaware of his dilemma: "Poor Janet, Clyde felt; except for the interval of himself—his splendid, perishable self—she would never see the light" (14). But Clyde needs corrective lenses, too. Faulty eyesight affects his ability to cope. He tells Dr. Pennypacker that his twitching eyelid makes it difficult for him to think. For example, he admits to Janet that he is "incredibly happy" with his wife, yet he acts as if he still has an adolescent crush on her: "Happiness," he says, "isn't everything."

The description of Pennypacker's examination goes to the heart of the matter: "Clyde, blind in a world of light, feared that Pennypacker was inspecting the floor of his soul" (19). Clyde's soul may be stale. Told that he may lose his eyelashes due to a fungus, he worries more about vanity than disease. Similarly, he is upset that Janet has forgotten what he remembers as an intense teen-age romance. In his conceit, he imagines that by marrying another woman he has deprived her of something special which is, of course, himself. Thus he glories in the guilt that he may have mistreated her. His vanity requires confirmation by his memory that he has made Janet unhappy by breaking off the affair. When she responds that she does not hate him, he is angry because her reply does not corroborate his view of the past: "Son of a bitch, so I'm a bother. I knew it. You've just forgotten, all the time I've been remembering; you're so *damn* dense. I come in here a bundle of pain to tell you I'm sorry and I want you to be happy, and all I get is the back of your neck" (22). The narrator's suggestion that Clyde resembles a thirsty blind man begging for sustenance makes the point. His nostalgia is too close to sentimentality.

Pennypacker, however, is a no-nonsense man dealing with the present. His job is to supply corrective lenses which, he cannot realize, Clyde needs in more ways than one. His prescription punctures at least some of Clyde's illusions: Drops for the fungus, adjustable nose pads for the strain despite Clyde's vain but expected protest that they leave ugly dents, and instructions to wear glasses all the time because he is no longer in the third grade. "Thus Clyde was dismissed into a tainted world where things evaded his focus" (25).

But not quite yet—Janet is still in the waiting room. Placing a note into his pocket, she slips out the door. Clyde, of course, thrills to this touch of conspiracy, to what he imagines is a promise of things to come which ironically will be a return to what he remembers of things long ago. But Updike knows better. Describing Clyde as an "actor snug behind the blinding protection of the footlights," and as a man who can no longer see the face of the new clock, he stresses the childlike blindness of Clyde's faith in the memory of desire. Eyes blurred by Pennypacker's drops, Clyde cannot read Janet's note. He wiggles it. He holds it at arm's length. He moves it toward his defective eyes. The note will not yield a single word. Nothing. Unwilling to give up and unaware of his problem, he decides that he can nevertheless detect Janet's identity in the shape of the handwriting. Desire quickens. He returns the note to his shirt pocket as if it were the armor needed to shield his wounded heart. The point is that he wants not Janet but the boy who once loved her. The note means more to him than her body because remembered happiness is more sustaining than current pleasure. In Updike's fiction, love may make either a museum piece out of the vanished past or an improbable goal for the unrealized future, but in the present it loses its magic. Clyde cherishes the note as a passageway to the past. Eyes still distorted, he steps into the streets of his boyhood: "The maples, macadam, shadows, houses, cement, were to his violated eyes as brilliant as a scene remembered; he became a child again in this town, where life was a distant adventure, a rumor, an always imminent joy" (26). Nostalgia and the possibility of defeat go together. Unless he can use the note to purge his past and to face his present, the persistence of memory and the romance of desire will reduce him to a child.

Unlike many of Updike's stories about the allure of the past, "The Persistence of Desire" shows the main character confronting the object of his memory. The question left purposely unanswered at the end is whether memory will give way to reality. With the unreadable note in his pocket, a symbol of the unobtainable past of his life, Clyde will have to accept the distinction between the demands of the present and the lure of memory or else stop living, like the grandfather clock. Although these stories are not specifically about Updike, he has his own adolescence in mind when he writes the Olinger tales. Those years, he explains, provide a sense of unity to his canon:

In a sense my mother and father, considerable actors both, were dramatizing my youth as I was having it, so that I arrived as an adult with some burden of material already half-formed. There is, true, a submerged thread connecting certain of the fictions, and I guess the submerged thread is the autobiography.... My own sense of childhood doesn't come from being a father, it comes from having been a child. We're all so curiously alone. But it's important to keep making signals through the glass.[21]

The signals are not clear when Updike steps away from Olinger in *Pigeon Feathers*. Although the stories set in England draw upon his experience as an art student at Oxford, he is not as committed to that part of his past and thus he does not bring to these tales the complexities of emotion and perspective which make the Olinger fictions so effective. In "Still Life," for example, his sensitive young man is in London, but Leonard Hartz is out of place. A slender, earnest American with "an unromantically round head" studying in the British Constable School of Art, he is alone in a strange city where chemists' shops are not drugstores and where tea parlors are not luncheonettes: "The American movies so readily available reaffirmed rather than relieved his fear that he was out of contact with anything that might give him strength" (29). Leonard is the kind of unconfident art student who, when he attempts to draw copies of cast classical statuary, neglects his own idealism to sketch in even the casting seams.

His lack of confidence unfortunately extends to his relationship with the female students. Updike's quiet comic touch shapes the description in which Leonard sizes up Robin not as a potential lover but as an artist checking over a model: "like a piece of fine pink ceramic her ankle kept taking, in Seabright's phrase, his eye" (34). "Still Life" stresses their differences and, by extension, the culture gap between the two countries. He is calm, patient, quiet; she is bouncy, breathless, blithe. Yet when Leonard is about to be embarrassed by an American acquaintance from his hometown, Robin rescues him with a "presposterous" lie. Unfortunately for Leonard, his lack of confidence with Robin is so pronounced that he inadvertently begins to assume a fatherly role with her. When she asks his advice about painting technique and then about modeling in the nude for the American friend Jack Fredericks, he fears that he is being "neutralized." His still life with Robin decays as quickly as the cabbage and onions they have arranged together. Reassigned to the classical statuary, she tells him that she never posed for Fredericks because he is a "dreadful bore." But her dismissal of Fredericks does not leave the way open for Leonard. The culture gap is too great. All he can do is agree that "All Americans are bores." Their tentative romance never gets beyond the state of still-life objects: Shy American boy, confident British girl. Arrange, focus, and paint. "Still Life" is competent but not distinguished, perhaps because the tone of wistful loss and the theme of the always receding past are absent. One suspects that Updike is too far removed from the story to care with more than his skill. Such is not the case with "Flight."

Charles Thomas Samuels calls "Flight" perhaps the "most brilliantly written of the autobiographical tales," and I certainly agree.[22] Although it is the first story in the collection told in the first person, "Flight" is a companion piece with "The Persistence of Desire" and "A Sense of Shelter." Updike is especially good in suggesting the dual perspective of the boy going through the unsettling competition with his mother and of the mature man looking back on the experience. Not only does Allen Dow recall the time when he speaks of himself in the third person; he also remembers that the struggle with Mother has been going on for years. "Years before, when I was eleven or twelve, just on the brink of ceasing to be a little boy, my mother and I..." (49). From the vantage point of maturity, he now realizes that at age seventeen he was poorly dressed, funny-looking, and conscious that "a special destiny made me both arrogant and shy" (49).

His sense of being special is ambiguous. Partly the result of Mrs. Dow's own frustration with her drab life, Allen's supposed specialness is also her most important dream for herself and her son. If we accuse her of trying to live through Allen, we must also recognize that her aspirations for his escape from the small town of Olinger save him from a similar frustration. "Flight" is the story of a mother-son relationship at a time in the boy's life when the father seems busy or asleep. Mrs. Dow prefigures the complex Mrs. Robinson in *Of the Farm* just as Mr. Dow becomes the Centaur. "Impulsive and romantic and inconsistent," the mother grudgingly accepts her static life in Olinger only because she is convinced that her son is going to "fly." But getting him into flight is her problem and his despair. She tells him at age twelve that he is special, and he thus becomes "captive to a hope she had tossed off and forgotten" (50). Since she fears his "wish to be ordinary," she protests when he tries to fly the nest with Molly Bingaman without abandoning the limits of Olinger. This point is crucial to the story. Mrs. Dow is not so much against Molly as she is fearful that Molly will tie Allen to his hometown.

Updike is especially perceptive in capturing the uneasy ambivalence of Allen's predicament. He sketches in the sense of generations by describing in a few paragraphs the tensions that identify Allen's ancestors as far back as his great-grandfather. "Perhaps," says the mature Allen, "prolonged fear is a ground of love" (52). Wondering if "each generation of parents commits atrocities against their children," he uses the memory of his adolescent love of Molly to ponder his relationship with his mother. The genius of "Flight" is that Allen's recollection of Mrs. Dow is as inconsistent as he claims she is. His descriptions hit the mark: She is precocious yet believes in ghosts; handsome, she has a deprecating smile; a fabric snob with a generous clothes allowance, she marries the penniless son of a minister; and though she obeys her own father, she, like Allen, tries to escape Olinger. The key to the relationship between Allen and his mother may be found in the mature Allen's realization that he has misunderstood her attitude toward her own father all along, that she fights with him not because of desperation or anger but because she cannot leave him alone. The same is true in the mutual relationship between mother and son. Allen needs to tell this story in order to understand a past which continues to puzzle him. Without the past, of course, there is no meaningful present and thus no basis for growth and knowledge. Allen's story is paradoxically both his most strenuous flight from and his most determined effort to know his roots. Plunging into the past in order to tell his tale, he hopes to soar from memory toward the future. He realizes now that he has successfully found his role in his mother's dreams for him, for Mrs. Dow is above all a mythmaker, a frustrated woman who gives those closest to her "mythic immensity." Allen is her phoenix. Believing that she and her father have been destroyed by marriage, she raises her son as a hero who will fly from the desolation of her domestic life and thereby redeem her.

No wonder she discourages his attraction to teen-aged girl friends. The second half of "Flight" details Allen's journey with three girls during his senior year in high school to debate at another school over one hundred miles from Olinger. There, away from mother and the inhibiting routine of home, Allen discovers the "beautiful skin, heart-breaking skin" of Molly to whom he has before not paid the slightest attention. He mistakenly thinks she frees him. He jokes with Molly, dances with Molly, and for the first time in his life stays up past midnight talking with Molly. From today's perspective, he has forgotten the details of what must have been a pivotal night in his adolescence: "What did we say? I talked about myself" (61). Yet the experience lodges in his memory, and we suspect that his attraction to Molly has itself become mythologized in his mind as the first serious step away from mother.

How wrong he is at the time. Mrs. Dow sees the ostensible out-ward–bound footprint for what it is, a step toward married life in Olinger. Still clinging to the dream that her son will somehow soar from the small town and thereby atone for her own disappointing life, she counterattacks as soon as Allen returns from the trip: "Don't go with little women, Allen. It puts you too close to the ground" (65). Unfortunately for the teen–ager, but luckily for the man, friends, teachers, and both sets of parents conspire to separate him from Molly: "The entire town seemed ensnarled in my mother's myth, that escape was my proper fate. It was as if I were a sport that the ghostly elders of Olinger had segregated from the rest of the live-stock and agreed to donate in time to the air" (67). His youthful vanity, as he now remembers, is so great that he believes all of Olin-ger focuses upon his plight. In his bewilderment, Allen criticizes Mol-ly because the affair makes him see an "ignoble, hysterical, brutal aspect" of his mother (68). But things are not that simple. He recog-nizes now, although he fails to do so as a teen–ager, that Mrs. Dow's apparent pettiness results as much from the daily presence of her dying father as from her desire for Allen's flight. The competing tensions from two generations of men nearly exhaust her.

Like Clyde Behn, Allen Dow returns to memory to discover who he was all those years ago, but unlike Clyde, he does not like all that he finds.

[Molly] gave herself to me anyway, and I had her anyway, and have her still, for the longer I travel in a direction I could not have taken with her, the more clearly she seems the one person who loved me without advantage. I was a homely, comically ambitious hillbilly, and I even refused to tell her I loved her, to pronounce the word "love"—an icy piece of pedantry that shocks me now that I have almost forgotten the context of confusion in which it seemed wise. (69)

Allen inadvertently conspires with his mother to hurt Molly, and he realizes now that his attraction to her was not only desire but also rebellion. Innocent Molly is the injured loser. His angry retort to Mrs. Dow that he will reject a girl she disapproves of only this one time prompts her reply, "Goodbye, Allen." She launches him into flight.

But this dismissal to the world is partly ironic, for, as we know from the story, Allen's flight takes him both forward into adult-hood and back into memory where the tensions remain and the wounds do not heal. The key phrase in the above quotation is his realization that he has traveled a direction in which he "could not have taken" Molly. We may not like Mrs. Dow, but her vision for Allen, no matter how selfish, is correct. Molly would have tied him down. Only Mrs. Dow knows that potential artists have to soar.

The genius of stories like "Flight" is that Updike fashions ambiguity about time and memory out of sketches of unextraordinary domestic life. Recognizable people do ordinary things. He shows the unresolvable complications that often rest at the center of mundane relationships. Nothing much happens in "Flight," but the story reveals a lifetime. So does "A Sense of Shelter." A companion piece to "Flight," this story has attracted many critics who continue to disagree about the ending: What is William Young's future as he leaves Mary Landis at the end of the story? Surely Arthur Mizener's reading is questionable: "He succeeds, and escapes back into the warm, stuffy world of the high school."[23] R.W. Reising disagrees, suggesting that William escapes from the high school toward his happy future.[24] A.S.G. Edwards and Robert L. Welker and Herschel Gower seem more correct when they note the irony of the ending.[25,26] William's "humiliated, ugly, educable self" may feel "clean and free" as he thinks about the days ahead, but the details of the story undercut his sense of a carefree tomorrow.

As in "Flight," Updike mentions the mother (who this time likes the girl), the confused high-school boy trying to come of age, and the sweetheart who represents a first step away from home. There are differences, however, which make "A Sense of Shelter" not a retelling of "Flight" but its own tale. The primary distinction is point of view. Told in the third person as William lives the experience, "A Sense of Shelter" does not touch as much on the processes of memory which frame many of the stories in *Pigeon Feathers*. We see William's high-school world as he does, but the point of view is omniscient enough to encourage irony created by narrative distance. In addition, "A Sense of Shelter" focuses not on a boy and his mother but on a boy and his girl. Finally, William Young and Allen Dow have different attitudes toward school, home, and the demands of small-town life. While Allen hopes to take flight toward his future, William struggles into his present. He loves the protection of familiarity too much. Note his reaction to the gloomy schoolroom on a dreary day: "The feeling the gloom gave him was not gloomy but joyous: he felt they were all sealed in, safe... the smells of tablet paper and wet shoes and varnish and face powder pierced him with a vivid sense of possession" (84).

Yet no matter how snug and secure he feels behind the protective walls of the school, the outside beyond the window must eventually beckon. William resists the invitation. Not only does he see the parking lot as a blackboard in reverse; he also rejects the fresh air coming in from the barely opened window. William has the kind of mind which deals in precise observations. He knows, for example, that the temperature is "exactly" thirty-two degrees, but we notice that the snow fails to cover the tire tracks which William sees as scars on the possibility of perfection. He is poised, in effect, between thawing and freezing.

It is not as if William is exceptionally popular or admired and is thus reluctant to abandon the domain of acknowledged successes. He is a senior, a teacher's pet, and an occasional winner of a school election, but according to the student's definition of success, he does not fit in: No girl friend, no gang of buddies, no seat on the bus. Within his self-defined world, he is king, a benevolent master to unappreciative but respectful subjects. Yet his definition of life is so insular that his notion of kingship is ironic. "A Sense of Shelter" tells of William Young's effort to invite someone else into his world:

So, his long legs blocking two aisles, he felt regal even in size and, almost trembling with happiness under the high globes of light beyond whose lunar glow invisible snowflakes were drowning on the gravel roof of his castle, believed that the long delay of unpopularity had been merely a consolidation, that he was at last strong enough to make his move. Today he would tell Mary Landis he loved her. (85)

From the initial description of Mary, we know what William will have to learn: She has grown beyond him. She approaches adulthood with her full breasts and poise while he looks at her from an angle of vision shaped by a second-grade memory when she grabbed his schoolbag and outran him. William has loved her, so he thinks, ever since, but she is still way out in front. Closer now to flawed maturity than to childhood perfection, Mary is the reality on the other side of the classroom window. Her hardness is suggested by her reputation as being sexually initiated, but she is also sympathetic, patient, and kind. She is the heroine who has stepped outside of the shelter, a character we may not wish to emulate but one we should respect. William, however, wants to make her the queen of his sheltered world. Updike needs only one sentence to show how far apart they are. When Mary enters a teen-age hangout, buys cigarettes, and steps back outside, William "yearned to reach out, to comfort her, but he was wedged deep in the shrill booths, between the jingling guts of the pinball machine and the hillbilly joy of the jukebox" (90). He has yet to give up childish things, whereas she has left shelter to enter the world of snow. William prepares thirty lines of Vergil and answers all of the questions in Social Science, but Mary dates a man she meets while working as a waitress in a nearby town.

One suspects that William has never been there. A womb-like retreat, the school is coziest to him when the halls are nearly empty after hours, leaving him free to wander without the crowds of unappreciative "casual residents." His plans for the future depend upon school, for he romanticizes earning a Ph.D. and teaching at college, "section man, assistant, associate, *full* professor, possessor of a dozen languages and a thousand books, a man brilliant in his forties, wise in his fifties, renowned in his sixties, revered in his seventies, and then retired, sitting in the study lined with acoustical books until the time came for the last transition from silence to silence, and he would die, like Tennyson, with a copy of *Cymbeline* beside him on the moon-drenched bed" (92). Mary is not of this world, and she knows it.

Holding on to the past and his crush on Mary, William fails to see that life is passing him by. He is alienated from girls, peers, parents, and self. The deflation of dreams begins when she calls the school an idiotic building which she longs to leave. Thus it is significant that when he bungles his declaration of love, he senses a panel pushed open in his world of closed surfaces. We suspect that he will never walk through it, but Mary wears a scarf, likened to a halo, and is ready to step through the door. As his myth of king and queen together dissolves following Mary's gentle refusal of his love, he takes the opposite direction toward the school basement: "Between now and the happy future predicted for him he had nothing, almost literally nothing, to do" (101). Updike's juxtaposition of "happy" and "nothing" suggests a clue to the unanswered question about William's future: Will he ever walk outside to live, or will he graduate from nothing to nothing, a copy of *Cymbeline* beside his bed instead of an experienced woman in it? Nothingness seems to be in store for him, for *Cymbeline* supports his tendency to idealize his lover. A king within his imaginary world, William loses his queen when he refuses to acknowledge the door opening from shelter to snow. He exchanges an illusion of his past for an illusion of his future.

The prospects for maturity and love are far more promising in "Wife-wooing." A widely anthologized, justly praised piece, "Wife-wooing" is more a lyrical meditation than a conventional short story. Like the traditional tale, it has character, movement, and resolution, but it is much more concerned with patterns of language and nuances of tone than dramatic action. In one sense, the play on words is the plot of "Wife-wooing."

Young adults often admit that they are stunned by this story, that they reread it aloud to savor the pleasures of Updike's rhythmical prose and the luxuriance of sustained love. Not everyone agrees. Richard H. Rupp calls "Wife-wooing" "Browning gone wild," a "silly" description of an experience in which Updike "resorts instead to self parody."[27] These comments miss the mark. What attracts readers to this poetic account of adult love is that the principals are a married couple with children. Many young adults are on the threshold of their own marriages when they read this meditation, and they find in it the promise of domestic difficulties overcome, of romance alive beyond the first years together. How seriously they take the line, "Courting a wife takes tenfold the strength of winning an ignorant girl" (112). Even at an age when most are still exchanging fraternity pins and engagement rings, they know the truth of that comment and hope that the word "wife" does "not end the wooing."

"Wife-wooing" appeals, however, to all kinds of readers. The meditation is much about art as about sex, and in an indirect way, it is Updike's homage to James Joyce, an author who could express the eroticism of "smackwarm woman's thigh" as well as "feel the curious and potent, inexplicable and irrefutably magical life language leads within itself" (110). In this sense, women resemble language. Both are mysterious, powerful, and above all creative. Yet the husband's language is also partly a parody of Joyce. The soaring prose, full of alliteration and caesura, adds to the humor as the husband suggests an affinity between modern lover and Anglo-Saxon poet. Gently mocking himself while seriously declaring his love for the bare-thighed woman beside him, he likens his family eating hamburgers in front of the fireplace to primitive lovers before the fire.

The narrator senses the creative unity of language and woman, but he feels let down watching his family eat the fast-food dinner. One reason is that he lacks Joyce's power. Like an Anglo-Saxon poet, he sings of his exploits: "I wielded my wallet, and won my way back" (110). But Joyce's "smackwarm" is better. Another reason is that he is not a hero, no Leopold Bloom enshrined in fiction, much less Ulysses enshrined in myth. Rather than wrestle meat from the forest and then circle back to his cave, he drives to the nearest hamburger joint. Although he is serious about his declaration of love, he can view himself with irony. Note the self-mockery in his mock-heroic description of the diner: "a ferocious place, slick with savagery, wild with chrome; young predators snarling dirty jokes menaced me, old men reached for me with coffee-warmed paws" (110). One cannot help but like such a narrator.

Most of all he worries that erotic love no longer binds man and wife after seven years of marriage and three children. Looking at his wife's exposed thighs as she sits with knees drawn up in front of the fireplace, he is aware of the demands which the children beside her make. The little girl asks questions, "enunciating angrily, determined not to let language slip on her tongue" (112). The two-year-old boy cannot quite grab language which the husband describes as "thick vague handles swirling by" (112). He has a similar problem: How does he communicate the mystery of love and sexual desire to a "cunning" woman he has known for so long? Where is the pleasure of surprise when "we sense everything between us, every ripple, existent and non-existent; it is tiring" (112)? The point is that all of these expressions are in his mind. Unlike Joyce, he has not yet found a way to translate his emotion into language equally fervent: "Once my ornate words wooed you." When the wife ignores his unspoken invitation to sexual love in order to read a book about Richard Nixon, he is angry and then glad when, the next morning, he notices that, not yet dressed, she is drab.

One can only marvel at the end of "Wife-wooing." Returning home from a day's run with the rat race in the city, so preoccupied with a business problem that his wife serves his supper as "less than a waitress," he hardly notices when once more she goes upstairs with the book about Nixon:

So I am taken by surprise at a turning when at the meaningful hour of ten you come with a kiss of toothpaste to me moist and girlish and quick; the momentous moral of this story being, An expected gift is not worth giving. (115)

The quiet irony is that she woos him. Surprises are still possible, even after seven years of marriage. She acts with her body and creates a love scene for him; he reacts with words and creates a love story for us.

The religious implications which inform much of Updike's non-fiction prose and which direct the thematic content of many of his short stories as early as "Dentistry and Doubt" in *The Same Door* are especially important in "Pigeon Feathers."[28] The most ambitious story in the collection, "Pigeon Feathers" explores an identity crisis as adolescent David Kern faces the idea of his mortality for the first time. The theological implications are impressively worked out, but the story does not seem to me as memorable as "Wife-wooing," "Flight," or "The Persistence of Desire."[29]

Mundane events produce crises of the soul: David and his family have moved away from the relative security of the past. The move from town to country farm, recalling Updike's own childhood move from Shillington to Plowville, becomes a metaphor for David's suffering as a spiritual refugee and, in turn, for the alienation of all men who bother to think about their condition. The story suggests that formal religion is little more than a refuge against the shock of recognition but that personal faith may sustain the soul. As David realizes immediately, things are "upset, displaced, rearranged" (116). Disorientation in the world of the quotidian thus becomes a metaphor for questions in the world of metaphysics. What better way to regain order than by arranging the books that have been hastily switched from moving crates to library shelves? But as David handles the books, most of which date back to his mother's college days, he senses the "ominous gap between himself and his parents, the insulting gulf of time that existed before he was born" (117). Dipping into volume two of H.G. Wells's *The Outline of History*, he stares into "unreal and irrelevant worlds" (118). His displacement gains momentum when he reads Wells's account of Jesus' death which denies Christ's divinity and which accounts for the genesis of a new religion called Christianity by discussing the "credulous imagination of the times." Jesus, says Wells, was just another political rebel. Convinced that this account of history is false, David is initially more outraged than frightened: "This was the initial impact—that at a definite spot in time and space a brain black with the denial of Christ's divinity had been suffered to exist" (119). The problem is that David cannot supply rational objections to Wells's story of Christianity. It is not so much that he worries about the challenge to Christ's divinity but that his faith in God's ability and willingness to touch his life has been shaken. David finds the steps too easy from questions about Jesus to hints of his own oblivion to, worst of all, doubts about the existence of God. His "enemy's" point seems impregnable: "Hope bases vast premises on foolish accidents, and reads a word where in fact only a scribble exists" (120).

His parents cannot help. They seem to have more troubles than he does. Preoccupied with their own domestic squabbles because Mr. Kern does not want to live on a farm, they argue whether the land has a soul. Mr. Kern's insistence that the soil is nothing but chemicals seems to ally him with H.G. Wells, while Mrs. Kern seems to echo David's faith by attributing mysterious essence to the farmland. Yet she unwittingly increases his fear by advising him about the present when he needs assurance about eternity. She fails to understand his belief that God has to be different from His creation and thus is not just *in* the land.

David needs proof. Triggered by the move to the farm, his disorientation so affects him that he begins to have visions not only of his own death but also of final extinction. He seems surrounded by possibilities of annihilation: His father's condemnation of alcohol and cholesterol, his mother's comments on heart attacks and dead earthworms, his grandmother's Parkinson's disease,[30] the pigeons he is later asked to slaughter. The point is that he unwittingly illustrates Wells's argument that men read a word where only a scribble exists except that in his confusion he interprets everything negatively. Even his science fiction novels seem to confirm "his impending oblivion." Worst of all is his horrifying revelation while sitting in the outhouse:

Without warning, David was visited by an exact vision of death: a long hole in the ground, no wider than your body, down which you are drawn while the white faces above recede. You try to reach them but your arms are pinned. Shovels pour dirt into your face. There you will be forever, in an upright position, blind and silent, and in time no one will remember you, and you will never be called. (123)

Surely Updike has in mind here the famous story about Martin Luther who is reported to have had his epiphany about matters of doctrine while seated in the privy.[31] David consults, after all, a Lutheran minister about his despair. His problem is that his thoughts in the outhouse lead him to fears of personal annihilation. Questions of

Christ's divinity suddenly seem secondary. He needs to learn Luther's message that not reason but faith leads to salvation. His mother's explanation about the soul's presence in the land is ridiculous to a boy who now associates the land with privy holes, graves, and the tunnel to final death.

At first his defenses hold. An unabridged dictionary, for example, defines "soul" in a way to confirm its separate existence. His prayer suggests at least the possibility of reassurance: "All he needed was a little help; a word, a gesture, a nod of certainty, and he would be sealed in, safe" (128-129). He hopes that Reverend Dobson, whom Mr. Kern has described as too intelligent for a bunch of farmers, will be his major defense, but David is too smart for Dobson. One need only read the exchange between the Lutheran minister and the searching boy in catechetical class to note Dobson's inability to discuss the resurrection of the body or to sense David's despair. In David's eyes, the minister's obtuseness betrays Christianity. Defining heaven as like Abraham Lincoln's goodness living on does not settle crises of metaphysical disorientation. David cannot explain what he wants heaven to be, but he hopes that it is something. As he says in response to his mother's comment that Dobson may have made a mistake: "It's not a *question* of his making a mistake! It's a question of dying and never moving or seeing or hearing anything ever again" (137). Mrs. Kern's offer of the farm's beauty as proof of God's existence is not enough. Neither is Plato's Parable of the Cave. David is alone.

Ironically, he has his religious experience when he is asked to kill. Pigeons foul the furniture in the barn, says Grandmother. She wants them shot. Note Updike's description of the barn as if it were a rustic church: "A barn, in day, is a small night. The splinters of light between the dry shingles pierce the high roof like stars, and the rafters and crossbeams and built-in ladders seem, until your eyes adjust, as mysterious as the branches of a haunted forest" (144). The irony is that as he begins to shoot the pigeons in the mysterious old building, he finds that he enjoys the slaughter. From despair to delight, he is suddenly a master, a "beautiful avenger," God-like in his ability to sweep away creatures that dirty the beauty of creation. While he is shooting, he may not realize the allusion to dying humans, but we do: "Out of the shadowy ragged infinity of the vast barn roof these impudent things dared to thrust their heads, presumed to dirty its starred silence with their filthy timorous life, and he cut them off, tucked them back neatly into the silence" (146-147). Examining the dead bodies before burying them, David sees for the first time the gorgeous designs of color and feathers, the intricate unity of pattern and flesh, the proof of care on the part of the creator. This experience means much more to him than his earlier investigation of his dog's ears, for he associates the animal's odor with holes in the ground and thus death: "And in the smell of the dog's hair David seemed to descend through many finely differentiated layers of earth: mulch, soil, sand, clay, and the glittering mineral base" (142). Beautiful designs on creatures of the air are different.

Still, the ending is ambiguous. David's faith is restored because he is now convinced that the God who "had lavished such craft upon these worthless birds would not destroy His whole Creation by refusing to let David live forever" (150). One may indeed accept his revelation of eternal life. In "Archangel" the angel offers gifts which are "as specific as they are everlasting." The message of the angel is the promise of God's love. Offering no proof of his truth, the angel only urges man to accept. For those who read "Pigeon Feathers" in this light, David is fortunate to take the message in the feathers on faith. How much better a dead pigeon is than Lincoln's goodness when it comes to looking for proof of God's love. At least he may touch the feathers as perhaps God touched the bird. H.G. Wells may not care about Christ, but God cares about David. Additional support for an affirmative reading of the story may be found in Updike's superb essay on Karl Barth, entitled "Faith in Search of Understanding," in which Updike shows his knowledge of theological arguments which explain the non-rational basis of faith.[32] But in spite of this evidence, one should not dismiss the possibility for irony. David makes a leap of faith from pattern in the feathers to design in the universe, but the fact remains that he does not gain his insight until he kills. His act is not a matter of losing one's life to save it but of slaughtering defenseless birds. If David is supposed to learn the lesson that faith thrives on acceptance instead of reason, he may fail when he interprets the pigeon feathers as if they were rational proof. Perhaps his violent road to faith is as absurd as Wells's determined attempt to nullify it. In either case, the paradox of slaughter and salvation lifts this story beyond the simplicity of religious formula.

Later in the collection, in "Packed Dirt, Churchgoing, A Dying Cat, A Traded Car," we learn that David Kern survives the adolescent religious crisis to become the regular adult churchgoer.[33] But in the last section of this four-part story, he confronts another religious dilemma: Are men judged by the soul's convictions or the body's deeds? Is the sensation of lust the same as the sin of adultery? David now suspects that a universe which would permit adultery would also sanction death—his death. Updike shows that contemplation of annihilation is not limited to the naive questioning of adolescents. David Kern has grown up, but he is still afraid: "I seemed already eternally forgotten. The dark vibrating air of my bedroom seemed the dust of my grave; the dust went up and up and I prayed upward into it, prayed, prayed for a sign, any glimmer at all, any microscopic loophole or chink in the chain of evidence, and saw none" (260-261). The minute intricacies of pigeon feathers will not help him this time. Reasoning that the God who permits his fear is unworthy of existence, he totters on the brink of despair. David has lost touch with the packed-dirt paths made by children and suggestive of grace.

Thus he has little to answer his mother with when, visiting her and his hospitalized father, she tells him that Mr. Kern no longer believes. Her telephone call on his birthday turns out to be a summons to death. Unexpectedly, he feels relief at the message, for he still has a childlike confidence in his father as a man who can defeat all adversaries. How, then, can he accept his dad's loss of faith? He learns that the beauty of his father's life is that he gives others faith, not so much in the specifics of religious mystery but in the grace of a job well done. David hurries to help his sick father but leaves buoyed by the old man's humor. His journey back home in an old car about to be traded is a renewal of the soul's voyage. Death and life are one, a truth he learns in England when he helps a dying cat on the night of his child's birth and which is reinforced here when the father falls ill on David's birthday. Mr. Kern may have lost religious faith, but as the doctor points out, the old man's heart is not yet blocked. Thus the strong gain from the weak: "I felt I would ascend straight north from his touch" (277).

More important, he learns a lesson which sustains him as a writer and which in turn supports us. Earlier, he is asked by a hitchhiking sailor to explain the reason for writing. He cannot answer then, but now, following the visit to the ailing father, he can: "We in America need ceremonies, is I suppose, sailor, the point of what I have written" (279). His first crucial ceremony takes place when, as a boy, he handles the dead pigeons. But as an adult, he needs more than one revelation. Grown now from adolescent to author, he uses his art to keep us in touch with our rituals, our memories, ourselves. Writers preserve the ceremonies which sustain humanity. They show how things which have served well in the past are not to be sloughed off in the present as easily as a traded car, "dismissed without a blessing, a kiss, a testament, or any ceremony of farewell" (279). Driving back through the dark, he is consoled as his old car brings him safely home to a vision of permanent stars in the black night of the soul.

The metaphysical considerations of "Pigeon Feathers" give way to the deceptive simplicity of "Home," an exquisite sketch not to be interpreted as much as admired for its mastery of the small detail. Returning home from England with his wife and newly born child, Robert notices that his mother has "the face of a woman whose country has never quite settled what to do with its women" (154). His father, who has lost his teeth to age, stands "perfectly erect, like a child that has just learned to stand" (154-155). Updike *knows* how mothers kiss returning sons on the cheek while father and son shake hands with averted eyes. He may be our master of the fiction of domestic crisis because he knows the way the kitchen looks and what the family says.

Robert's problem resembles that of most of the young men in this collection: What to make of memory and the persistence of the past. It is as though Updike writes these stories in order to answer the problem that Robert poses to himself when he reveals that they will spend a month with his parents in Pennsylvania before he begins teaching college girls in New York: "He had looked forward to this month; it would be the longest he would have been in Pennsylvania with his wife, and he had a memory of something he had wanted to describe, to explain, to her about his home. But exactly what that was, he had forgotten" (157). Robert is David Kern grown up, returning to the same farm where epiphanies are found in dead pigeons and where parents always squabble. Although he has escaped the small town and the outhouse through education, marriage, and travel, the landmarks of the past are still home to him. Flight may have been necessary, but it leaves him "feeling hollow, fragile, transparent." He needs to return to touch base with his heritage much the same way Updike needs to write to prop open the door to memory. Updike knows that the trip home is always engaged with a sense of "guilty urgency" which quietly but painfully exacerbates the prodigal with "disappointment, apology, and lost time." When we learn that Robert, as if still a child, is upset because his aging parents cannot solve the many mysteries of life, we know that his flight from home has not been dramatic or final.

But "Home" is not all nostalgia and loss. Renewal is as important to the process as guilt. The confrontation between the furious, vulgar, squat Pennsylvania Dutchman in the florid Hawaiian shirt and Robert's calm father, standing as tall as Uncle Sam while trying patiently to understand the source of the fury beneath the obscenities, is a master stroke of comedy. The father wins the battle of cross-purposes but only because each misunderstands the other. Laughter is directed not so much at the angry driver as with Robert's bewildered father. "Home" is his story after all. Criticism is mixed with admiration, similar to our feelings about George Caldwell in *The Centaur*, and we sense that Updike sees the father as a kind of flawed saint muddling through one more catastrophe. The father's awkward innocence, so earnest in its expression, refreshes the tired son and reacquaints him with the security of continuity which has been threatened by a foreign country and a new child. As if he were a boy again, looking up to his dad, Robert is excited as the car approaches the familiar folds of land. He is almost home.

Variations on the validity of a sense of shelter and its contrasts with the more impersonal outside world are also important to "A & P" and "Lifeguard." Very little happens in either, but both are about the demands of heroism. William Young refuses to leave the warm shelter of the school, Robert crosses an ocean with a wife and baby before returning home, and Sammy, the hero of "A & P," finally steps outside to the parking lot.

"A & P" is one of Updike's most popular and anthologized tales.[34] Told in the first person from Sammy's point of view, the story calls attention not to the tone of nostalgia but the brashness of his colloquialism. The first sentences suggest his confidence: "In walks these three girls in nothing but bathing suits. I'm in the third checkout slot, with my back to the door, so I don't see them until they're over by the bread. The one that caught my eye first was the one in the plaid green two-piece" (187). Sammy's sympathy with the teeny boppers is established immediately by the contrast between the girls and the typical cash-register watcher, "a witch about fifty with rouge on her cheekbones and no eyebrows" who gives him a hard time for ringing up a box of HiHo crackers twice. Admiring the three girls for daring to enter the grocery store dressed in bathing suits, he especially likes the one who wears her straps down and her head high. He also enjoys the shock on the faces of the housewives in pin curlers who do a double take to corroborate this breach in decorum: "these are usually women with six children and varicose veins mapping their legs…there's people in this town haven't seen the ocean for twenty years" (191).

The sketch turns on the offhand comment that his parents think the outcome sad. We know then that despite the colloquial immediacy of the tale, "A & P" is the record of an incident which Sammy has already lived through but not forgotten. His response to the situation has made an impact upon him which he continues to ponder. When Lengel, the store manager who teaches Sunday school, criticizes the three girls with the comment, "this isn't the beach," Sammy's sense of heroism is aroused. Lengel utters his sarcasm as if the A & P were a great sand dune and he the head lifeguard, but no one is saved. Like a hero in a story by J.D. Salinger performing a quixotic gesture, Sammy accepts the role of the girls' unsuspected hero and announces to Lengel that he quits.

He does not agree with his parents that the outcome is sad. Someone must stand up for embarrassed teen-agers in bathing suits with straps down. But this quixotic gesture does him no good. The girls never hear him declare himself their protector, and they do not wait for him in the parking lot with favors and thanks. Indeed, when he steps outside, he is in the ugly world of harried housewives with varicose veins: "There wasn't anybody but some young married screaming with her children about some candy they didn't get by the door of a powder-blue Falcon station wagon" (196). Sammy does not want to quit his job, but he believes that he must go through with the gesture. His protest throws him out of the artificially ordered world of the A & P, where the third checkout slot looks directly up the row to the meat counter, and into the parking lot where mothers yell at children while pretty girls in bathing suits do not notice small acts of heroism. Worse, they do not care.[35]

Sammy's brash slang covers his sentimental act which neither the teen-agers nor the world accepts. His sacrificial action is incongruous but nevertheless mildly moving. The irony is that the girls never need his help. They stand up well under the Victorianism of Lengel and the stares of the other shoppers. As one of the girls retorts, "We *are* decent." Sammy learns that no one welcomes or even tolerates idle idealism. Rather than insist on a principle, he has merely shown off: "My stomach kind of fell as I felt how hard the world was going to be to me hereafter" (196).

The world is just as hard on the unnamed narrator of "Lifeguard," but he misses both the point and the irony of his position. Once again Updike explores the complexities of mundane heroism in a sketch based on an elaborate analogy between a lifeguard and God. The first-person narrator is a divinity student nine months of the year, but although his occupation is more intellectual than Sammy's job in the A & P, he also finds himself surrounded by teen-aged girls in bathing suits when he assumes his lifeguard duties in the summer. Yet this lifeguard is no Sammy. His tone is different. Confident, haughty, and conscious of the image he projects, he ponders problems while Sammy acts hastily. His first statement throws the reader: "Beyond doubt, I am a splendid fellow" (211). Is he egotistical? Pedantic? Childish? One suspects Updike's irony in the opening sentence, for if the lifeguard is beyond doubt, he has no need of faith. He seems too smug. Perhaps he unwittingly loves himself more than the sun-bathing masses he would comfort. If they do not need him he will praise himself.[36]

The lifeguard's language is a parody of the religious sermon, and his stilted rhetoric stands between himself and those he hopes to convert, including the reader. Calling his elevated guard's station a throne, he explains that he is disguised by the sun in the summer so that he no longer resembles the pale student of divinity who spends most of the year in seminary libraries wrestling with the complexities of Paul Tillich, Karl Barth, and Kierkegaard. Is he God disguised as Christ when he ascends to his summer throne to cast a watchful eye over those who may one day be in danger? He at least thinks so. The teeny boppers say that his tan contrasting with the white pith helmet gives him a "delightfully edible appearance." One hears echoes of "this is my body." His lifeguard's chair is decorated with a red cross, and his daily ascent to the throne reminds him of climbing "into an immense, rigid, loosely fitting vestment." As if anticipating protests against his analogies, he hastens to define the point of his monologue which he calls a sermon: "I rest my eyes on a sheet of brilliant sand printed with the runes of naked human bodies. That there is no discrepancy between my studies, that the texts of the flesh complement those of the mind, is the easy burden of my sermon" (213).

He is indeed hard-pressed to justify his sexual desire, so he cloaks lust in rhetoric. Arguing that discrepancies exist between the ways ancient theologians and modern thinkers discuss God's relationship to the world, he suggests that humanism erodes the demands of divinity. Just as the sea is no longer a metaphor of divine mystery but only a place to play, so God is no longer an awe-inspiring idea but a lifeguard watching, as opposed to watching over, bathing suits and bodies. Humanity parades before his throne. The old, the matronly, the young with toddlers—they all come. But most of all the young women in skimpy bathing suits catch the eye, especially the lifeguard's. Who can miss the irony of a would-be God ogling "the dimpled blonde in the bib and diapers of her Bikini, the lambent fuzz of her midriff shimmering like a cat's belly. Lust stuns me like the sun" (216). Lest any reader accuse him of emulating Elmer Gantry, of confusing godliness and the desires of the flesh, he hastens to explain that lust is related to love and that love is the sister of salvation: "To desire a woman is to desire to save her.... Every seduction is a conversion" (216, 217). He would like to convince us that sexual intercourse which is neither predatory nor hurried unlocks the shadows of the soul, that in sex all lovers approach the immensity of immortality, but we are not so sure. For immediately following his effort to link sex and salvation, he defines his calling to lift the masses into eternal life: "It is not a light task; the throng is so huge, and its members so individually unworthy" (217–218). One hears again his opening statement with the echo that only he is worthy.

Yet one of the delights of "Lifeguard" is the ambiguity. If the story is not ironic, the shepherd correctly seeks his flock at the beach where they congregate instead of in church. They take his presence for granted, yet he is always there. Bidding them to be joyful, he awaits their call for help, "a call, it saddens me to confess, that I have yet to hear" (220). But irony seems to apply. He has not heard their call because they cannot understand his rhetoric. Perhaps it is ironic that he is not in church either, but surely his contorted effort to justify lust in terms of salvation smacks of sophistry. The answer to the question of irony depends upon how the reader reacts to the opening sentence. If the lifeguard is a pompous ass, boasting about his greatness and deluded about his worthiness, then his monologue is suspect, an elaborate analogy by a puffed-up would-be hero. God is absent. But if he utters a truth in the first statement, a truth he must speak himself since no one hurrying to the beach will acknowledge him, then his meditation is a sermon from a mount marked with a red cross and well stocked with suntan lotion. God loves. The former reading seems more acceptable. This divinity student fails to see that intellect and reason, which he has in abundance, do not replace love and faith.

In both "A & P" and "Lifeguard," the first-person narrators are defined largely by their tones and vocabularies. No one else supplies background information or details to round out character. Updike experiments with opposite extremes of voice, for Sammy is casual and colloquial while the lifeguard is pompous and pedantic. Sammy initially seems so confident that he may irritate some readers. Surveying the three girls as they wander the aisles, he assumes that his perspective and judgment are naturally correct. When he describes the girls, we wonder if his lyrical flights of language expose the inadequacy of his slang as he stretches to show why these teen-agers deserve his sacrifice: Breasts, for example, become two smooth scoops of vanilla. We can see him longing to ring up the purchase of *that* ice cream. Yet the end of the story suggests that all is not self-righteousness and slang. Sammy has sympathy and a sense of outrage. However ironic, his sacrificial gesture is as refreshing as his colloquial candor. We finish the story sensing that he is more than just another A & P employee with an eye for cute behinds. An observer of his social world, he resolves not just to record but also to act upon his impressions.

The lifeguard's language is just the opposite. A student of theology and thus a reader of abstract ideas expressed in abstruse prose, his tone is stilted and his vocabulary formal. Many readers are so taken aback by the opening sentence that they can only assume the lifeguard's monologue echoes the academic jargon he has heard in the classroom and read in the library. At least Sammy's two scoops of vanilla are real. Perhaps the lifeguard's words parody the theologians' by showing how meaningless intellectualisms can be disguised in important sounding language. Reading on, however, we suspect a contrast developing between the erosion of theological speculations once designed to define the relationship of God and man, and the lifeguard's need to reconcile religious convictions and the demands of the flesh. He speaks largely in abstractions, the way he has been trained to think, but he hopes that his concern for religious speculations will not nullify the goal for which they are conceived in the first place. Language may belie his conviction, but it also unfortunately hampers his communication.

Jack faces a similar problem in the exquisite five-page sketch "The Crow in the Woods." One of the most moving pieces in *Pigeon Feathers*, this story joins "Walter Briggs" and "Should Wizard Hit Mommy?" as the three Jack and Clare tales. The domestic tension forecast for this marriage in "Walter Briggs" is not yet an open sore, but Jack's sense of intimacy with his family and nature at the end of "The Crow in the Woods" does not ward off the possibility of alienation. We linger in Updike's luxurious gift for natural description and domestic detail when we follow Jack through the early dawn with a slight hangover and a child who needs attention. Note the sense of security and magic as Jack awakens to a world suddenly white: "All the warm night the secret snow fell so adhesively that every twig in the woods about their little rented house supported a tall slice of white, an upward projection which in the shadowless glow of early morning lifted depth from the scene, made it seem Chinese, calligraphic, a stiff tapestry hung from the gray sky, a shield of lace interwoven with black thread" (221). Nearly stunned by the beauty, Jack is ready for a vision despite the demands of his child and the desire for sleep.

Against the wondrous backdrop of nature's surprise, Jack tries to do a favor for Clare. She may sleep while he cares for the baby. There is no crisis in this sketch, only gently comic snapshots of Jack's domestic inadequacy and the poignancy of resolution when his vision of universal love finds a mundane balance in Clare's declaration of pragmatic routine. Leaving her in bed, he manages to change the baby's diaper. But he cannot find the cereal. He cannot fit the tray to the high chair. He cannot place the little girl's legs in the chair. Inadequate to the tasks but proud that he has tried, and relieved when Clare, unable to sleep and thus unable to accept his gesture, appears in the kitchen, he watches her deliver without effort warm baby cereal and orange juice. To his eyes already full with the beautiful snow, Clare is magical like the earth which has blessed them with last night's unexpected gift. It is as if heaven has visited them with grace in the guise of snow: "Like her sister the earth, the woman puts forth easy flowers of abundance" (225). Surrounded by a white world, they seem insulated in a world of love.

No longer in charge of necessary domestic duties which he is unequipped to perform, Jack turns to the window and looks at the snow-covered earth. For him the hour, the morning, the world are magic. Yet the apparently inviolable surface of whiteness is shattered when a huge crow dives to land on a high branch, its black bulk destroying the lacy patterns like flak. To Jack's surprise, the crow settles down as if uniting with the white world. Harmony is inexplicably restored in the mystical balance of extremes suggested by white and black, ephemeral vision and domestic routine. Stunned again, Jack calls to Clare to look: "The woman's pragmatic blue eyes flicked from his face to the window where she saw only snow and rested on the forgotten food steaming between his hands. Her lips moved: 'Eat your egg'" (226). Thus are we called back to the things of this world.[37]

Meditations like "The Crow in the Woods" illustrate the advance that Updike has made in *Pigeon Feathers* over *The Same Door*. The tone is surer, the pursuit of the past more fervent, and the prose more lyrical, all signs of Updike at his best. Richard H. Rupp, no fan of Updike's work, says that in *Pigeon Feathers* Updike cannot "close the gap between style and emotion, between the outside and the inside."[38] But it seems to me that Updike is a master at revealing the possibilities for ever-expanding mystery in the homeliness of the ordinary detail. "The Crow in the Woods" does indeed illustrate the unity of the "outside and inside," literally in terms of outdoors and indoors, artistically in terms of style and emotion, and thematically in terms of reality and vision. Those who believe otherwise might read "The Blessed Man of Boston, My Grandmother's Thimble, and Fanning Island" in which Updike mentions the importance of details to the author who hopes to celebrate the mystery in the mundane: "But we would–be novelists have a reach as shallow as our skins. We walk through volumes of the unexpressed and like snails leave behind a faint thread excreted out of ourselves. From the dew of the few flakes that melt on our faces we cannot reconstruct the snowstorm" (228-229).

The narrator decides that he will never write a novel about the blessed man of Boston because while he can fix the exact detail, he cannot fathom the man's life. Yet Updike does admirably well turning out dozens of short stories, many of which pivot on his genius for catching precisely the minute detail which mirrors a snowstorm or a lifetime: "Details are the giant's fingers" (245). Much of the business of *Pigeon Feathers* is with memory and the necessity of scraping the skin to crawl through the always narrowing door of time. The little moments of the past matter. Often no larger than a grandmother's thimble, the apparently insignificant details of the past loom large in the present when they fill in a bit of the mystery about where we have been and who we are. The writer's duty—and privilege—is to honor the delicate task of transporting these details and moments to the page for all who will accept the gift. Art redeems. Thus the writer's request: "O Lord, bless these poor paragraphs, that would do in their vile ignorance Your work of resurrection" (229). Updike knows what Jack learns in "The Crow in the Woods": "that we have no gestures adequate to answer the imperious gestures of nature" (232). But the man of imagination tries. *Pigeon Feathers* is Updike's homage to the relentlessly closing door of memory and the mysterious detail of now. Then other memories come, tap his elbow, and lead him away.

Notes to *Pigeon Feathers*

1. Charles Thomas Samuels, "John Updike: The Art of Fiction XLIII," *Paris Review*, 12(Winter 1968), 93.
2. Frank Gado, "Interview with John Updike," *First Person: Conversations on Writers and Writing* (Schenectady: Union College Press, 1973), p. 92.
3. Jane Howard, "Can a Nice Novelist Finish First?," *Life*, 4 November 1966, p. 74 D.
4. Howard, p. 82.
5. Lewis Nichols, "Talk with John Updike," New York *Times Book Review*, 7 April 1968, p. 34.
6. Eric Rhode, "Grabbing Dilemmas," *Vogue*, 1 February 1971, p. 185.
7. R.B. Larson, "John Updike: The Story as Lyrical Meditation," *Thoth*, 13(Winter 1972–73), 33.
8. Granville Hicks, "Mysteries of the Commonplace," *Saturday Review*, 17 March 1962, p. 21.
9. Arthur Mizener, "Behind the Dazzle Is a Knowing Eye," New York *Times Book Review*, 18 March 1962, pp. 1, 29.
10. Mizener would agree with Alice and Kenneth Hamilton that in *Pigeon Feathers* Updike writes with a surer touch than in *The Same Door*, with less cleverness and more perception, and with the ability to show how the mysteries of sex, art, and religion are inseparable from the ambiguities of the commonplace. *See* Alice and Kenneth Hamilton, *John Updike: A Critical Essay* (Grand Rapids: William B. Eerdmans, 1967), p. 27. *See also* J. Mitchell Morse, "Fiction Chronicle," *Hudson Review*, 15(Summer 1962), 303, who writes that *Pigeon Feathers* is one book he can recommend; and Donald Emerson, "Three Perceptions," *The Progressive*, 26(Au-

gust 1962), 35, who praises Updike's ability to uncover portentous reality in ordinary incidents.

11. Stanley Edgar Hyman, "The Artist as a Young Man," *New Leader*, 19 March 1962, p. 23.

12. J. M. Edelstein, "The Security of Memory," *New Republic*, 14 May 1962, p. 30.

13. Stanley J. Rowland, Jr., "The Limits of Littleness," *Christian Century*, 4 July 1962, p. 840.

14. The anonymous reviewer for *Time* concurs with Rowland. Disagreeing with Hyman and calling "A & P" the best story in the book, the reviewer argues that Updike is not interested in exploring "time and soul, but merely in finding some minimal core to be crusted with his magnificent words." *See* "Put and Take." *Time*, 16 March 1962, p. 86.

15. Alfred Chester, "Twitches and Embarrassments," *Commentary*, 34(July 1962), 77.

16. Thomas Molyneux, "The Affirming Balance of Voice," *Shenandoah*, 25 (Winter 1974), 40–41.

17. Reactions to *Pigeon Feathers* in British Journals reflect these general opinions but from different perspectives. Richard G. Stern complains about Updike's fondness for detail not because it shows a lack of vision or is merely luxuriating in catalogues of objects but because, understandably, the things named mean little to British readers. [Later generations of American readers may have the same problem as the nuances of the time lose currency.] Similarly, Christopher Ricks suggests that while the collection is "stylistically magnetic," the stories dealing with England are weak. Ricks also joins Chester and Molyneux in criticizing Updike's penchant for the quotable ending as a "recurring and brief embarrassment." Barry Pree says that *Pigeon Feathers* shows Updike to be one of the best writers of the day who, even failing, exhibits a superior talent. Malcolm Bradbury praises his ability to find security in the precise understanding of a moment. Finally, the anonymous reviewer for the *Times Literary Supplement* says that *Pigeon Feathers* shows Updike handling bigger subjects with a surer touch. *See* Richard G. Stern, "The Myth of Action," *The Spectator*, 27 September 1963, p. 389; Christopher Ricks, "Tennysonian," *New Statesman*, 8 February 1963, p. 208; Barry Pree, "Special Notices," *London Magazine*, 3(April 1963), 88; Malcolm Bradbury, "New Fiction," *Punch*, 13 February 1963, p. 247; "Bigger and Better," London *Times Literary Supplement*, 1 February 1963, p. 73.

18. John Updike, *Pigeon Feathers and Other Stories* (New York: Knopf, 1962), p. 170. All further references will be noted in the text.

19. The stories in *Pigeon Feathers* are arranged in the order in which they were written.

20. Robert Detweiller, *John Updike* (New York: Twayne, 1972), p. 71.

21. John Updike, *Picked-Up Pieces* (New York: Knopf, 1975), pp. 497–498, 519.

22. Charles Thomas Samuels, "John Updike," in *American Writers: A Collection of Literary Biographies*, ed. Leonard Ungar (New York: Scribner's, 1974), p. 222. *See also* Robert W. Cochran, "The Narrator Then and Now in Updike's 'Flight,'" *Rendezvous*, 10(Fall 1975), pp. 29–32.

23. *Modern Short Stories: The Uses of Imagination*, Revised Edition, ed. Arthur Mizener (New York: Norton, 1967), p. 428.

24. R. W. Reising, "Updike's 'A Sense of Shelter,'" *Studies in Short Fiction*, 7(Fall 1970), 652.

25. A.S.G. Edwards, "Updike's 'A Sense of Shelter,'" *Studies in Short Fiction*, 8(Summer 1971), 468.

26. *The Sense of Fiction* , eds. Robert L. Welker and Herschel Gower (Englewood Cliffs, New Jersey: Prentice-Hall, 1966), p. 46. *See also* Thomas Molyneux, "The Affirming Balance of Voice," for a negative evaluation of "A Sense of Shelter" in terms of what Molyneux calls its "precious" language and undramatic ending.

27. Richard H. Rupp, "John Updike: Style in Search of a Center," *Sewanee Review*, 75(October–December 1967), 698.

28. Updike includes an essay on the religious aura associated with pigeons in *Assorted Prose* (New York: Knopf, 1965), especially p. 54.

29. Not everyone agrees. Robert Detweiller says the story "exemplifies Updike at his best"; *see John Updike* (New York: Twayne, 1972), p. 163. Robert Alton Regan examines "Pigeon Feathers" "from a neo-Kantian point of view"; *see* "Updike's Symbol of the Center," *Modern Fiction Studies*, 20(Spring 1974), 77–96.

30. But *see* "The Blessed Man of Boston, My Grandmother's Thimble, and Fanning Island" for a sympathetic portrait of the grandmother.

31. For an excellent analysis of the impact of Martin Luther's history on "Pigeon Feathers," *see* William H. Shurr, "The Lutheran Experience in John Updike's 'Pigeon Feathers,'" *Studies in Short Fiction*, 14(Fall 1977), 329–335.

32. This essay was first published in the *New Yorker*, 12 October 1963, and then collected in *Assorted Prose*.

33. David shows up again in "The Christian Roommates" and perhaps in "The Dark"; *see The Music School* (New York: Knopf, 1966). For a perceptive reading of "Packed Dirt...," *see* Michael Novak, "Updike's Quest for Liturgy," *Commonweal*, 10 May 1963, pp. 192-195. Novak calls the story "one of the most perfectly worked pieces of prose in the English language, perhaps even overworked, too elaborate."

34. But *see* William Peden, *The American Short Story* (Boston: Houghton Mifflin, 1964), p. 70. Peden dismisses the story as "deftly narrated nonsense... which concerns nothing more significant than a checking clerk's

interest in three girls in bathing suits."

35. For a discussion of Sammy's act in light of Emersonian non-conformity, *see* M. Gilbert Porter, "John Updike's 'A & P': The Establishment and an Emersonian Cashier," *English Journal*, 61(November 1972), 1155-1158.

36. Alice and Kenneth Hamilton try too hard, it seems to me, to fit the tale to conventional Protestant theology. *See The Elements of John Updike* (Grand Rapids: William B. Eerdmans, 1971), p. 89.

37. For a discussion of Updike's views on love as explained by Denis de Rougemont, *see* his essay in *Assorted Prose*, 283-300.

38. Richard H. Rupp, "John Updike: Style in Search of a Center," 698.

Olinger Stories:
A Selection

"The hero is always returning, from
hundreds of miles finally."

—Foreword to *Olinger Stories*

Following the appearance of *The Same Door* and *Pigeon Feathers*,
Updike selected three stories from the former, seven from the latter,
added a previously uncollected tale, and published the collection as
Olinger Stories: A Selection (1964). Thus ten of the eleven stories
had been published twice, once in the *New Yorker* and once in a
volume. Only "In Football Season," the last sketch in *Olinger Stories*,
had not yet been collected in book form. Although the tales may
have been familiar territory to critics of his first two books of short
fiction, many readers responded favorably because he had finally
acknowledged formally what had always been implied: That in creating his male narrators and giving them various names, he was nevertheless writing about the same person in the same town.

In both *The Same Door* and *Pigeon Feathers*, Updike had arranged
the stories not chronologically but in the order in which they were
written. In addition, of course, not all of the tales in these two earlier
volumes had focused on the local boy growing up in Olinger, Pennsylvania. He made no effort, in other words, to define a small town
world which he returns to again and again in order to depict various
stories from various perspectives. Yet the sense of that special milieu
was always present to readers who followed all of his fiction to the
publication of *Olinger Stories*. Even when scattered in several jour-

nals and volumes and narrated by a male with different names, the short fictions had too many references to Olinger, too many allusions to the mother's farm and the father's teaching to be ignored. Most of all, there were many stories about what seemed to be the same boy's bafflement when faced with the demands of family, school, and the awkwardness of aging.

With *Olinger Stories*, Updike consciously acknowledges the existence of this special world. The eleven stories are arranged chronologically according to the narrator's age. In the first, "You'll Never Know, Dear, How Much I Love You," ten-year old Ben offers his fifty cents to the world's crassness at the carnival. In the middle tale, "A Sense of Shelter," seventeen-year old William finally confesses his love to a girl he has had a crush on since the second grade. In the final story, "In Football Season," the nameless man recalls his high-school days. In addition to the conscious arrangement, Updike supplies a foreword in which he admits the special unity and urges the reader not to confuse Olinger with his own home town of Shillington: "He wears different names and his circumstances vary, but he is at bottom the same boy, a local boy .... The name [Olinger] is audibly a shadow of 'Shillington,' the real name of my home town, yet the two towns, however similar, are not at all the same. Shillington is a place on the map and belongs to the world; Olinger is a state of mind, of my mind, and belongs entirely to me."[1] These stories are not autobiography but fiction. Indeed, Updike says that in writing the Olinger stories he has made his own autobiography impossible.[2] Some readers believe that he is too close to his material, that, as Nadine Overall writes, he "is still tied to his ego-strings" in *Olinger Stories*.[3]

The idea of a special collection of previously published tales consciously arranged to suggest chronology and order did not at first appeal to Updike. To begin, he reveals, *The Same Door* and *Pigeon Feathers* were still in print. An anthology derived from them seemed "fussy." More important, he knew that the chronological order designed to emphasize consistency of tone and material would also expose inconsistencies of detail. In addition he argues that "not all of the stories whose spiritual center is Olinger take place there" (vi).

Serious objections notwithstanding, Updike agreed to the collection. His doubts "succumbed to the hope that a concentration of certain images might generate new light, or at least focus more sharply the light already there" (vi). His assumption seems justified, for reading these stories in the chronological order of the narrator's age encourages not only a different perspective but also a deepening sympathy. This boy could be any one of us. Many readers have been there. Yet a more significant motive prompted Updike to publish the selection. Suggesting that he collects these stories as one who binds a packet of love letters just returned, he tries to say farewell to one part of a fictional world which will continue to have special meaning but which is now behind him. "Olinger has receded from me. Composition, in crystallizing memory, displaces it, and the town and the time it localizes have been consumed by the stories bound here" (vi). His point is well taken, for in the last story Olinger is described as "like a town in a fable." The processes of memory which often determine the tone and theme of the short stories seem concluded. Yet not quite, for Updike returns to that packet of love letters in the novel *Of the Farm* (1965) and in the poems of *Midpoint* (1969) and *Tossing and Turning* (1977) in order to explore this familiar territory from the perspective of middle age. Although imaginary New England towns like Tarbox primarily dot the map of Updike's fiction after 1965, Olinger seems more and more precious as the special province of innocence and grace because the specter of mortality now beckons the middle-aged man.

"In Football Season" is the one story in this book not previously collected and thus deserves mention here. Not everyone likes it. Charles Thomas Samuels, for example, calls it a "valentine," a piece so slight that Updike must force the significance with a "terminal infusion of spiritual dread."[4] Stanley Kauffmann charges that the second sentence "runs away from him."[5] Yet tone is the key. Wistfulness and memory hang heavy, as anyone knows who returns years later to a football game in a town or at a school where he once belonged and was welcomed. As Updike says in the foreword: "Olinger is haunted—hexed, perhaps—by rural memories, accents, and superstitions.... It is beyond the western edge of Megalopolis, and hangs between its shallow hills enchanted, nowhere, anywhere; there is no place like it. Its children, however dispersed by military service and education, almost all return. I have returned often, though seldom bodily..." (vii). In "In Football Season," he returns once more, a mature man engaged with the ghosts of his past.

This tale, more a meditation than a conventional story, is a perfect climax to the Olinger cycle. The first sentence invites the reader to join the narrator and take his own plunge into the past. The invitation is as personal as the narrator's tone: "Do you remember a fragrance girls acquire in autumn?" (186). Refreshing our memories as well as his, urging us to relive that magical time when as highschool students we all attended the Friday night football games and experienced the excitement of adolescent love and athletic tension, Updike completes the invitation with a description of that special fragrance: "This fragrance, so faint and flirtatious on those afternoon walks through the dry leaves, would be banked a thousand-fold and lie heavy as the perfume of a flower shop on the dark slope of the stadium" (186). The reader knows that he has been there, and he knows that John Updike has too.

Updike recalls a time of petty jealousies, group cheers, no driver's license, and the awkward grace of adolescent immaturity. Although the point of view of this story is that of a grown man, the narrator reenters the world of Friday nights to provide the double perspective of maturity and youth. He does not condescend. He remembers. Updike's ability to evoke the details of the past as if they were just experienced, and yet convey the loss of those moments to time, accounts for the gentleness, the nostalgia, the sheer joy of memory which make many of his stories special. Updike possesses what Willa Cather called "the precious, the incommunicable past."

Yet "In Football Season" is not about fragrance and football but about transition and time. The narrator's comments on time keep the reader in touch with the mature point of view of the tale. For this is not a story of adolescence, after all. It is, rather, an acknowledgment of the difference between the years of childhood when time can be abused with a "luxurious sense of waste" and those later years when time is a black hole infinite and immortal:

For as children we had lived in a tight world of ticking clocks and punctual bells, where every minute was an admonition to thrift and where tardiness, to a child running late down a street with his panicked stomach burning, seemed the most mysterious and awful of sins. Now, turning the corner into adulthood, we found time to be instead a black immensity endlessly supplied, like the wind. (190)

The more time forces us to grow away from adolescent female fragrance and Friday night football, the more, the narrator reminds us, we all sink into time's chasm. Introducing an awareness of death to the Olinger cycle, Updike alters the perspective by which both he and the reader view the tales.

Now no longer of the age when he is permitted to linger at the edge of the black immensity, the narrator comes face to face with his mortality. He may return to Olinger all he wants. He may peer through the same door and down the long corridor. He may even attend a Friday night game. But he will never again be admitted to that special fragrance of the past: "Now I peek into windows and open doors and do not find that air of permission. It has fled the world. Girls walk by me carrying their invisible bouquets from fields still steeped in grace, and I look up in the manner of one who follows with his eyes the passage of a hearse, and remembers what pierces him" (191). All he can do is remember, be grateful, and regret.

Notes to *Olinger Stories*

1. John Updike, *Olinger Stories: A Selection* (New York: Vintage, 1964), v. Further references will be to this edition.
2. But *see* the "First Person Singular" section of *Assorted Prose* (New York: Knopf, 1965) for autobiographical essays.
3. Nadine W. Overall, review of *Olinger Stories, Studies in Short Fiction*, 4 (Winter 1967), 197.
4. Charles Thomas Samuels, "John Updike," in *American Writers: A Collection of Literary Biographies*, ed. Leonard Ungar (New York: Scribner's, 1974), 219.
5. Stanley Kauffmann, "Onward with Updike," *New Republic*, 14 September 1966, p. 15.

The Music School

"We are all pilgrims, faltering
toward divorce."

—"The Music School"

The Music School (1966) is Updike's most impressive volume of short stories. As readers of Updike and probably Updike himself now expect, critical opinion of this book is widely divided. *The Music School* marks a transition in his canon, for it looks back toward the first tales of adolescence and nostalgia before confronting the more contemporary world of maturity and loss.

For this collection, Updike chooses as an epigraph the nine-line second stanza from Wallace Stevens' poem "To the One of Fictive Music." The poem invokes and celebrates the artistic muse, and it concludes with a plea that man be reunited with the imagination as the only way of knowing reality. In the second stanza, Stevens observes how man's birth paradoxically separates him from nature yet leaves him in it. Thus the muse must find expression through humanity, for only in art, created by man, may mankind and nature be reunited. The fertile imagination, always adhering to reality, is the key to all meaningful expression.

In *The Music School*, Updike begins his celebration of the imagination with a reprise. "In Football Season" is the first story, a meditation that had previously been published only in *Olinger Stories*. Placing it first, he pays homage to the inspiration of his earlier collections, Olinger/Shillington, before turning to acknowledge the new source of imagination, Tarbox/Ipswich. Although the stories are arranged in the order in which they were written, there is a progression from the initial to the last tale which suggests a changed emphasis away from reminiscence toward irony. Lyricism still operates, and nostalgia is not entirely forsaken, but Updike's concerns in *The Music School* are those of middle age and marriage rather than adolescence and youth. "In Football Season" is his bow to the rural world of relative innocence before focusing on the suburban experience of increasing defeat. The opening address to the reader, "Do you remember a fragrance girls acquire in autumn?", leads to a fond memory of a peaceful time which in turn gives way to the despair of the final story in the collection, "The Hermit."[1] The rural world is the setting in both tales, but the distinction in tone between the mood of love in the one and the detail of defeat in the other is startling enough to suggest the difference between *The Music School* and the earlier collections. Taking a cue from the last paragraph of "In Football Season" which emphasizes a movement from the innocent waywardness of youth to the inevitable loss of grace, the rest of the stories illustrate the toll time takes through the relentless encroachment of mortality.

Updike is aware of the transition. The difference between Olinger and Tarbox is not a variation on a map but a distinction between youth and adulthood. He explains: "The trauma or message that I acquired in Olinger had to do with suppressed pain, with the amount of sacrifice I suppose that middle-class life demands, and by that I guess I mean civilized life... these stories... they are dear to me and if I had to give anybody one book of me it would be the Vintage *Olinger Stories*."[2] This is not to say that he will never again write about his boyhood but only to suggest that many of the stories published after *Olinger Stories* are about marriage and divorce. Adultery is now much more an achieved fact than an anticipated pleasure. Norman Cousins even paraphrases Updike explaining to a group of Russian authors that the novel cannot exist without adultery.[3] The point is not that infidelity is conspicuous in the stories of *The Music School* and after but that at middle age Updike alters his perspective while continuing to look at middle-class America with the insight and freshness we have come to expect. Common details are still worthy of praise, and Updike is still grateful.

Most critics notice the change but are divided about its value. The disagreement about his stories is astonishing. Those who praise *The Music School* are enthusiastic indeed. J. Mitchell Morse, for example, says that Updike writes some of the best stories "of our time" by showing an artistry and "compass of vision" that will make him a major writer.[4] Josephine Jacobson praises his "poet's practice of capturing an essence, and then allowing it to infuse the total tone."[5] The brilliant metaphors may occasionally overshadow the development of the tale, but at his best Updike shows how the bleak sense of defeat may be tempered by the slightest promise of hope. Unexpected epiphanies reveal character, and loss of faith not only in religion but also in the stability of the middle ground illustrates an emptiness which Updike insists must be met. Aware that the stories in *The Music School* may not appeal to readers who look for the obvious drama of development and climax, Peter Meinke observes, "Critics keep telling him to cut loose, but—should a surgeon take off his gloves?"[6] Finally, Charles Thomas Samuels' essay is the most appreciative of all. Calling *The Music School* Updike's most polished volume, Samuels admits that the *New Yorker* formula makes the author impose structural neatness on materials which might seem more authentic if given free rein, but he recognizes that Updike usually "infuses his story with meaning not by commenting on the action but by always finding the right gesture or word for his people so that their significance is the satisfying accumulation of all they have said or done."[7] Updike's celebrated genius with language, a gift which disturbs some readers who believe it overshadows the fictional situation, is not a sign of technique trying to do the work of theme but proof of his commitment to the seriousness of his art. Reverence for language and homage to the ordinary moments of the day show that he cares. To try to separate language from subject matter in order to praise the art while lamenting the topic it brings to life is to deny this commitment.

Yet some reviewers do just that. A sense of impatience is apparent in many of the more important commentaries on *The Music School*. If the graceful use of language is one of Updike's major contributions to fiction, what happens to his art when he seems to lose control of it? Those who worry about his "growth" or "development" are not the perennial disparagers who review his books for *Commentary* but readers who generally wish him well. Granville Hicks is one. Although he appreciates Updike's fiction, as shown in his review of *Pigeon Feathers* and in his comments about "The Christian Roommates" and "Harv Is Plowing Now" from *The Music School*, his essay on this collection amounts to cautious praise. He does not want to criticize Updike's fiction because he thinks too highly of the successes, but he would be more comfortable if Updike wrote something challenging enough to lift him above the general level of contemporary writing: "None of the stories in *The Music School* is a bold step forward, but most of them measure up to Updike's standard, which is not low."[8] Yet this comment amounts to a step backward, for Hicks had seen in *Pigeon Feathers* potential for a breakthrough in short fiction.[9]

The recurring lament in most of the analyses of *The Music School* is that Updike does not challenge the reader, does not ask him to risk being disturbed or exhilarated as much as he delights him with the triumph of delicate prose. Only Robie Macauley apparently dismisses the collection on these grounds, arguing that the too fancy writing circles too long around the too familiar themes.[10] In the best review of *The Music School*, Stanley Kauffmann criticizes those who try to separate technique from content. His essay is another left-handed compliment, for while he defends the collection, he wishes that Updike would grow beyond the art of the miniaturist. The point, says Kauffmann, is not the prose which is occasionally flawed or the content which is occasionally challenging, but that Updike seems reluctant to choose material that might threaten the perfect shape of the technique: "He wants to understand, but we are rarely convinced that he wants to understand everything."[11] Kauffmann admits that negative evaluations of an author as prolific as Updike may be unfair because one will finally have to wait until the canon is nearly completed before judging the quality of the career.

Surely it is useless to ask an author as gifted as Updike to do more without first thoroughly discussing what he is doing now. Like most collections of short stories, *The Music School* has weak spots. "The Indian" and "Four Sides of One Story" are not among his best, but "The Music School" and "Harv Is Plowing Now" are. Read in the context of his achievement thus far, the volume is his most satisfying collection, for it joins the pursuit of memory of a lost past to the recognition of disturbances in a fleeting present. The commonplace event remains a catalyst for insight, and the tiny cracks in the surface still reveal a potential for serious loss, but the gradual change of emphasis from Olinger to Tarbox illustrates the broadening of vision that Updike's uneasy admirers fervently want him to have.[12]

The technique has also changed. He continues to engage the reader's sense impressions through the evocation of detail, but he often steps outside the boundaries of the traditional short story with its developing character and dramatic rise and fall of action to create meditations which linger over rather than activate a scene or person. This change is first apparent in sketches such as "Wife-wooing" and "Lifeguard" in *Pigeon Feathers*, but in *The Music School* he is even more insistent in his move from the dramatics of conventional story-telling toward the meditations of imagination. A shift of emphasis accompanies the wider scope and altered technique. A small crisis in a little life still results in a recovered or missed moment, but the resolution is not always affirmative. Many of the characters in *The Music School* strive not to restore the past but to live with a loss. Tenaciousness is hope in these stories. The alterations are understandable, of course, for at the time Updike wrote the collection he was as much involved in approaching the new demands of middle age as he was concerned with youth and the beginning of married life in *Pigeon Feathers*.

The opening sentence of "The Indian," the second story in the volume, specifies the change in location from the Olinger of "In Football Season" to the Tarbox of many of these tales. Updike is now in New England, so he begins with a historical sketch of Tarbox and its founding. In the 1960s, the present moment of this story, Tarbox survives but nevertheless has failed to fulfill the promise which the first settlers from Boston thought it had in 1634. If its street front of shopwindows is not as desolate as those in some of the larger mill towns to the north and west, its rivermouth and bay have never developed into a port once expected to rival Boston. This failure is a kind of blessing, for if twentieth-century prosperity never quite finds Tarbox, neither do the crises of superhighways and overpopulation. Many of the unheated houses date back to the seventeenth century, and the Indian still sits in the window of the newsstand and by the wall of the drugstore. The villagers do not approve of him, and he himself prefers to be known as a typical run-down Yankee. He may not be as noble as his ancestors, but he is their link to the past and one source of their common imagination: "the imagination, surprised by his silhouette as he sits on the hydrant gazing across at the changing face of the liquor store, effortlessly plants a feather at the back of his head" (15). To guess his age is to place him between forty and sixty, but old Miss Horne recalls that the Indian was that old when she was a tiny girl in gingham. Like Tarbox and its salt marshes, like the nation itself, he degenerates but survives.

In a special editon of *The Blue Cloud Quarterly* (Volume 17, No. 1), Updike published both "The Indian" and a commentary in which he says that Tarbox is "the arena of the Decline of the West." Among other things, the Indian suggests America's original man waiting in the shabby downtown areas for the current world to collapse and thereby "restore to him—primitive man—his primal inheritance." *The Music School* does not focus primarily upon one location as *Pigeon Feathers* and *Olinger Stories* do, but "The Indian" is an entry into Updike's new milieu and beyond. The tale is more a sketch than a story, a historical essay which establishes the background of the Tarbox fictions much as "In Football Season" illustrates the tone of the Olinger tales. "Giving Blood" is the first of what will turn out to be eleven accounts of marriage and the constant threat of divorce in *The Music School*.

First introduced in "Snowing in Greenwich Village" in *The Same Door*, the Maples now fulfill their penchant for domestic trouble originally suspected when Richard walks their tempting neighbor home. His attraction to Rebecca in "Snowing in Greenwich Village" turns into doing the Twist or, as he tells Joan, gliding chastely to "Hits of the Forties" all evening with equally tempting Marlene Brossman. Richard's immaturity and inability to know himself have grown to crisis proportions. The responsibility which, Updike suggests, marriage requires seems too demanding for him. The images are appropriate: Richard giggles a lot and thinks of Joan and himself as Hansel and Gretel; Joan thinks of childhood diseases and doll pillows. Unlike the characters in *Pigeon Feathers*, the Maples are not involved with the demands of memory and the pressures of the past. When they recall yesterday, they hope not to scrape the skin on the narrow door of memory but to see their failing marriage from the perspective of relative innocence. This glimpse of the past is not nostalgia but a different angle of vision which helps them judge their present crisis.

Unlike Clyde Behn ("The Persistence of Desire"), the Maples are very much up-to-date, taking full advantage of the cosmopolitan opportunities in the 1960s, exacerbating their differences as they drive to Boston to give blood for "a sort of cousin." In need of their own kind of transfusion, the Maples are especially adept at reopening old wounds.[13] Richard particularly resents the obligation of marriage. More immature than Joan, he longs for his younger days when he is "king of his own corner" working with teletype machines.

Now married nearly ten years, he no longer feels royal, and thus he illustrates what might have happened to William Young of "A Sense of Shelter" who rejects a chance to mature in order to remain king of a secret world in high school. Note Richard's accusation once Joan puts him on the defensive by seeing through his pose: "It's your smugness that is really intolerable. Your stupidity I don't mind. Your sexlessness I've learned to live with. But that wonderfully smug, New England—I suppose we needed it to get the country founded, but in the Age of Anxiety it really does gall" (20). No tone of nostalgia here—he seems out for blood. Nine years have worn this marriage.

The key to Joan's reaction to this kind of harangue is a porcelain expression "even to the eyelashes." Seeing it, Richard knows that he is in the wrong and perhaps has been for several years. The scene in what he calls the blood room is well done, as Updike captures Richard's uneasy attempts at comedy which reveal his nervousness at donating blood as much as his uncertainty over this latest flare-up of marital tension. The simple irony is that while they give blood to save a barely known distant relative, their marriage is bleeding to death from years of verbal lacerations. He, especially, is reluctant to give, to part with some of his life sustenance in order to shore up the lives of others. The point is clear. Richard Maple resembles a smaller version of the King of Arabia who enters the hospital with four wives and eye trouble. With only one wife to care for, Richard is just as blind. The suggestion of sacrifice is also ironic, for each has tried to sacrifice the spouse to his own need: "the mystical union of the couple sacrificially bedded together."

Yet for a few moments all seems well. Stretched out at right angles on separate beds, Richard watches his blood mingle with Joan's. He imagines that this physical merger signifies some kind of renewed spiritual unity as the act of love consummates and consecrates the sacrament of marriage: "His blood and Joan's merged on the floor, and together their spirits glided from crack to crack, from star to star on the ceiling" (27). Thus "chastely conjoined," he declares his love to Joan as they leave the hospital.

Here Updike writes the pivotal sentence in the story and perhaps in the entire collection: "Romance is, simply, the strange, the untried" (31). Mystery, the sense of unfulfilled pursuit, is essential. Love has a kind of purity about it which is soiled by human activity and the progress of time. Although Updike is not at all Victorian about sex, he does suggest that ideal love totters if fulfilled.[14] In the case of the Maples, the illusion of starting over is encouraged by the unexpected opportunity to drive along together in midday without the children and with time to stop for pancakes and coffee. Richard senses this strangeness and responds to it when he asks Joan to lunch as if he were inviting his secretary for a date. To his delight, she reciprocates: "I do feel sort of illicit." They shyly enjoy each other's company, but the bloodletting has been too grievous. The love does not grow. The wounds have not healed. When the conversation returns to the Twist and the accusation of Joan's sexlessness, Richard tries to regain the momentum that the unexpected lunch date has supplied. He assumes the comic role of the dumb suitor and offers to pay the check. The illusion cannot hold—he has only one dollar in his wallet, perhaps an indication of the value their marriage now has. Note the change in Joan's face as her expression again becomes blank: "Her hands dropped to the pocketbook beside her on the seat, but her gaze stayed with him, her face having retreated, or advanced, into that porcelain shell of uncanny composure. 'We'll both pay,' Joan said" (34).

Needless to say, they will both pay in blood. Their romance is no longer strange, and their efforts to gain a new perspective on a deteriorating situation by assuming the guise of past innocence result only in judgment and implied accusation. Updike does not try to imbue their moment of reckoning with tragedy, but he does suggest a link among domestic crisis, declining culture, and loss of religious faith. The word "king" is mentioned several times in "Giving Blood," and in the context of the story it recalls the Elizabethan notion of a great chain of being. Usurping a king threatens God and in turn reverberates all through creation. Chaos ensues. Richard Maple, an immature domestic king, is tottering.

Yet his surrogate has not yet fallen in "A Madman." The narrator and his bride, perhaps Richard and Joan Maple in happier times, perhaps the couple returning from Britain in "Home" (*Pigeon Feathers*), are in Oxford where the strangeness of an utterly new locale is personified in the charming, learned, but daffy Mr. Robinson. "A Madman" illustrates Updike's ability to focus all of the details on a single mood so that the tale becomes not a short story in which things happen but an evocation of a few moments lived and remembered. The first sentence directs the rest: "England itself seemed slightly insane to us" (35). The pentameter rhythm is fitting for a tale set in Oxford and dominated by an old man who effortlessly quotes poetry, but the point is the phrase "slightly insane." This is not a story of raving lunacy but rather an offbeat comedy. The nameless American couple's sense of strangeness combines with Mr. Robinson's daffiness to produce the sensation that everything is slightly out of kilter. The narrator and his wife are even a little strange to one another. Married less than a year with the wife now three months pregnant, and stuck in a foreign country with no place to stay (they make the same mistake in France in a later story, "Avec la Bébé-sitter"), the couple is all but primed for a meeting with a genteel madman.

Updike is a master here at uniting all of the details. The English meadow seems "deliriously" green, "obsessively" steeped in color. Looking at it, the narrator's "excited and numbed" brain recalls Falstaff's final babbling of green fields. London seems a gigantic literary shrine to them. The taxi driver in Oxford cannot believe that the Americans would be crazy enough to arrive at a destination at evening without a place to spend the night. Breakfast the next morning—half a cooked tomato on a slice of fried bread—is "an insanity." In the midst of all this displacement, they are given tour after tour of Oxford by eccentric Mr. Robinson who promises to find for them, but who never produces, a flat. They break with the old man only after they regain their bearings. A sense of stability brings a calmer perspective. "A Madman" is both a delight and a kind of writing lesson in how to organize details to create a sketch in which nothing much happens.

Yet by contrast "A Madman" is much closer to the conventional short story than the unusual "Leaves" and "The Stare." They should be read together, for both illustrate Updike's technique in the lyrical meditations. Action is subordinated to questions of its effect or meaning and, in "Leaves," of how to write. Description of guilt replaces dramatization of its causes in "Leaves" as Updike unifies the purity of nature and the narrator's despair.

Despite the dazzling performance of "Leaves," the tale has been criticized as an example of Updike's inability to control his lyrical language, as no more than, according to Robie Macauley, a piece of lace.[15] This story is, however, one of the few which Updike defends in print. Contributing an introduction to an anthology for which he selected "Leaves," he defines it as written in a mode of his called "the abstract-personal," and he admits that it is not a favorite form with his critics. Moreover, he shows that he is aware of the negative criticism when he indirectly refers to Macauley's dismissal of "Leaves" as "fine lace":

Well, if "Leaves" is lace, it is taut and symmetrical lace, with scarce a loose thread. It was written after long silence, swiftly, unerringly as a sleepwalker walks. No memory of any revision mars my backwards impression of it. The way the leaves become the pages, the way the bird becomes his description, the way the bright and multiform world of nature is felt rubbing against the dark world of the trapped ego—all strike me as beautiful, and of the order of artistic "happiness" that is given rather than attained.[16]

His claim that the meditation was written, as it were, with one stroke of the pen without revision is beside the point; many authors say as much. What is important is his comment on the proximity of the world of nature and the pain of ego, for his ability to unify such diverse effects makes "Leaves" both unusual and impressive.

In "Leaves" and "The Stare," Updike sketches first from a rural and then from an urban setting the reactions of a nameless man who has split with his wife and mistress. Guilt and loss surround him, and he is desperate with the need to be forgiven. It makes little difference if these people are the Maples finally spilling the blood that was clearly foreshadowed in the earlier tale. What does matter is Updike's precision in describing a man who has "behaved wantonly" and who thus suffers both shame and regret.

In the rural "Leaves," he is so absorbed in the long darkness of fear and loss that his only relief is to discover how the beauty of the natural world maintains its equilibrium while his own bearings are thrown out of whack: "that things are beautiful, that independent of our catastrophes they continue to maintain the casual precision, the effortless abundance of inventive 'effect,' which is the hallmark and specialty of Nature" (52). Aware of himself as a fabulist, he writes this meditation as an imitation of that same precision and thus as a testimony to his determination to maintain his mental balance. "Leaves" is an homage to the restoring power of art. In a passage which irritates Updike's negative critics as narcissistic, but which strikes me as integral to a meditation on how a guilt-ridden man attempts to transfer the order of nature to his own art for the purpose of regaining control, Updike writes:

A blue jay lights on a twig outside my window. Momentarily sturdy, he stands astraddle, his dingy rump toward me, his head alertly frozen in silhouette, the predatory curve of his beak stamped on a sky almost white above the misting tawny marsh. See him? I do, and, snapping the chain of my thought, I have reached through glass and seized him and stamped him on this page. Now he is gone. And yet, there, a few lines above, he still is, "astraddle," his rump "dingy," his head "alertly frozen." A curious trick, possibly useless, but mine. (52-53)

Drawn to nature because he defines it as existence without guilt, he follows Walt Whitman's lead, whose *Leaves of Grass* he has just dipped into, and he concentrates on the intricacy, the sheer inventiveness of leaves. Nature invites him from fear and shame into the warmth and breeze. He would like to respond, to accept the invitation with gratitude, but this is not a sentimental story of Nature's balm healing man's wounds. As much as he senses the serenity of the leaves, he cannot block out the guilt which has become the sun to his universe of inner darkness.

Updike is our chronicler of suburban tension. His fictional children are usually healthy, his wives are educated, stylish, and available, and his husbands are successful and alert. In the world of Tarbox, snug houses sit on kept lawns, and the next cocktail party or cookout is just hours away. How can love thrive when these surfaces are illusions? The narrator of "Leaves" is so hurt that he cannot stop the pain. Most of all, he is honest. Admitting that his impression of "unqualified righteousness" mingles with his self-awareness of wanton behavior, he wonders if, like Whitman, he can give his miscalculations to nature to be absorbed by the perfection of the leaves. The answer is "no" except through the imaginative process of art. The natural world which he shares for awhile with his wife cannot withstand the onslaught of his inner darkness which breaks through when divorce is literally upon him: "There is no more story to tell. By telephone I plucked my wife back; I clasped the black of her dress to me, and braced for the pain. It does not stop coming. The pain does not stop coming" (55). Now trying to exorcise the guilt by writing "Leaves," he paces in front of his desk and confronts a spider engaged in its own artistic handiwork. Nature and man inhabit contiguous but unbridgeable worlds. The leaves on the cottage floor are dead.

But the leaves of his pages have the eternal life of art. Order is restored through the energy of the imagination, and sunlight breaks through the darkness in the closing sentences. "Barbaric shadows" give way to a new "angle of illumination," and he opens the door to the warmth. As Updike himself comments, "The last image, the final knot of lace, is an assertion of transcendental faith scaled, it seems to me, nicely to the mundane."[17]

The same scale applies to "The Stare." Now from the perspective of third person, the narrator adjusts his focus to the mistress who may have been rejected in "Leaves." Nothing happens in this story, but that is the point as the narrator's excited anticipation of meeting once again the former lover with the unusual stare is negated by his tendency to find the glance on the faces of strangers. Updike is especially adept at handling the counterpoint between the man's memory of his time with the mistress and his current effort to find her again in the anonymous city. The leaves, sunlight, and spider of the country in "Leaves" become here the crowds, neon lights, and a "wrinkled painted woman with a sagging lower lip," but none of the details diverts his shame. Although he has bluntly but honestly confessed that he does not love the woman with the curious look enough to leave his wife, he fantasizes that an unexpected meeting will begin gracefully with her accepting his apology. Yet guilt continues to dog him: "But she took it as a death blow, and in a face whitened and drawn by the shocks of recent days, from beneath dark wings of tensely parted hair, her stare revived into a life so coldly controlled and adamantly hostile that for weeks he could not close his eyes without confronting it—much as a victim of torture must continue to see the burning iron with which he was blinded" (61). The relationship between the lover's unusual stare and the narrator's sense of blindness is an example of Updike at his best with metaphor.

His ability to narrow the distance between himself and his narrator despite the creation of ironic situations encourages the reader's sympathy for his guilt-ridden and often self-deceived characters. Updike understands that this narrator wants his need for forgiveness to be fulfilled magically. If he can neutralize the guilt, he can declare his love once more to the woman who has become unexpectedly lovely during the affair. His desire for forgiveness is so great that he feels justified when his unsuspecting wife recognizes the change in the mistress. He acts like a creator who takes pride in his offering of beauty, but unlike the narrator's pages in "Leaves," his "art" smacks too much of rationalization. He cannot, for example, bring himself to define the stare: "It was accusing, yet that was not its essence; his conscience shied away from naming the pressure that had formed it and that, it imperceptibly became apparent, he was helpless to relieve. Each time they parted, she would leave behind, in the last instant before the door closed, a look that haunted him, like the flat persisting ring of struck crystal" (60). Throughout the story he refuses to name the quality which shapes the memory of his mistress and haunts the nature of his narrative.

Perhaps it is knowledge of eventual betrayal. Thus his guilt is intensified because he understands that she has suspected his desertion all along. His refusal to admit his deception, his egotistical but natural need for forgiveness, and his childish longing for one last chance to retract his denial of love all combine to expose him as a weak but hopeful man. Updike has caught, by a combination of metaphor, irony, and sympathy, the middle-aged adulterer in mid-century suburban America.

"The Stare" and especially "Leaves" illustrate Updike's variations on the conventional short story. Closer to "Wife-wooing" and "Lifeguard" (*Pigeon Feathers*) than to "Ace in the Hole" (*The Same Door*), they depend for their success upon the subordination of action to the demands of description and meditation. On one level they are about art and its processes, about how imagination and creativity forge order from the confusing crises of mundane dilemmas. As the narrator says in "Leaves," "And what are these pages but leaves? Why do I produce them but to thrust, by some subjective photosynthesis, my guilt into Nature, where there is no guilt?" (56). Similarly, the husband in "Wife-wooing" creates patterns of language to seduce his wife, while the divinity student in "Lifeguard" fashions an apologia and a sermon from a short story. The possibilities of language and the nuances of the narrative voice take the place of patterns of action and details of character as Updike steers the traditional tale toward essay, meditation, and what he calls the "abstract-personal."

Not all of the stories of marital crisis are as experimental. Assigning his couples various names, and defining them at different stages of emotional disarray, often by the number of children they have, Updike takes his husbands and wives from Tarbox to Boston to London and Oxford and, in "Avec la Bébé-sitter," to Cannes. These stories with specific locales and developed characters are nearly always in the traditional mode. In the latter story, the wife is exhausted, shy, and hurt, and the husband is, as usual, guilty and confused. Struggling to fulfill the promise of the love of which they have so much in the beginning, they travel to southern France in the wrong season and without knowing the language in order to postpone the alternative of divorce. There in a strange land and to an adult baby-sitter he does not know, the husband is reduced to a child learning to talk as he confesses in fumbling French his love for another woman. Although he can hardly believe that indiscretion can be committed in an unknown tongue, he nevertheless hopes that confession has eased his burden: "Locked in linguistic darkness, he had thrown open the most intimate window of his life. He felt the relief, the loss of constriction, of a man glimpsing light at the end of a tunnel" (74).

How wrong he is. This marriage does not die, despite the adults' need of a baby-sitter, as Updike shows in the much better story which follows. Reappearing by name in "Twin Beds in Rome," Joan and Richard Maple continue to act out Updike's mini–drama of the contemporary American couple. This story is better than "Avec la Bébé-sitter" because the husband's point of view includes his understanding of the wife's perspective and because all the details unify with the action. The Maples now openly discuss the separation hinted at in "Giving Blood" but which never seems to happen. Like the narrator in "Leaves," Richard and Joan find that a caress postpones efforts to part. Their hostilities may seem absurd, but they are knit "ever tighter together in a painful, helpless, degrading intimacy" (76).

"Twin Beds in Rome" is extremely well done. Updike shows how the trip to Italy, which for most married couples would be a second honeymoon, is for the Maples a chance to break from familiar surroundings in order to define amid strangeness the intangibles which urge them to stay together even as they strain to part. Perhaps they make the mistake of trying to salvage a vague ideal of marriage rather than working to shore up their lives within the institution. Richard admits, for example, that he has wearied trying to reach the deepest recesses of the secret woman who is his wife. He also confesses the sorrow he causes when he verbalizes his paradoxical needs to leave and yet love Joan, to feed her "simultaneous doses of honey and gall." His immaturity mingles with his insecurity, and he resorts to the unmanly condition of picking fights with a wife who refuses to fight back. Yet we sympathize because he recognizes his weakness. He insists on knowing if she is happy: "He wished her to be happy, and the certainty that, away from her, he could not know if she were happy or not formed the final, unexpected door barring his way when all others had been opened. So he dried the very tears he had whipped from her eyes, withdrew each protestation of hopelessness at the very point when she seemed willing to give up hope, and their agony continued" (77). Unlike Victor Emmanuel, whose monument they visit, Richard cannot unify his kingdom.

Updike sets up the story so that nearly every detail illustrates the dilemma. Their lovemaking continues satisfactorily, but the Rome hotel provides them with twin beds. Recall that they lie on separate beds in "Giving Blood" whereas in the first Maple story, "Snowing in Greenwich Village," their double bed is a prominent feature. Another allusion to both "Giving Blood" and their current predicament is the metaphor of their bodies collapsing "together as two mute armies might gratefully mingle, released from the absurd hostilities decreed by two mad kings" (76). The monuments in Rome are grand but deteriorating. The tours are informative, but the walking hurts Richard's feet. He thinks that he sleeps soundly, but he unknowingly shouts out for Joan to leave him alone. Finally, his severe stomach pain suggests the crisis before the calm. Those who have read "Giving Blood" will recognize the irony of his blaming the need to give large tips as the source of his agony. Richard is unable to give willingly, especially himself. Waking, he tells Joan that the stomach illness is gone, and we know that he means the marriage. The periodic sicknesses exhaust him, just as their years together do. The source of the illness is mysterious, but it nevertheless hurts. Intimate for so long with the mutual pain of their love, Joan also senses that they have finally parted.

But Updike is not through. The nuances of love which both fulfill and torment are not so simply resolved. Once again, the key line from "Giving Blood" is relevant: "Romance is, simply, the strange, the untried." They need to renew the sense of the chase, the illusion that love is perfect when pursuit is all. Apparently free of the twin burdens of guilt and shame following Richard's recovery from the psychosomatic stomach illness, the Maples find during their last days in Rome something strange, a return to courtship. They are now "courteous, gay, and quiet." The shared acceptance of a likely end of the affair renews the natural freedom which Updike shows to be necessary to erotic fulfillment. Strolling through Rome, they walk out of a trapped marriage and into the possibility of love. Communication flourishes once again, and Joan is finally happy, free, a separate person in a separate bed.

Updike's final twist is not the surprising, melodramatic reversal often expected in a short story but the observation of an artist who watches the progress of adult love with an understanding not found anywhere else in contemporary American literature. The difficulties of separating are just as formidable as the burdens of togetherness. More is involved than twin beds and, finally, a tearful visit to an attorney. Richard's final thought illustrates Updike's grasp of the complexity. Authorial commentary is unnecessary: "She was happy, and, jealous of her happiness, he again grew reluctant to leave her" (86). He will not divorce her if she is not happy; he cannot do so when she is. No more need be said.

Further reading in *The Music School* confirms what a study of the first eight or so tales suggests: That the tensions within marriages which still support love, and the increasing need for extra-marital lovers are the general themes in many of these stories. The young boy from Olinger, bewildered by the awkwardness of maturing and the fear of religious doubt, grows into the middle-aged man from Tarbox, baffled by the simultaneous need to cling to and spurn his first woman. In "Four Sides of One Story," Updike creates narrators who offer generalities on the difficulties of adult love. The story is an artificial retelling of the Tristan-Iseult legend and is unsuccessful, but some of the comments apply to the dilemmas of Updike's married couples:[18]

... the syllogism that (major premise) however much we have suffered because of each other, it is quite out of the question for me to blame you for my pain, though strictly speaking you were the cause; and, since (minor premise) you and I as lovers were mirrors and always felt the same, therefore (conclusion) this must also be the case with you. Ergo, my mind is at peace. That is, it is a paradoxical ethical situation to be repeatedly wounded by someone *because he or she is beloved.* (92)

The narrator argues that the natural course of love is "passion, consummation, satiety, contentment, boredom, betrayal" (93). How fervently Richard Maple or the narrators of "Leaves" and "The Stare" would agree.

Yet unlike Richard's discussion with his wife of their predicament, this narrator is writing to his mistress. To talk with a wife of marital betrayal takes more than syllogisms. The female narrator of "Four

Sides of One Story"—Joan Maple as it were—knows that the dilemma calls not for theory but communication. The husband's tormenting effort to hold on to both wife and mistress so as not to hurt either frustrates her. Updike presents the woman's point of view sympathetically: "If I had any dignity I'd be dead or insane. I don't know if I love him or what love is or even if I want to find out" (94). Jealous of his misery, and truly afraid, all she can do is wait. These stories look forward to Updike's more complete exploration of the various possibilities of the marital predicament in *Marry Me* (1976), a novel which focuses more directly on the adulteries in two families than does *Couples* (1968), a novel which dissects all of suburbia.

Despite these gentle portraits of the betrayed woman who continues to inspire love, Updike's many short stories of American marriage are effective primarily because of his empathy with the male's point of view. Guilty, shamed, unfair, idealistic, and loving—all of these descriptions apply to his man caught between commitment and contentment. Blessed with what initially seems perfection in the woman loved, the narrator is unable to accept his good fortune. He is determined, as if by compulsion, to seek improvement through change. We salute his idealism even as we condemn his selfishness. Guilt and the pursuit of happiness are inextricably mixed in many of Updike's stories. The male character often recalls Aylmer of Hawthorne's "The Birth-mark," an allusion to an earlier author of love stories which is not far-fetched as readers of *A Month of Sundays* (1975) know.[19]

The reference to Aylmer, not ever obvious or developed and thus perhaps deserving only this one mention, seems especially pertinent in the sketch "The Morning." If the reader wishes to identify the nameless character as Richard Maple, he understands that divorce has finally ended the marriage. Yet Updike reveals that the man is a student, probably a graduate student, and thus we may assume that he is not old enough to have experienced both marriage and divorce. His identity does not matter, but his situation does. For this man is lucky enough to be loved by a woman who so stuns him with her beauty and grace that he literally cannot tolerate the hours without her. Blond, fragrant, and beautifully clean, the woman—a nurse—reminds him of a triptych. Street clothes and the nurse's uniform compose the side panels; her nude body is the all important center. He especially loves her in the meticulous white of the uniform. Note the religious allusions: "There was, in her rising from beside him to don white, something blasphemous and yet holy, a reassumption of virginity emblematic of the (to a man) mysterious inviolability of a woman. It was like nothing else in his experience. A book, once read, can only be reread; a machine, used, imperceptibly wears out. But she, she came to him always beautifully clean, and unexperienced, and slightly startled, like a morning, and left, at noon, immaculate" (105).

His idealism bordering on worship is unmistakable, and that is the flaw in his concept of love. Utterly in love with what she represents, he has trouble accepting what she is. When she takes off the uniform and dresses in green or brown, she is like other women. She eats in restaurants, nervously crosses her legs, and sometimes drinks too much: "The woman separated from him by a restaurant table was a needless addition to the woman who was perfect; she wished to add needlessly to the love that needed nothing but endless continuance" (106). When she hints at marriage, he responds that he is unable. She never returns, of course.

Updike depicts the man's foolishness and blindness dispassionately. Confining the point of view to the narrator's mind as it gropes around the enclosed space of the dingy apartment, he uses the technique to show how restricted the young man's life has become. The title of the story is obviously a pun on "mourning," but the suggestion that he uses the nurse to administer to psychological as well as physical needs is more important. The lovely woman to whom he endows religious connotations nurses his inability to live outside the apartment or the affair. He resembles both an emotional and physical cripple, as if he were the narrator of "The Stare" now holed up in a small room following the failed search through the city for the girl with the curious glance. Healthier, able to function beyond the apartment as the narrator is not, and caring for others while he mourns for himself, she leaves him to his silence and lament. The third person monologue illustrates the claustrophobic confines of his apartment and his mind.

As is often the case in these stories, nothing melodramatic or sudden occurs. Updike's tales are not usually the stuff of mid-afternoon soap operas. At first the man is angry at the nurse's failure to explain that her gift of love in the morning is an extravagance she could always curtail. Later he returns to classes. He laughs and answers questions. He does not visibly collapse. We are not even sure that he has learned a lesson. But Updike's ability to encourage the response of criticism mixed with sympathy makes the story moving. Like Hawthorne's Aylmer, Updike's nameless narrator fails to look beyond the shadow of time to find "the perfect future in the present."

The narrator in "Harv Is Plowing Now" turns to the past. Along with the title story, this lyrical meditation, or what Updike calls the "abstract-personal" mode, is one of the two best tales in the collection. Yet it is generally ignored. One of the few good discussions of it is by R.B. Larsen who notes correctly that a conventional short story could not convey the "density of such a piece" because it would have to abandon the meditative, lyrical qualities for the development of action and character.[20] Creating an elaborate but effective analogy between his memory of the boyhood neighbor plowing a field and his need today to plumb the depths of his still painful divorce from his still lovely wife, the first person narrator of "Harv Is Plowing Now" identifies his life with the earth that piles layers upon the remnants of the past. This story, more than "In Football Season," unites the pastoral past of the Olinger tales with the bedrock of Tarbox. From the suburban vantage point of a broken marriage, the narrator digs back through memory to posit Harv as his metaphor for the cyclical ritual of plowing and rebirth, a cycle he must believe in following the loss of wife and home.

The story begins with a conundrum: "Our lives submit to archeology" (175). The puzzle is not immediately explained in this eight-page meditation, for the narrator first recalls his days on the Pennsylvania farm, fully described in *Pigeon Feathers*, and we know that Richard Maple *et. al.* have momentarily assumed again the guise of David Kern *et. al.* Harv's plowing "winter-faded" fields parallels the narrator's need to turn over his present to examine his roots: "It seemed to be happening *in me*; and as I age with this century, I hold within myself this memory, this image unearthed from a pastoral epoch predating my birth, this deposit lower than which there is only the mineral void" (177).

The unexpected transition to the English excavations at Ur is startling until Updike, describing the painstaking removal of strata of rubbish, clarifies the opening conundrum: "My existence seems similarly stratified" (178). At the top is the trash of his current minutes and days.[21] At the bottom is the memory where Harv eternally plows. In between is the "dense vacancy where like an inundation the woman came and went" (178). For all of the allusions to Olinger, this meditation is not a comment on the memories of adolescence.

The successive layers of life which he longs to excavate all point to the void left by the loss of his wife: "She is not there. But she *was* there: proof of this may be discerned in the curious hollowness of virtually every piece of debris examined in the course of scavenging the days" (178). All lives are stratified like the earth, but his life will make sense only if Harv's plowing remains the bedrock of his memory. Notions of innocence support feelings of guilt.

Updike's elaborate metaphor illustrates the definition of history as more than a random progression of events upon which man imposes order by excavating. Harv, Ur, divorce, this tale—all make sense together through, in this case, the storyteller's art. The reader soon recognizes the appropriateness of the analogies: The Biblical flood and the "inundation" of the marriage, digging at Ur and Harv's plowing, archeological probes and the narrator's reentry to his past. The cyclical ritual which the narrator needs in order to affirm his present is available to him in art. Harv plows, the English archeologist digs, and the author writes; all reaffirm the present by recovering the past. As his memories of childhood center on the farm, so today his returns to memory veer toward the woman of the void. Her hair still engulfs him. He senses a hollowness from which he might reshape her presence. Hearing guitar music, he turns to ask if she notices, but she does not. She is no longer there.

The last movement of the story details a final meeting, perhaps imaginary, between narrator and former wife. The brief confrontation is significant, for when he realizes that the old love is indeed dead, he feels bereft of all bearings: "Where am I? It has ceased to matter. I am infinitesimal, lost, invisible, nothing" (182). But despair is unnecessary. Buried beneath the strata of guilt and pain and loss, he awaits, as he says, resurrection. Just as excavations reaffirmed Troy and Harappa, so art confirms his life. The love he has left behind is readily unearthed by the archeology of memory. Transforming the loss of love into the permanence of art, he structures his life through metaphor. His final evaluation of the ruined marriage is not that destroyed love leads to guilt but that his life and all of history are more than randomly piled stratifications of rubbish: "Having fallen through the void where the woman was, I still live; I move, and pause, and listen, and know. Standing on the slope of sand, I know what is happening across the meadow, on the far side of the line where water and air maintain their elemental truce. Harv is plowing now" (182). His current life has stability because it is founded upon the solidity of a memory fashioned in the concrete form of art.

Updike's tone is so sure here, so affirmative. One hesitates to mention biographical influences, but one wonders if the mixture of loss, guilt, art, and "resurrection" stems at least in part from Updike's own life. He knows that for all their value the artifacts of archeology are not the realities of today. Peering into the void where the woman was, he sees that he still lives. Painful loss does not mean death. Harv can plow, and he can remember, and the demands of today are faced. He picks up his pen and writes this tale.

More important, under the name of Alfred Schweigen (which means, to keep silent), he writes "The Music School." Although perhaps not obvious at first reading, the two stories are companion pieces. Mutually concerned with a theology of marital guilt, both meditations use metaphors of time, of the sacrament of communion, and of geology to communicate the complexities of managing a marriage. The first person narrator in "Harv Is Plowing Now" is already divorced, while Alfred Schweigen is still an adulterer, but Updike suggests, as he does all through the collection, that each narrator is a variation of the same suffering man, perhaps even the author himself.

The first sentence of each tale illustrates the preoccupation with time: "Our lives submit to archeology" and "My name is Alfred Schweigen and I exist in time." The need in "Harv Is Plowing Now" to strip away the layers of one's life to recover for examination the bits and pieces of the core event becomes in "The Music School" the assurance that "in the end each life wears its events with a geological inevitability" (184). Finally, the paradox that material distinctions between physical and spiritual worlds reflect metaphorical similarities confronts both narrators: "What is bread in the oven becomes Christ in the mouth" (176), and bakeries being instructed to make a "host, in fact, so substantial it *must* be chewed to be swallowed" (184).

Yet for all of these parallels, and there are others, "Harv Is Plowing Now" is not the equal of "The Music School." The latter is superb. It is the best in the collection, and it may even be Updike's finest story. Selected by the Public Broadcasting System for dramatization in the 1977 television series "The American Short Story," "The Music School" transforms to fiction in only seven and a half pages Updike's contemplation of what may be called the theology of marriage and the inevitability of ensuing guilt. He asks a serious question which may be unanswerable: If life, itself a sacrament, is God-given and thus meant to be confirmed in joy, how does one explain the pain and shame which love and marriage, other sacraments, inadvertently cause to challenge the confirmation? Many of Updike's stories ponder this dilemma, but the effect in "The Music School" is stunning.

The school itself is a metaphor for life where Schweigen ponders the harmonies of the universe while sitting in the basement of a church, only to realize that experience leads not to visions of universal order but to a necessity to know the self. The story, in a phrase, celebrates active participation in the world. Just as the communion wafer should no longer melt passively but must be chewed, so the complexities of living must be met. The tension between religion and science provides the structure. Unlike the science of archeology in "Harv Is Plowing Now," computer mathematics in "The Music School" suggests not the foundations of human life but atheistic humanism. Although Alfred Schweigen, a non-believer, needs a glimpse of universal harmony, the computer scientist does not believe in anything except the proved propositions of science, and he is thus unprepared for the impact of the unforeseen event which, in this case, kills him. All of these metaphysical complications go on in Schweigen's mind. As Joyce Markle notes, the scenery in "The Music School" is not external but internal.[22] The story is the narrator's silent dialogue with himself.

The contrast between the religious and secular worlds is established in the first two paragraphs in a connection the narrator does not understand "though there seems to be one." A young priest's explanation of the change in Roman Catholic attitudes toward how to receive the Eucharistic wafer is juxtaposed to a newspaper article reporting the murder of a computer expert. Schweigen knows both the priest and the dead man, and his effort to understand the connection revolves around his confrontation with his own guilt: He is an adulterer. Apparently cheered by the priest's explanation that the communion host is now to be chewed rather than allowed to melt in the mouth, Albert realizes that "to dissolve the word is to dilute the transubstantiated metaphor of physical nourishment" (183). Theology must transform into action. Life must be physically, not passively, lived. The computer scientist, on the other hand, has no use for the imprecise and thus incessantly reinterpreted nuances of religion. A family man truly at home in the secular world of numbers and science, he seems, before his murder, agreeable and free of guilt, as if he participates "not in this century but in the next" (185).

Yet his murder is as mysterious and unexplained as transubstantiation. If the Eucharistic wafer transforms the physical bread into the spiritual body of Christ, surely the assassin's bullet changes the victim from material to immaterial. There must be a connection, but Alfred does not understand it. Faith gives meaning to what might be otherwise merely a life with "geological inevitability."

Alfred may be stranded in the middle of these theological speculations, but he is connected to both extremes. Trying to locate the associations, he sits in the music school waiting for his daughter to complete her lesson, and he understands how nourishment is involved in both mysteries. The scientist is eating dinner when the bullet pierces his temple. Just as an immaterial hatred results in the material phenomenon of death, so the immaterial theology results in the material phenomenon of the wafer which promises eternal life. Spiritual and physical reflect each other; do religion and science, art and computers, vision and numbers? Schweigen believes that the young priest and the computer scientist mirror each other since both find harmony in what Alfred sees as a disorderly universe. Yet their kind of harmony is not what he seeks. Described as translucent, they resemble the thin wafer which is now inappropriate to a coarse world.

Music is another attempt to locate harmony. The priest plays the guitar, and Schweigen's daughter practices the piano, but Alfred himself has never learned despite taking lessons for years. Yet he loves the music school in the basement of the Baptist church. Art, religion, and human effort merge in his description of the various lesson sounds he loves: "hints of another world, a world where angels fumble, pause, and begin again" (186). How more appropriate is the relationship of these novices to the discordant world than that of the priest and the computer expert who seem to assume a benevolent order. The parallel between the murdered scientist's domain of arcane numbers and the notations for a musical score is significant. Each language, music and computer, seems at first improbably opaque and complex, just like theology, but all result in the unity of vision. "How great looms the gap between the first gropings of vision and the first stammerings of percussion! Vision, timidly, becomes percussion, percussion becomes music, music becomes emotion, emotion becomes—vision. Few of us have the heart to follow this circle to its end" (186–187).

Alfred never completes his novel about a computer programmer, but this does not mean that he abandons the circle before returning to vision. Judging from the few excerpts of manuscript he supplies, the story in his novel would have been an unsatisfactory metaphor for his own dissolving marriage. Unlike the murdered scientist, Alfred the artist is of this world and does feel guilt. He has the habit of confession although he exchanges the sacrament he recalls from childhood for the confessional fiction he attempts to write. More important, he has always chewed the communion wafer, tasting the physical to know the spiritual. Chewing the host and violent death are variations on transubstantiation. Eating itself is the primary image in this story and thus the connection among religion, music, and fiction: The discussions of chewing the wafer; the scientist murdered at dinner; the daughter not asking for candy because her lesson fills her like a meal. Pondering the opaque relationships, Alfred realizes that his failed novel resembles the discarded wafer, too translucent to serve his needs in a coarse world. His more appropriate fiction is this story about himself. Thus while he confesses that he is neither musical nor religious in the conventional sense, he learns to hear, see, taste, and know. The murdered scientist dies at the feet of his children; Alfred notes that his daugher's smile "pierces my heart, and I die (I think I am dying) at her feet" (190). One is reminded of the final lines of "In Football Season" when the narrator recalls the fragrance of the innocent girls and "remembers what pierces him."

Alfred finally understands the connection between these abstract ideas and his dissolving marriage. Just as vision leads to percussion, music, emotion, and back to vision, so perhaps love leads to marriage, dissension, lawyers, divorce, and back to love. "We are all pilgrims," he says, "faltering toward divorce." Updike's final metaphor is perfect. Recalling again the party with the priest, Alfred describes a woman in the process of divorce arriving late, taking two baffled steps backward in embarrassment at seeing the priest, and then regaining composure to move forward toward the group. She elects to complete the circle, to seize, as it were, life. Like the children in the music school, she fumbles, pauses, and begins again. Her courage is a grace note to Alfred's tale, providing him with his coda:

"The world is the host; it must be chewed" (190). Each person confronts life as he will.

Not all of the stories in *The Music School* dissect the irregularities of adult love. "At a Bar in Charlotte Amalie" is an observation piece of color, music, and conversation.[23] A testimony to Updike's ability to watch and listen, this tale has no conventional plot or hero. The main character is the narrative voice who reports the scene and describes the patrons of the bar with such precision that the sketch resembles finally a sharply focused color home movie with sound, taken by a tourist who knows how to handle his camera and who wants to make sure that the neighbors back home in Tarbox see something better than the usual vacation snapshots. The first several lines illustrate the minuteness of Updike's observation: "Blowfish with light bulbs inside their dried skins glowed above the central fortress of brown bottles. The bar was rectangular; customers sat on all four sides. A slim schoolteacherish-looking girl, without much of a tan and with one front tooth slightly overlapping the other, came in, perched on a corner stool, and asked for a Daiquiri-on-the-rocks.... The green sea was turning gray under round pink clouds" (110). The patrons of the bar seem at first glance to be eccentrics, but close observation reveals the pathos of their humanity. Reading this sketch, one is reminded of Ernest Hemingway's advice to supply all of the pertinent details including how the weather was.

When Updike does write what is generally called a conventional short story complete with beginning, middle, and end, characters in conflict, and resolutions of plot, he downplays his penchant for lyrical meditation and the accompanying emphasis on mood and tone. The result is a story such as "The Christian Roommates" which, in my opinion, is not as impressive as "The Music School" but which has its admirers. Granville Hicks names "The Christian Roommates" his favorite in the collection, and Charles Samuels says flatly that it is Updike's best story to date.[24] The tale has nothing wrong with it. Indeed, it is the work of a professional who is sure of his art. Dialogue is natural and pacing apt. But the nuances of memory and regret, the tone of lingering guilt painfully earned, and the poetic descriptions all associated with an Updike short story are missing. Perhaps point of view is an issue. Although the third person narrator is largely connected with Orson's angle of vision, it seems detached, uncaring, as if reporting the squabble in a Harvard dormitory from a vantage point on high. There is nothing technically wrong with narrative distance, of course, but the sense of identification which Updike often encourages between reader and point of view is missing in "The Christian Roommates." The intimacy with the subject matter, that closeness which the reader senses in, say, "In Football Season" or "Harv Is Plowing Now" is not possible in this story which ends with a catalogue of what happens to the principal characters.

Still, this story is significant for those readers who urge Updike to step beyond what Samuels calls the "essentially domestic walls of his universe." Although one could quibble with this comment by pointing to earlier non-domestic stories such as "Dentistry and Doubt" (*The Same Door*) and "A & P" (*Pigeon Feathers*), the point is that in "The Christian Roommates" Updike does not write about "faltering" toward divorce or the narrowing door of memory. The theological debates recall the discussions in "Dentistry and Doubt" and between Hook and Conner in *The Poorhouse Fair* (1959), and Rabbit and Eccles in *Rabbit, Run* (1960). A primary difference is that unlike Burton's or Rabbit's searching, Orson Zeigler has each step of his life already planned. He never finds Burton's bird feeder or Rabbit's "it" because he is too sure of himself to break out of his sense of decorum. No wonder his roommate Hub's quest for God does not impress him. Yet one wonders if the final resolution, that the now successful Orson never prays, is earned. The narrator implies that the lapse of religious conviction, although shallow to begin with, results from Orson's crisis with his roommate, but the connection seems tenuous. David Kern's spiritual turmoil in "Pigeon Feathers" is more convincing. "The Christian Roommates" works best as a picture of the nervous, excited, and finally bumbling steps toward knowledge and experience suffered by countless college freshmen, a picture Updike captures with precision and refocuses later in the poem "Apologies to Harvard" (*Tossing and Turning*).

The Music School ends with "The Hermit," a story set, like the penultimate "The Family Meadow," in the relative peace of rural America. Yet the pastoral quality of both is ironic, for in this volume irony often replaces nostalgia as a technique for insight. Here is no fond memory of the farms and small towns around Olinger but a commentary upon the defeat of the rural perspective. The sense of peace, the tone of nostalgia, and the photographs of yesterday which make up the first story in *The Music School* have all disappeared in the last. Although one realizes that Updike orders the stories according to when they were written, the arrangement of this collection suggests nevertheless that the shift in focus from Olinger to Tarbox spells doom for the pastoral angle of vision. Just as the first story, "In Football Season," looks back toward *Pigeon Feathers* and *Of the Farm*, so the last tale, "The Hermit," points toward *Couples* and *Museums and Women*.

The failure of the attempted retreat to the rural world in "The Hermit" illustrates the impossibility of regaining a time of grace when life was gentle and people cared.[25] Stanley the would-be hermit fails to understand the lesson that to flee in space is not to escape in time. He may indeed learn to see the "overwhelming fineness in things; the minute truth of bark textures, the many-layered translucence of leaves," but he gains his clarity at the expense of his ties with the community (258). Unlike Thoreau, Stanley cannot accept the proposition that he must eventually leave the woods because he has other lives to live. The word "translucence," important in "The Music School," is Updike's hint that Stanley's method of coping is too thin, too tenuous, too unsuited to the demands of a rough world. For those who resist reading one tale in terms of another, Updike makes the same point when he describes the tiny stream in which Stanley tries to immerse himself. He cannot plumb the depths of his being, much less Walden Pond, in a trickle of water too shallow for a bath. His family and friends are criticized for not understanding him, but Updike also shows that Stanley's solution to daily pressures is unacceptable. Kafka's ever-closing door to the past which Updike uses as an epigraph to *Pigeon Feathers* has slammed shut for the hermit. He does not know the lesson which Updike illustrates in his fiction: That the only way to pry it open is through art.

Notes to *The Music School*

1. John Updike, *The Music School* (New York: Knopf, 1966), 3. The first edition, first issue of *The Music School* has transposed lines in the quotation of poetry on page 46. Further references will be to this edition.
2. Charles Thomas Samuels, "John Updike: The Art of Fiction XLIII," *Paris Review*, 12(Winter 1968), 93.
3. Norman Cousins, "When American and Soviet Writers Meet," *Saturday Review*, 24 June 1978, p. 42.
4. J. Mitchell Morse, "Where is Everybody?," *Hudson Review*, 19(Winter 1966–67), 682.
5. Josephine Jacobson, "Books," *Commonweal*, 9 December 1966, p. 300.

6. Peter Meinke, "Yearning for Yesteryear," *The Christian Century*, 7 December 1966, p. 1512.

7. Charles Thomas Samuels, "A Place of Resonance," *Nation*, 3 October 1966, p. 328.

8. Granville Hicks, "Domestic Felicity?," *Saturday Review*, 24 September 1966, p. 31.

9. Bernard Bergonzi is not as generous. Recognizing that Updike is too gifted to be read with anything other than respect, he nevertheless admits that he finished *The Music School* with discomfort tempering admiration. Bergonzi separates language from content. He wonders if Updike's celebrated patience which permits him to reveal multiple nuances in the ordinary is in danger of being nullified by his facility for the sharp, often stunning effect. The action in these stories is too familiar, the language too narcissistic, and the author too prone to preen "himself on his verbal wizardry." Robert Martin Adams agrees when he asks about *The Music School*, "Is the art of fiction here reduced to fine writing? Not altogether, but dangerously close to it." Yet Adams likes the collection. He calls it "beautifully written" and "exquisitely artful," and he recognizes that it is much better than most of the work by Updike's contemporaries. Still, Adams wants him to do more. *See* Bernard Bergonzi, "Updike, Dennis, and Others," *New York Review of Books*, 9 February 1967, p. 28; and Robert Martin Adams, "Without Risk," New York *Times Book Review*, 18 September 1966, p. 5.

10. Robie Macauley, "Cartoons and Arabesques," *Book Week*, 25 September 1966, p. 4.

11. Stanley Kauffmann, "Onward with Updike," *New Republic*, 14 September 1966, p. 16.

12. The British reaction to *The Music School* often echoes the American. Neville Braybrooke likes the collection, but he believes that only the meditative pieces like "Harv Is Plowing Now" demand rereading. Simon Gray argues that Updike is a minor writer who dazzles the reader into "an ungrateful irritation because he so relies upon the bright surfaces that he refuses to let the reader glimpse the heart of the matter." The *TLS* reviewer repeats the old claim that Updike cannot find a form to match his talent. *See* Neville Braybrooke, "New Novels: Meditations," *Spectator*, 23 June 1967, p. 744; Simon Gray, "Myth and Magic," *New Statesman*, 16 June 1967, p. 840; "Keeping It Short," London *Times Literary Supplement*, 24 August 1967, p. 757.

13. Charles Thomas Samuels argues that the puns in "Giving Blood" smack too much of the slick formula story. *See* "A Place of Resonance."

14. *See* his essay on Denis de Rougemont's *Love Declared* in *Assorted Prose* (New York: Knopf, 1965).

15. *See* the reviews by Bernard Bergonzi, Robie Macauley, and the London *Times Literary Supplement*.

16. John Updike, Introduction to "Leaves," in *Writer's Choice*, ed. Rust Hills (New York: David McKay, 1974), 391.
17. Updike, Introduction to "Leaves," 391–392.
18. Many readers agree that the story fails. Robert Detweiller, for example, says that the use of the legend is a "clever gimmick"; *John Updike* (New York: Twayne, 1972), 123. Stanley Kauffmann says that the tale is Updike at "his clever–clever worst": "Onward with Updike," 17.
19. Hawthorne is specifically mentioned in "The Bulgarian Poetess."
20. R.B. Larsen, "John Updike: The Story as Lyrical Meditation," *Thoth*, 13(Winter 1972-73), 36.
21. Considering the epigraph to the collection from Wallace Stevens, one might read Stevens' "The Man on the Dump" along with this story.
22. Joyce B. Markle, "On John Updike and 'The Music School,'" in *The American Short Story*, ed. Calvin Skaggs (New York: Dell, 1977), 391.
23. The anonymous reviewer for *Time* calls the story "a tense little moral essay on true and false innocence." *See* "Madrigals from a Rare Bird," *Time* 23 September 1966, p. 105.
24. Granville Hicks, "Domestic Felicity?," 31; Charles T. Samuels, "A Place of Resonance," 328.
25. For a complete reading of "The Hermit" in light of pastoral literature, *see* Larry E. Taylor, *Pastoral and Anti-Pastoral Patterns in John Updike's Fiction* (Carbondale: Southern Illinois University Press, 1971), 118-121.

Museums and Women

> "All around us, we are outlasted."
> —"Plumbing"

Museums and Women (1972) corroborates the claim on the dust jacket that it is Updike's most varied book of stories. Whether or not it is his best is still debated. Many familiar names and situations are here, including the tormented marriage of the Maples whom we last saw in "Twin Beds in Rome" (*The Music School*), the longings of middle-class, middle-age life in suburban America, and lyrical meditations.

The religious undercurrents present in much of Updike's fiction throb throughout, although never to the extent that the stories may be called strictly theological.[1] The epigraph from Ecclesiastes 3:11-13 provides a link to the religious nuances of the title story in the previous collection of tales, *The Music School*. "The world is the host," says Alfred at the end of that story; "it must be chewed." His admonition to live, to seize the day, is one message in the third chapter of Ecclesiastes:

> He has made everything beautiful in its time; also he has put eternity in man's mind, yet so that he cannot find out what God has done from the beginning to the end.
>
> I know that there is nothing better for them than to be happy and enjoy themselves as long as they live;
>
> Also that it is God's gift to man that everyone should eat and drink and take pleasure in all his toil.

Man should be happy as long as he lives, but he will never understand the infinity of God's plan or plumb the depths of His eternity.

162

The irony of these sentiments is readily apparent to Updike's readers. Seizing the day, chewing the metaphorical host, his suburbanites often find that pleasure is momentary but memory long. As one character says, he has been "merely happy." What is the value of love with a mistress if one is tormented by pain for the wife? How can one enjoy the attractions of adulthood when he feels the pull of desires from the past? A master of the glance over the shoulder, of making the reader feel the magic of that little moment shared long ago, Updike communicates the tension between the act of pleasure and the lack of fulfillment. Gifts are offered joyously, but man bungles the job of unwrapping the packages.

Some commentators on *Museums and Women* would have us believe that the collection is merely repetitive and unusually precious. Yet an examination of approximately two dozen reviews and essays reveals that reactions to Updike's short fiction remain extremely varied. Guy Davenport, Elmer F. Suderman, Dorothy Rabinowitz, and Doris Grumbach, for example, all but dismiss the volume.[2] Grumbach's negative reaction is the most complete, for she criticizes both content and style. Calling the tales merely "superb snippets" and the style "adolescent superfluity," she insists that his descriptive passages lack inevitability and thus force the reader to strain for connection:

The individual terms of these sentences, the separate parts of speech as they come on, are fine, colorful, vaguely suggestive. I carp, as I find myself doing so often with Updike's allusory writing, at the failure of the addition, the relegation of so many valuable insights to the mangle of style. One is often left with the sense that his sensibility is too private and too highly developed, too special for one's more pedestrian expectations, and the progress of his thought and narrative too eccentric for comfort.

One can only grant these negative commentators their say and then remark that one does not pick up an Updike book for comfort.

The stories in *Museums and Women* are not repetitions of his earlier collections if only because of the distinction between Olinger and Tarbox. Updike's characters are now so far removed from the desires of the Olinger tales that they face the future with as much dread as the narrator of "The Happiest I've Been" (*The Same Door*) faces it with hope. The young John Nordholm races joyfully toward tomorrow even though he knows that he has just experienced "the moment of which each following moment was a slight diminution."

In *Museums and Women*, today's diminution overwhelms yesterday's confidence. The characters are older, more tired, and worst of all, not wiser. When they remember the past, they are still grateful but now afraid. The critics with mixed reactions to this collection recognize some of these distinctions.

Tony Tanner, for example, praises Updike's ability to convey children quarreling, the insecurity of moving to another city, the misery of participating in the excitement of an affair which lacks the stability of a marriage, and most of all the growing fear that once on the downside of middle age each life rushes toward death and the terror of annihilation. But even though Tanner responds to a story like "I Am Dying, Egypt, Dying" as a welcome leap beyond "the rather wearisome boundaries of Tarbox," he insists that Updike seldom persuades him "of the genuineness of his experience of love."[3] The response to this criticism, as Tanner himself admits, is that in this volume Updike is especially convincing about the erosion of once hopeful lives, the sense of inevitable decay tempered with an acceptance that all men are eventually outlasted. Surely these are not the themes of *The Same Door* and *Pigeon Feathers* and thus not the "same old stuff." Ever since the final tales of *Pigeon Feathers* in which he steers the short story away from its traditional reliance upon dramatic plot and developed character toward experiments with lyricism, meditation, and essay, Updike has provided variations on the short story form.[4]

The critics mentioned thus far have serious reservations about *Museums and Women*, but the majority of reviewers thinks it a fine volume indeed. The point is that those familiar with the entire canon see this collection as one more substantial addition to what is rapidly developing into a truly significant achievement. Admiration for the career is occasionally tempered by nagging doubts of its importance, but many astute readers are grateful. Richard Todd is one such reader. Suggesting that Updike's stories are his minor work, Todd lauds his ability to communicate the enormity of loss even when the thing lost is not extraordinary: A moment of happiness, a rabbit, a new car. Updike sets up an ironic contrast between history and the present moment so that the sense of personal diminution poignantly felt underscores the character's awareness of his own impermanence in the face of all that will outlast him. What happens, asks Updike, to one's longing for immortality when one realizes that even the plumbing pipes are more permanent? As Todd observes, the narrative distance between the meditative voice of the stories and the experience it describes affects the reader's reaction with a kind of assurance despite the general tone of melancholy. Unlike the negative critics, Todd praises Updike's style: "The delicacy of Updike's style derives from the sense that you had better keep your eyes on the small task at hand; look around the room and you'll see pointlessness."[5]

The small task at hand concerns empty swimming pools, plumbing fixtures, and Christmas carols. Updike's people, says Peter Rohrbach, are not leading Thoreau's "lives of quiet desperation."[6] Occasionally content but often bewildered, they live lives in which being merely happy is somehow not enough. The characters in *Museums and Women* cannot define the missing cog, but they sense the incompleteness. Lacking a body of belief to sustain them, they turn the corner toward middle age in Tarbox and experience the tension between fear of the future and thanks for the past. Critics who accept the importance of this theme praise the collection. Joseph Kanon, Charles Deemer, and William Pritchard judge the book to be exceptional.[7] Updike's skill is shown in his ability to make connections, to find a whole in the part, to connect, as it were, his characters with an object such as a deck of cards in order to suggest the importance of a moment which without his help might have been dismissed as insignificant. Emphasizing the necessity for acute perception and the relative stability of little things, a theme he also offers in the poetry, especially *Telephone Poles* (1963), he directs many of his stories away from confrontation toward what Pritchard calls "the musing retrospections of a narrator." Pritchard concludes on a note of high praise: "He is putting together a body of work which in substantial intelligent creation will eventually be seen as second to none in our time. 'Do you really think he's *that* good?' a voice will say, has said. I do, I really do."[8]

The critical reception of *Museums and Women* with its ups and downs, praise and doubts, affects, as one might expect, the reactions to specific stories. Just as the first tale of *The Music School*, "In Football Season," looks back to Olinger before turning to Tarbox, so the title story of *Museums and Women* picks up William Young from *Pigeon Feathers*. Like most of the characters in the collection, William is now old enough to begin descending the other side of what Updike calls the Hill of Life in the poem "Midpoint." The problem, implies Thomas Molyneux, is that Updike's growth is as stagnant as William's. Updike is too pictorial, too literal, and thus he does not grow: "In William's world, as I suspect in Updike's, perception and acknowledgment are all."[9] This criticism seems unfair, since "Museums and Women" is meant to be not a dramatic situation but a lyrical meditation.[10] The letters *M* and *W* from the title words which William muses upon are joined by the central letter *e*. *M* and *W* are thus two halves of a larger whole which consists of museums and women at the extremes with William in the middle. The story is an account of his musing upon this equation and not a dramatic rendering of it.

The tale also illustrates the religious aura suggested by the epigraph to the collection: "Every one should eat and drink and take pleasure in all his toil." But William Young is not joyous because he fears that he has left radiance behind. The trees surrounding his first museum are tagged as if just christened by Adam, yet the museums and the women in the story remain nameless. William is no namer, no Adam figure confronting the wonders of the garden, but he is burdened with Adam's sense of guilt and loss. In his journeys through the museums of his life in search of radiance, beauty, and surprise, he is aware of completing a circle. The fountain which splashes unseen in the small, home-town museum visited with his mother reappears in the New York museum entered with his mistress. The mistress in turn recalls the fine-arts student who becomes his wife as well as the freckled girl from grammar school: Both sit in the front of the class and feel confident in museums while William lingers back and says little. All of these women reflect his mother and, of course, Eve, each being a "mystery so deep it never formed into a question."[11]

Updike's point is that museums encompass all the reverence and ritual of religion. Museums are not churches, but we enter both as searchers: "What we seek in museums is the opposite of what we seek in churches—the consoling sense of previous visitation. In museums, rather, we seek the untouched, the never-before-discovered; and it is their final unsearchability that leads us to hope, and return" (12). William steps into each museum and finds love. Thus the words "museums" and "women" merge for him. "Both words hum. Both suggest radiance, antiquity, mystery, and duty" (3). But if radiance, antiquity, and mystery are the gifts of museums and women, so duty is the legacy of Adam. Never in a position, even as a schoolboy, to declare his love to the freckle-faced girl, just as he postpones for too long his pledge of love to Mary in "A Sense of Shelter," William realizes now that he is "condemned by nature to be dutiful and reverent" (7). He may worship, even love, but never claim. Thus he is forever caught between mother and wife in, as it were, one museum, and between freckled girl friend and mistress in the other. Condemned by duty, he remains steadfast to the former; urged by reverence, he longs to possess the latter.

His dilemma illustrates the irony of the epigraph, for William recognizes how shame and guilt pursue those who separate reverence and duty. Once entered, museums and women lose part of their mystery, yet the lure that attracts him in the first place remains. His mistress is as fully possessed as the museum is fully searched. Although he knows her in the Biblical sense, she will forever remain as unobtainable as the smooth statuette of a nude asleep on a stone mattress which reminds him of his childhood fascination with small statues and which he likes to believe only he has discovered. But ideals are never attained, at least not in this world. William will abandon his quest to find the perfect woman through possession of many. As his wife points out, the female body of one near perfect statue is in a Boston museum, but the head resides in the Louvre. Reverence, William learns, leads to love which in turn is countered by duty. Despite his desire for the mistress, he will not leave his wife whom he also meets in a museum. Before parting from the mistress for the last time in the museum, he glances back toward the splendid entrance of both the woman and the building. The broad stairs lead "upward" into "heavens knows what" treasure, but he is now condemned to stop short of possessing the ideal. His search for radiance will fade, and the enchantments will cease to beckon. William may enter more and more museums, but he will do his duty. Desire and loss and the mysteries of memory give special poignancy to Updike's meditations.

This story is crucial to a reading of the Maple tales at the end of the collection, for in it Updike suggests why Richard and Joan have not yet crossed the line to divorce. Pursuit of eros, as in "Eros Rampant," may illustrate the quest for ideal love as shown in the nude statuette, but marriage is earthbound and thus imperfect. Divorce denies duty. For all of their frustrations, the Maples struggle to combine love and commitment. Richard may be unable to accept the fundamental differences between male and female, and Joan may finally take her own series of lovers, but they realize, like the man in "Solitaire," that the children are with them always. The mistress in "Museums and Women" is associated with a "translucent interval," a phrase which, as Updike says in "The Music School," suggests something too fine for this world. At the end of the sketch, William Young walks out of the building with its statues of ideal females and presumably goes home to his wife. The generation of his children is described in the next meditation, "The Hillies."

A cross-reference to "The Indian" from *The Music School*, "The Hillies" is another chapter in Updike's history of mythical Tarbox, Massachussetts. Yet it is a mistake to think of Tarbox, as some readers do, as a typical suburban enclave in mid-century America. For one thing, it has a sense of the past. Founded in 1634, it can point to the sixth church building built on the site of the original Congregational church. This town is not a new commuter development sprung up around shopping centers and motels. In addition, Tarbox has its local Jesuit, lone Indian, and single black who is a crack golfer and horseman. A town so WASP-dominated cannot serve as a microcosm of middle-class suburbanites.

Updike's point is not that Tarbox mirrors reasonably affluent America but that like much of the nation it does not know what to make of its turbulent present. As many of the Olinger stories recall the 1950s, so the Tarbox of *Museums and Women* reflects the Viet Nam decade. The differences between Olinger and Tarbox are as significant as those between *Rabbit, Run* (1960) and *Rabbit Redux* (1971), and it seems likely that in decades to come Updike will be celebrated as a kind of social historian of post–World War II America. He understands the dilemmas of the 1960s. The city fathers, for example, may be able to point to the old post office built in 1741, more than a century following the founding of the town, but they do not know how to assimilate history and hillies, young adults who congregate just above Tarbox to take dope and discuss the war. (Similar problems of communication are discussed later in "The Corner.") At first tolerating the drugs and recognizing that these young people take seriously both the Preacher's message in Ecclesiastes and the First Fathers' proviso about the pursuit of happiness, the populace nevertheless does not know what to do with those who will not work.

"The Hillies" is a kind of historical memoir while the Olinger tales are often personal meditations, but both types of stories document an era. In this tale, Updike catches a mood of America: Baffled populace versus pacifist subculture; "bone-chilled" policemen clearing out non-resisters. Reminding us that the 1960s were never so simple

as "them against us," Updike shows how the hillies are just as stratified as the more conventional people who use the letters-to-the
editor column to reveal surprisingly varied responses to those in their
midst who pose a threat merely because they are different. The hillies differ just as much in their attitudes and actions as those who
lead more orthodox lives. Most of all, Updike knows the origin of
hillies. To those who scream, "Push 'em back where they come from,"
the narrator replies that they come from us. They are our children,
yet we fear them. Rejecting our gods of industry and acquisitiveness,
they erode our definitions of self-respect and the flag. Both sides begin to consolidate. Tolerance loses face in a town identified with the
historical foundations of the nation's freedom. Fear breaks through
in middle America, and the parable of the Prodigal Son no longer
seems to apply.

With these two modes of history established, as meditation and as
memoir, Updike dramatizes the process of linking past and present
in the more conventional tale "The Day of the Dying Rabbit." For
all of the resonance of its title, "The Day of the Dying Rabbit" is
not one of his impressive stories. Too many characters are thrown at
the reader in too short a space; the quiet but strongly felt tension between husband and wife is better developed, not to say more poignantly expressed, elsewhere; and the camera metaphor may be asked
to do too much. The matter at hand is not to dissect the story but
to suggest how it provides another angle of vision for Updike's tales
of memory and loss.

The narrator is a professional photographer just as Updike is a
writer. Both capture spots of time in still life and then offer the art-
work to posterity. But is the offering a record of the past or an artifact for the present? Strictly speaking, only the latter, suggests the
narrator, for "the camera does lie, all the time. It has to" (30). The
processes of memory do not mirror the truth of the past because the
lens limits the vision. Even the photographer admits that "what is
captured is mostly accident" (26). By extension, all stories about the
past have the same limitation: "the shadows would be lost, the subtle
events...would be vapid blobs. There is no adjustment, no darkroom
trickery, equivalent to the elastic tolerance of our eyes as they travel"
(38). Yet the viewer often wants to recall what the eyes see. Thus the
photographer employs one of the tricks of the trade and plans "a lot
of takes," while the author writes many stories about the same past.
None is wholly true, but neither photograph nor tale wholly lies.

In this sense, then, both are flawed records of the past. Even the injured rabbit sees through a damaged eye as through a glass darkly, and the photographer has no lens to duplicate the animal's fuzzy vision or his son Godfrey's (nicknamed God) reaction. When the older son tries to hide his frustrations at the rabbit's suffering by "thumping God," the reader understands the religious implications in the narrator's effort to peer through the darkened glass. Human vision is better than the camera.

The photographer finally describes the day of the dying rabbit as a singular day of gallantry as opposed to other "merely happy" days. How can this be, asks the reader who recalls the mauled animal, the marital tension, the crying son, and the girls growing too obviously and too soon? Yet Updike emphasizes not irony but the way the past is etched on memory: "the dying rabbit sank like film in the developing pan, and preserved us all" (40). The children learn about death, although some are indifferent, some squeamish, some emotional. A sign of life in the rabbit awakens a dormant sexual activity in the parents. Tennis with the neighbors causes jealousy in the wife and longing in the husband. Marital difficulties contrast with the first budding of adolescent attractions. As the narrator recalls this day, he sees that all the various emotions and unspoken communications seem to derive from the moment the cat offers the rabbit through the malfuctioning door. Memory lies, too, all the time. It has to. But not totally. Preservation of the past means preservation in the present. Despite its limitations, we need what the camera gives us.

Yet Updike surprises the reader with another level of meaning. Peering through the observed past is a way of stepping toward the future. The rabbit's damaged eye is a metaphor for the Biblical description of looking through a glass darkly. The narrator's family learns a great deal on this day of gallantry. As they paddle back through the dark night with only a "single, unsteady star" to guide them, they reach safety "afloat on a firmament warmer than the heavens" (39). Light, "astonishing" impressions of phosphorescence, is unexpectedly all about them on the water. Dying, the rabbit becomes through the narrator's art an exemplum for living.

Updike's couples periodically need this lesson. Their lives are in a constant flow of demise and renewal. The sense of duty and reverence which he assigns to the middle-aged narrator in "Museums and Women" characterizes Tom Brideson of "I Will Not Let Thee Go, Except Thou Bless Me." Echoes of the epigraph from Ecclesiastes and of Jacob wrestling with angels are evident in the title. Making everything beautiful in its time, God nevertheless keeps motive and meaning hidden. Thus, says Ecclesiastes, man may take pleasure in his toil and yet never know the significance of his work.

The angel in the tale who appears to withhold her blessing is Maggie Aldridge, Tom's former mistress who arrives at a farewell party for the Bridesons wearing a white dress with "astonishingly" wide sleeves like wings. Apparently Lou Brideson does not consciously know of her husband's deceit, yet as she packs the family's accumulation of the ten-year stay in the town, she dreams of arriving in Texas without her husband. Both Tom and Lou somehow sense that "departure rehearses death" (50). They are not eager to leave.

Updike's reputation as America's keenest observer of middle-aged, middle-class suburban America is supported in this story. He sees, for example, how the adults try to adapt to their own needs and tastes the styles and standards of the largely rebellious youth culture described in "The Hillies." This is the era of the late 1960s and early 1970s. Attractive women wear mini-skirts which permit them "comfortably" to show their thighs; the less inhibited men turn "mod" with turquoise shirts and wide pink ties. More telling, perhaps, are their attempts to Frug "(or was it Monkey?) to the plangent anthems of a younger generation" which quickly give way to "the reeds and muted brass of an earlier time" (50). Updike knows the restlessness of these adults with healthy children and good jobs. They are the in-between generation "too young to be warriors, too old to be rebels," and significantly for the Updike canon, a long way from Olinger. They are also in-between youth and age. Too old to Frug, they are nevertheless too young to participate fully in the emotions of the big band music which dates from before World War II. Those who argue that Updike has nothing to say miss the resonance of these stories in *Museums and Women*. Apparently wanting him to write about the more newsworthy events of his day, they ignore these penetrating glimpses of affluent Americans who are uninvolved in the social unrest of their time but bored with the social intrigue of their lives. The distinctions between Olinger and Tarbox are crucial here as Tom muses on "a heap of organic incident that in a village of old would have moldered into wisdom. But he was not wise, merely older" (51). Compare the narrator in "The Day of the Dying Rabbit" who is merely happy. The sense of poignancy in these stories comes not, as it does in the Olinger tales, from recognition of the always closing door to the past but from awareness of the continually shrinking possibilities in the present.

As a group, Updike's suburbanites lack identity. All Tom Brideson can do is witness a progression of similar events acted out by a host of similar people with different names as they all grow older:

These women: he had seen their beauty pass from the smooth bodily complacence of young motherhood to the angular self-possession, slightly gray and wry, of veteran wives. To have witnessed this, to have seen in the sides of his vision so many pregnancies and births and quarrels and near-divorces and divorces and affairs and near-affairs and arrivals in vans and departures in vans, loomed, in retrospect, as the one accomplishment of his tenancy here. (51)

No wonder Tom is afraid to move. Since he no longer belongs to their group, his friends have all but dismissed him. He is in-between. The accumulation of ten years in New England has left him with hundreds of children's drawings and stacks of *Life* in the closet. He needs a blessing, but Maggie the angel resists.

Her face averted and stony, she accepts his invitation to dance and then paralyzes him with the comment that he is now nothing. Leaving the party later with his wife, however, Tom decides that Maggie's blessing has been offered indirectly. She warmly kisses Lou farewell instead of him. Tom wants to gloat, but he dutifully admits that Maggie may have been drunk. All the reader knows is that he has followed the command of Ecclesiastes without finding happiness in the momentary pleasure of his toil. His memories of Maggie are like the children's drawings: "each one a moment... impossible to keep, impossible to discard" (49). All blessings are not victories. As Lou explains and as Updike shows, they are all just "very tired."

Not all of the stories in *Museums and Women* illustrate the frantic turn of the decade from the 1960s to the 1970s. The Frug and miniskirts and the casualness of adultery give way in several tales to Joseph McCarthy, Eisenhower, and the "brinkmanship" of the 1950s. The adults of this generation are surely not in-between, for as the narrator of "The Witnesses" Herbie explains, their task had been to bring society across the chasm of World War II "and set it down safely on the other side, unchanged. That it changed later was not our affair" (70). Just as Viet Nam is a crucial reference point for the stories about the late 1960s, so World War II helped to shape an earlier generation.

Updike understands both. Herbie's group is "conservative and cautious," perhaps because of the willing sacrifices for the war. As a result, he belongs to a generation which expresses "affection through shades of reticence" (70). Values seem more easily agreed upon; emotions more easily shared. If his friend Fred Prouty cheats on his wife, he does so with more fear and uncertainty than the adulterer-lovers in the stories of the 1960s who are inclined to temper guilt with memory and desire. Herbie and his wife are embarrassed to offer Fred and his mistress drinks, and the mistress is embarrassed to accept. Surface proprieties must somehow be observed; one does not normally take his mistress to a friend's house without first divorcing his wife. Such conservatism and domestic stability seem a long way indeed from the casually accepted but rapidly occurring changes of the next decade.

As a snapshot of the 1950s, "The Witnesses" stands by itself as discussed. But Updike offers more. The title points not to Fred the adulterer but to Herbie the friend. Although Herbie and his wife find the visit embarrassing and even dreary, they learn that Fred has more in mind than just showing off. Later divorced from the mistress, he confesses to Herbie that he needed a witness to his moment of happiness: "I wanted somebody I knew to see us when it was good. No, I wanted somebody who knew me to see me happy. I had never known I could be that happy. God. I wanted you and Jeanne to see us together before it went bad" (77). His explanation resembles a prayer. But Herbie and his wife miss the silent plea for sympathy. Seeing only something dreary, they do not understand until too late Fred's effort to freeze a moment of happiness in order to make it last.

Nostalgia does not hover between the lines in "The Witnesses." It is more a story of Fred's inability to adjust to either decade than a mood piece reminiscent of many of Updike's meditations. Another sketch of the 1950s from the perspective of the 1970s, "When Everyone Was Pregnant," is different. Updike supplies virtually the same narrator from "The Witnesses" (both are "in securities") and lets him remember his Fifties which will never come back. Unlike Herbie, this narrator is secure in his feeling for yesterday as he sits in a moving train, a symbol of passing time, and jots down his notes on the past.

He would like to live it again. Yet as Updike observes in another context, "happiness... makes us afraid."[12] From the chaos of today, the Fifties send up an image of growth, of a time when everyone was pregnant and the years were beautiful and kind. The romance of consumption contains no room for the contemporary problems of pollution and population, for in the 1950s the cup seemed to fill to overflowing. In this moving meditation which has received such high praise, the narrator lists the highlights of that decade as if, like Fred, he needs a witness to his happiness. The horizon is blue and sparkling, and the babies are bubbly and fat. Laughter mixes with the beach and the aluminum chairs, and all the wives are pregnant. An absolute enemy may exist across the ocean, but possibilities of annihilation make them live all the more fully. They don't have time for apocalypse.

For as Updike correctly notes, this was the decade of guiltlessness. With the presence or absence of that one emotion, he pinpoints the distinctions between Tarbox and a not-too-distant earlier time. He knows that America may not have changed as much as the way it is remembered. Guiltlessness was a primary factor in the decade of the bomb. "The world's skin of fear shivered but held.... Viewed the world through two lenses since discarded: fear and gratitude. Young people now are many things but they aren't afraid, and aren't grateful" (93). Updike and his narrator still are.

His effort to probe memory for the foundations of his present is just as difficult as the epigraph to *Pigeon Feathers* says it is. He should remember the Fifties better: Innocent dancing with pregnant women in a mood so different from Tom Brideson's guilty dance with Maggie, picnics on the beach, hand squeezes, babies. But all that is now gone, never fully to be recaptured even in memory. All Updike can do is take notes for a story similar to his experiments with the short story form in the final two tales of *Pigeon Feathers*. The Sixties arrive, and the parties get wilder. The babies grow, and the couples divorce. His hand shakes, and the notes come to nothing. His babies are now the children in "The Hillies"—alienated, different, resentful. They accuse him. Guilt surfaces with the change of the decade, and the guests at the beach party are now polite enemies. "Did The Fifties exist? Voluptuous wallpaper. Crazy kid. Sickening sensation of love. The train slides forward. The decades slide seaward, taking us along. I am still afraid. Still grateful" (97).

This evocation of a lost time, so near and yet so far down the tunnel of memory, is one of Updike's greatest strengths. Writing these metaphors of irreversible flux and of the toll which time demands, he persuades us to see and hear. He comments on the change: "I think our lives really are solipsistic, self-centered. And perhaps, in part, because of a new sensibility about such things, the particular swing to life that we knew in the 'fifties is really not around anymore. The difference between the heroes elevated by the early 'fifties and those of 1970 reflects this."[13] Updike's details of the Fifties are always correct: The clothes, the catch phrases, and what the records were. But most of all he urges the reader to feel desire, change, and the poignancy of loss. Memory, like the camera, may lie, as he suggests in "The Day of the Dying Rabbit," but glimpses of truth always filter through. Communism, Korea, and the specter of the bomb all hover near the horizon in these tales of the Fifties, but the absence of guilt and the innocence of joy neutralize the threat. These people are not naive but happy. No wonder Updike remembers them as if through a golden glass.

The gold tarnishes in the domestic tales about the next decades, as the contrast between "When Everyone Was Pregnant" and "Solitaire" shows. In one sense this six-page story is pivotal in Updike's short fiction of love and loss, for it touches briefly on all three high-sports of his memory: Childhood, early marriage, and current bewilderment. "Solitaire" may even be the place to begin when reading his collections of short stories. The nameless narrator may be Richard Maple or Tom Brideson or Updike himself, but identity makes no difference in this case. What does matter is that the narrator has passed beyond Olinger and the guiltless decade of the Fifties to confront during a game of solitaire a dilemma he would prefer to avoid: Wife or mistress?

Stuck as he is in the silent house with wife at a meeting and children asleep, he knows that memories of childhood cannot resolve crises of maturity. Remembrance of his mother playing solitaire while his father attends a meeting reenforces what he suspected as a child—that he needs and loves both parents even if they live in tension. To lose one is to plunge toward "that black pool prematurely" (80). Thus he grows up in solitude and leaves the farm which his mother has forced on them, "where now his father and mother still performed, with an intimate expertness that almost justified them, the half-comic routines of their incompatibility" (80).

Although comedy no longer applies to his current dilemma, the narrator learns the lesson well. Escaping from the farm to embrace the Fifties, he dives not into a black pool but to a sunny beach of happy times when everyone is pregnant. Guilt does not apply. He gives his wife children to make remote the possibility of another escape and to spare the first child the punishment of solitude. But the children are now all born, and the Fifties recede to memory. How does he solve the stalemate, amid the shame and guilt of the Sixties, of "fair" wife versus "black-and-white" mistress? Perhaps, he thinks, his first inclination is correct, that "our lives are devoted to doing the contrary of what our parents did" (80). The choice is clearly defined: "prudence, decency, pity" on the one hand; "a doubtless perishable sense of existing purely as a man" on the other. Since his game of solitaire is headed nowhere, he will have to make a decision between the two remaining cards, a red ten (wife) and the missing ace (mistress). He chooses the ten and follows his parents' lead.

The choice is not pleasant, nor does the result bring relief. "He was a modern man, not superstitious even alone with himself; his life must flow from within. He had made his decision, and sat inert, waiting for grief to be laid upon him" (84). To abandon the security of a family for the freedom of a mistress is to lose identity. Perhaps he needs his trap to define himself. In either case he feels guilty. The Fifties do not return. His musing recalls Rabbit's thoughts in *Rabbit, Run*: "The fullness ends when we give Nature her ransom, when we make children for her. Then she is through with us, and we become, first inside, and then outside, junk."[4] Updike handles the metaphor of the card game well. Placing black eights on red nines, the narrator is a *"king uncovered, but nowhere to put him"* (82). The lonely husband playing solitaire in a quiet house is one of Updike's most effective metaphors of the post-1950s marriage. The transition from sunny beach to black pool, two of Updike's symbols of the contrasting decades, is explicit in the companion story, "The Orphaned Swimming Pool," when divorce splinters the family and turns the pool into "one huge blue tear." As Updike observes, "Marriages, like chemical unions, release upon dissolution packets of the energy locked up in their bonding" (85). "The Orphaned Swimming Pool" is a conventional story in the sense that it is more dramatic than many of the fictions in *Museums and Women*, but the meditation of "Solitaire" is more effective.

The longest, perhaps the most unusual, but not the most memorable story in the collection is "I Am Dying, Egypt, Dying." If we accept the dust-jacket blurb, commentary which Updike surely approved and perhaps wrote, the story concerns a "hallucinatory trip up the Nile" which "allegorizes our foreign policy." One suspects irony. The tale is not hallucinatory except in the sense of vision altered by merging stretches of shimmering light reflecting off blue Nile and gold sand, and by Clem's inability to sleep, but it does indeed suggest the ineffectual desire to be loved which often characterizes America's dealings with sister nations. Updike's ironic attitude may be glimpsed in his choice of names for the main character, for no matter how wealthy and well-traveled the man is, Clem is not a name associated with the sophisticated and stately.

If Clem represents America traveling the world with beneficence and wealth, then it is clear that America/Clem cannot give love. He has everything except that gift: "His pronunciation was clear and colorless, his manners impeccable, his clothes freshly laundered and appropriate no matter where he was, however far from home" (108). Rich but unmarried, showing perfect posture but walking without swing, Clem attracts and repulses others simultaneously because his apparent perfection flatters them and yet reveals no flaw in himself. He flirts but does not follow through; he drinks but never loses control; he attends costume parties but prefers not to dance. Insomnia may be the only weakness. "This also was a hopeful sign. People wanted to love him" (109).

They try to show their love. The Egyptians traveling with him offer insights into their mysterious culture, and one of the women makes known her availability. An Egyptian tailor and a blustering American solicit homosexual liaisons. The bikinied Scandinavian woman visits his bedroom, and an American widow invites him to play bridge. Significantly, the Russians remain unseen and unloving except for functional sex. Clem cannot reciprocate. Always polite, consistently tactful, he reflects but does not generate affection. Note Updike's appropriate description: "Glistening like a mirror, he slept in this gliding parenthesis with a godlike calm that possessed the landscape, transformed it into a steady dreaming" (109). Surrounding this mixture of tourism, love, and history is the Arab-Israeli war. Clem the attractive American sails right through its middle during a lull in the fighting. Museums are full of sandbags, and guards patrol the bridges. But Clem takes a luxury cruise down the Nile because a "tan would look great back in Buffalo" (111).

Although not arrogant about his position or ostentatious with his wealth, Clem makes minor but telling errors when purchasing souvenirs. He buys, for example, an inexpensive lapis-lazuli bug, but he makes the mistake of revealing his well-stuffed wallet while looking for the correct bank notes. When an Egyptian woman remonstrates him for "torturing" the beggars, he can respond truthfully but naively that he bought the bug only because he does not wish to be rude. The woman can say nothing except that rudeness is not an issue in these cases. Later he purchases a caftan even though the fit is too tight rather than demand satisfaction for his money.

Updike's point is clear. Clem is not a bad American, but though he travels far and often, he never assimilates other cultures. He spends money, but he does not understand different systems of bargaining. He tries to be polite but ends up being rude. Intent on encouraging love, he cannot give himself to those who would adore him. America, Updike implies, is the good-natured, well-mannered big spender who attracts others with a glistening sheen and yet repulses them with an unwavering dullness. As the Egyptian woman tells him with perhaps a reference to personalities as well as to language, English is "clear and cold," but French and Arabic have the nuances of passion. Ingrid, the Scandinavian girl, implies the same: "'I think the thaw, when at last it comes in such places, is so dramatic, so intense.' She glanced toward him hopefully" (120). The thaw, when it does come, is not as intense as she hopes. Confronting him with the evidence of his desire for her, Ingrid hears his excuse that he lacks the right to take things. He falls asleep when she assumes the initiative and offers herself in his stateroom.

Ingrid defines Clem's flaw as self-consciousness: "You are always in costume, acting, You must always be beautiful" (125). Similarly, the Egyptian woman snaps, "All countries are women, except horrid Uncle Sam" (135). They believe that the cold precision of the English language limits the activity of the heart. A fellow traveler tells Clem that American energy menaces the world and that although most countries love American movies, clothes, and music, they do so with their brains. Perhaps this reserve is why other nations turn to the Russians who appeal to the stomach. Besides, the unseen Russian couple at least makes love in the cabin next to Clem's while he leaves a party to sleep alone.

Thus, Updike has more in mind than a colloquialism when Clem apologizes to the willing Ingrid, "God, I'm sorry.... I told you I was dead" (140). He does not understand that in the language of the ancient Egyptians the word for life and death is the same. Enjoying the trip, which the narrator calls an "abyss," but never learning from the implications, Clem decides that he has been happy on the Nile. The reader wonders at the irony, for Updike juxtaposes Clem's declaration of happiness with a summation of his flaws: "His defect was that, though accustomed to reflect love, he could not originate light within himself; he was as blind as the silvered side of a mirror to the possibility that he, too, might impose a disproportionate glory upon the form of another. The world was his but slid through him" (140).

Updike's insights about the fallacies of Americans abroad are telling. Image, not politics, is the problem. Everyone wants to love us, but all we offer in return is money and an energetic, relatively benign presence. Americans tour the world to take souvenirs back to Buffalo. Why, then, is "I Am Dying, Egypt, Dying" not as impressive as "Wife-wooing," "The Music School," "Twin Beds in Rome," or "When Everyone Was Pregnant"? It is difficult to say, for personal preference often affects critical opinion. Yet it seems to me that Updike is at his best in the essays, sketches, and tales which reflect the domestic scene of America, especially the America of the mid-Atlantic and New England states. Born in 1932, and blessed with a discerning eye and a lyrical prose style, he was a child in the Depression, a student and young married in the innocent Fifties, and a middle-aged observer in the guilty Sixties. At the same time, he is a veteran of a small high school and an Ivy League university, as well as a resident of tiny towns and large cities. Thus when he calls upon memory in order to write about what he knows, he throws into relief contrasting states of American domesticity in such a way that the reader nods in agreement and feels the pang of loss implied by the contrast. The reader may be still afraid, still grateful, but the Fifties will never return. Neither, implies Updike, will America's innocence. One need only compare "The Hillies" and "When Everyone Was Pregnant" to survey the change and to witness the loss. The teen-agers and college students of Tarbox will not care to moor their memories to the debating contests, the football games, the dying grandparents, and the traded cars, all touchstones from the past which give Updike's stories their special grace. That quality of memory, made significant by the realization that America has passed beyond guiltlessness in its movement from the Thirties to the Seventies, is missing in "I Am Dying, Egypt, Dying." The story is not a failure. The comedy, the insight, and the prose are all confidently handled. The tale is also important to Updike's expanding canon, for it shows that he can write skillfully about locales other than Tarbox and Olinger. Yet the reader appreciates without participating. Clearly, reader involvement is not a criterion for all successful fiction, but in Updike's case it is often welcome. The result of its absence in "I Am Dying, Egypt, Dying" is that we like the story from a distance.

Enroaching age, pursuing death, the accretions in the pipes which will eventually burn out the pump—all these are part of Updike at his best as he confronts the erosion by time. For time is his true subject. When it grabs, memory must stand firm. Failure to do so means loss of the past, and loss of the past means dilution of the future. No wonder he scrapes the very skin from his body to crawl through Kafka's always closing door. The rewards are worth the pain. In *Museums and Women*, they come in short meditations or sketches like "The Corner," "The Carol Sing," and especially "Plumbing."

For all its delicacy, "Plumbing" appeals to me more than the ambitious "I Am Dying, Egypt, Dying." Solidly established on the literal level with his efficiency and craftsmanship, Updike's plumber has a full life on the figurative level as a metaphor for the remembering, preserving artist: "The old plumber bends forward tenderly, in the dusk of the cellar of my new house, to show me a precious, antique joint.... He knows my plumbing; I merely own it" (148). The key words are "tenderly," "precious," and "antique," for this plumber, like the author himself, is a caretaker of the past. He can point out the workmanship, the functionalism, the joints in need of repair. But what is only living space for the author is history, "an archeology of pipes" for the plumber. His art recalls "Harv Is Plowing Now" (*The Music School*) and the line that is crucial to Updike's best work: "Our lives submit to archeology." The digging and the repair work are expensive, for while replacement parts are cheap, labor is not. Closing as slowly and as surely by accretions like ancient plumbing beneath the house, the door to memory must be periodically cleaned and repaired. Updike shoves through and scrapes the skin, and he willingly pays the cost.

Time is the key, as both the plumber and the author know. "He is a poet. Where I see only a flaw, a vexing imperfection that will cost me money, he gazes fondly, musing upon the eternal presences of corrosion and flow" (149). The narrator becomes aware of the ubiquity of the quotidian when he recalls his former house while paying the plumber to repair the new one. When he and his family move in to that first house, he engages in the necessary business of archeology and digs in the backyard to find remnants of the previous owner, artifacts from a lost era. Now he has memories of his own yesterdays when he and his wife hide Easter eggs for the children and when, following a spat, they discuss "change, natural process, the passage of time, death" (153). Trying to hold on to his life in the midst of these inexorable powers of time, he recalls the moment when as a child he ate dirt, as if he were storing the fundamental ingredient of archeology within him for use in a later decade. Now a husband and father, he realizes that even his youngest daughter, a child almost nine, can recognize the toll of time's passing, the accretions in the pipe. She does not want a birthday because "then I will get to be an old old lady and die" (154).

All he can do in the face of such truth is admit that on this point all men are dumb. In the meantime, he can call in the plumber, that poet who will replace the blocked pipe and thus slow but not halt the demands of time. If the narrator leaves the pipe as it is, it will overwork and burn out the pump. Better to replace it with new hardware that will both save the pump and outlast the narrator's "time here," thereby preserving the house for a later family. Updike's final paragraph is emotionally true as he pinpoints the insignificance of man's threescore and ten: "My time, his time. His eyes open wide in the unspeaking presences of corrosion and flow. We push out through the bulkhead; a blinding piece of sky slides into place above us, fitted with temporary, timeless clouds. All around us, we are outlasted" (155). The metaphor of plumber for artist holds. Man's work is his immortality.

"Plumbing" ends Part I of *Museums and Women*, a collection in which Updike consciously arranges the stories instead of placing them in the book according to the order of composition as is his usual practice. Part II, titled "Other Modes," contains ten sketches averaging six pages each and not well received by critics. Alice and Kenneth Hamilton defend "Other Modes" as more than merely whimsical, seeing them as Updike's allegory for the truth that man, like the dinosaurs, must die so that nature may repeat itself.[15] But most commentators dismiss the section as too cute. Robert Phillips speaks for many when he describes "Other Modes" as "Updike riding a two-wheeler on a high wire and shouting, *Look, Ma, no hands!*"[16] There is indeed an element of showmanship about these ten sketches as if Updike were paying homage to one of his heroes, James Thurber. A comparison of the two writers confirms that Thurber does this sort of thing better and that Updike's more graceful bow to him is in the essays collected in *Assorted Prose*. Yet some of the pieces deserve comment as cross references to more substantial Updike stories.

The dust–jacket blurb explains that the ten tales in the "surreal" mode are ornamented with an array of "stolen" illustrations, and Updike provides a list of illustration credits at the conclusion of the book. Except for an imaginary interview with a Baluchitherium and a description of a cocktail party for dinosaurs, these short tales are not surreal at all. They are comic, well–informed essays intended to induce a smile. Many of them ponder mystical questions: "What is the source of language?; Does a baseball slugger in a slump experience Kierkegaard's "dread"?; Why is golf the most transcendent of all sports? Irony is occasionally at work here.

In "The Sea's Green Sameness," the most important of "Other Modes," Updike provides a cross reference to the brief discussion of language in "I Am Dying, Egypt, Dying" which leads him to the mysterious distinctions between art and nature. Art slowly reveals a meaning whereas Nature, like the sea, is always opaque. The problem, says Updike, is clear: Should the artist assume that the meaning in his work will be found? Does art always yield its secrets? In another sketch from this section, "One of My Generation," the narrator praises explication as an academic exercise "by now perhaps as obsolete as diagrammatic parsing" (178). Explication helps to clarify mysteries, even at the risk of creating the evidence. Similarly, the narrator of "The Sea's Green Sameness" wonders about the value of his writing if it, like the ocean, is never understood. In other words, should an author trust his readers:

It is a chronic question, whether to say simply "the sea" and trust to people's imaginations, or whether to put in the adjectives. I have had only fair luck with people's imaginations; hence tend to trust adjectives. But are they to be trusted? Are they—words—anything substantial upon which we can rest our weight? The best writers say so. Sometimes I believe it. But the illogic of the belief bothers me: From whence did words gather this intrinsic potency? The source of language, the spring from which all these shadows (tinted, alliterative, shapely, but still shadows) flow, is itself in shadow. (160)

How can he describe the ocean if he sees the externals but not the substance?

Insight in fiction is no substitute for narrative skill. Updike explains:

I wrote "The Sea's Green Sameness" years ago and meant, I believe, that narratives should not be *primarily* packages for psychological insights, though they can contain them, like raisins in buns. But the substance is the dough, which feeds the story-telling appetite, the appetite for motion, for suspense, for resolution. The author's deepest pride, as I have experienced it, is not in his incidental wisdom but in his ability to keep an organized mass of images moving forward, to feel life engendering itself under his hands.... Insights of all kinds are welcome; but no wisdom will substitute for an instinct for action and pattern, and a perhaps savage wish to hold, through your voice, another soul in thrall.[17]

Art is not nature. Updike thus trusts the adjectives much to the dismay of his negative critics who claim that he overwrites.

The metaphorical dilemma of sight and insight carries over to the next essay, "The Slump." Ostensibly a comment on why athletic prowess suddenly fails ("the reflexes," say all those trying to help), this "other mode" is more a discussion of the gulf between the will to achieve and the failure to perform. Just as the writer in "The Sea's Green Sameness" ponders the distinctions between sight and expression of what is seen, so the slumping slugger of "The Slump" wonders if the "spiral vagueness" affecting his ability to see the baseball as clearly as he used to is related to metaphysical concepts of blind spots. He calls his slump "panic hungry"; Kierkegaard calls it "dread." The results are the same: The body does not act as the performer wills. How can he hit a fast ball if alienation enroaches to the point where the batter is the only one "really there"? He cannot slug the baseball; the writer cannot describe the sea.

A companion piece to "The Slump," written in homage to a batter who did hit consistently well for many years, is "Hub Fans Bid Kid Adieu," first published in the *New Yorker* (October 22, 1960), later collected in *Assorted Prose* (1965), and then printed in a limited signed edition by the Lord John Press in 1977. This justly renowned tribute to Ted Williams does not require explication. It is discussed here as an extension of the metaphysical question probed in "The Slump," for "Hub Fans Bid Kid Adieu" looks at the problem from the other side of the blind spot. In this essay on the man who saw through the spiral vagueness to unite will and body, Updike writes an elegy to heroism in the guise of a history of baseball. The heroism described is peculiarly American with its swagger, arrogance, and bad manners coupled with its grace, strength, and endurance, all personified in the aging Williams who hit a home run in his last at bat in a game against the Baltimore Orioles on September 28, 1960, and who then retired. Updike was there: "But immortality is nontransferable. The papers said that the other players, and even the umpires on the field, begged him to come out and acknowledge us in some way, but he refused. Gods do not answer letters."[18]

Yet Updike can write letters to gods. In its own way, this essay is part of his continuing homage to the recent past which exists for him as a heroic time. He explains that he began following Williams' exploits while a boy of fourteen in Pennsylvania. His tribute to the retirement of a childhood hero is a hymn to the passing of his own youth. For Updike was twenty-eight when Williams last circled the bases, a writer about to enter the netherworld between youth and middle age. More important, "Hub Fans Bid Kid Adieu" is a farewell to American guiltlessness. Williams retired in 1960, the end of the decade when "everyone was pregnant" and the beginning of the years when everyone was hurt. Unlike the batter in "The Slump" who personifies the 1960s and who substitutes analysis for doing, Williams does not need to define his actions. He hits.

Updike's prose in praise of sports is consistently witty and well informed. One thinks immediately of "Ace in the Hole" (*The Same Door*), *Rabbit, Run*, and his description of the legitimate anxiety experienced when former basketball heroes can no longer send the ball through the net without getting winded. An excellent example of the extra dimension which Updike sees in sports is the golf game in *Rabbit, Run* when Rabbit points to his unexpectedly perfect tee shot as an illustration of the "it" he pursues but cannot define:

Very simply he brings the clubhead around his shoulder into it. The sound has a hollowness, a singleness he hasn't heard before. His arms force his head up and his ball is hung way out, lunarly pale against the beautiful black blue of storm clouds, his grandfather's color stretched dense across the east. It recedes along a line straight as a ruler-edge. Stricken; sphere, star, speck. It hesitates, and Rabbit thinks it will die, but he's fooled, for the ball makes this hesitation the ground of a final leap: with a kind of visible sob takes a last bite of space before vanishing in falling. "That's it!" he cries and turning to Eccles with a smile of aggrandizement, repeats, "That's it."[19]

One cannot miss the ecstasy of grace, the pride of accomplishment in the description of the long, straight tee shot. It is as if the little white ball connects the mundane with the eternal.

This sense of an extra dimension inherent in golf makes up the heart of "The Pro" from "Other Modes" in *Museums and Women* and of three essays on the sport collected in *Picked-Up Pieces*. In "The Pro," the first person narrator smiles at himself as he tells about his four-hundred-and-twelfth golf lesson and his urge to "clobber the bastard." But the pro is impassive and does not laugh. Golf is serious business, and a hurried backswing with too much right hand at impact is more than a miscalculation—it is a fundamental flaw. "You're blocking yourself out," says the pro. "You're not open to your own potential. You're not, as we say, *free*" (171).

The implications are clear. Unlike any other game or sport, and despite Updike's praise of George Steiner's essays on chess and Roger Angell's on baseball, golf demands the fulfillment of man's potential while it offers the prize of freedom. No wonder Rabbit shouts in delight. Indeed, the pro, Dave, is a surrogate psychiatrist, a healer of hooks and slices who instructs the narrator to stretch out on the fragile bent-grass greens while he listens to the novice's problems. When the narrator explains that he may give up golf lessons in order to enjoy life, Dave responds without irony but with "noble impassivity" and a smile, "Golf is life, and life is lessons."

How correct he is. Updike knows that the nuances of sports call humanity to the pride of performance. The demands of golf are inflexible and unforgiving, but stretching to meet them, man rises beyond himself. It may be that only in sport can middle-aged men in the last half of twentieth-century suburban America hope to approach the glories of heroism: "and the humps of his brown muscles merge with the hillocks and swales of the course, whose red flags prick the farthest horizon, and whose dimmest sand traps are indistinguishable from galaxies. I see that he is right, as always, absolutely; there is no life, no world, beyond the golf course—just an infinite and terrible falling-off" (174). Watching the flight of a perfectly struck golf ball, he touches, for a moment, the heavens.

And yet, the narrator realizes, there is just the slightest chance that he is being taken. After all, Dave is a pro. He smiles and shows a dimple when he announces that golf is life. Besides, after four-hundred-and-twelve lessons, the narrator is still shooting 108. Is he a sucker? But the demands of the sport are worth the possibility of irony. It is not what he scores that counts; it is how he plays the shots. Lessons are forever necessary.[20]

The metaphysical dimensions of golf are fully explored in three essays in *Picked-Up Pieces* which are cross references to "Other Modes": "The First Lunar Invitational," "Tips on a Trip," and the appropriately titled "Is There Life After Golf?" The union of the mundane and the eternal exemplified by the soaring golf ball is comically suggested in the first of these when Updike commemorates Alan Shepard's golf swing on the moon with a piece of whimsy about a lunar invitational tournament. Spiro Agnew is still a victim of the shanks, and East-West politics in Africa scuttle plans for a second tournament, but golf has entered the galaxy. In the second essay, Updike explains with tongue partly in cheek that golf is not a hobby, profession, or pleasure, but a trip: "golf so transforms one's somatic sense, in short, that truth itself seems about to break through the exacerbated and as it were debunked fabric of mundane reality."[21] Cause and effect seem suspended on a golf course, for the success of a shot does not always depend upon the execution of the stroke. Only here are men truly free. Finally, in "Is There Life After Golf?", written in praise of Michael Murphy's *Golf in the Kingdom* (1972) and William Price Fox's *Doctor Golf* (1963), Updike celebrates the essential enigma of this sport which, he implies, is man's closest analogy to Life itself, "an outward projection of an inner self." As the "most mysterious, the least earthbound" of games, it narrows the distance between man and the supernatural while it reveals a psychosomatic sensitivity to his moods. Updike lauds Murphy's sentence as a beautiful description of golf and life: "We are spread wide as we play, then brought to a tiny place."[22] As Bill Fox writes, "the *swing is the man*."

Updike's meditations on the most mysterious sport may provide at least one answer to the question posed at the very beginning of the section "Other Modes." Recall that in "The Sea's Green Sameness," the narrator ponders the value of writing if art can never accurately describe nature and thereby unite man with it. Golf may bridge the gap.

Part III of *Museums and Women* is titled "The Maples." This section contains five stories about the continuing crises of Joan and Richard Maple, Updike's middle-class and now middle-aged couple swirling from love to adultery to near divorce and back to love in the mixing bowl of suburban marriage. These stories illustrate what Updike calls in another context "the irremediable grief in just living, in just going on."[23]

The Maples are his late twentieth-century couple who, in suburban parlance, are trying to hang in there. Their chances are slim. Although the following comment is not about them explicitly, it does suggest something of their dilemma: "I wonder if twentieth-century man's problem isn't one of encouragement, because of the failure of nerve, the lassitude and despair, the sense that we've gone to the end of the corridor and found it blank."[24] The Maples may not fall to despair, but the ends of their corridors are increasingly empty.

Not everyone approves of these stories. Robert Phillips, for example, says that Updike condescends to the Maples.[25] Charles Thomas Samuels admits that Updike's marriage tales are admired, but he finds them "trivial in situation," "no more complicated than his bittersweet little valentines," and proof only of his professionalism.[26] Some of them may be slick, but these stories are effective portraits of middle-class domestic crises. Marital hesitancy has never been more poignantly, even personally glimpsed. "I feel about the family as I do about the middle class," explains Updike, "that it's somehow fiercer in there than has been assumed."[27] Updike uncovers the ferocity.

He introduced the Maples in "Snowing in Greenwich Village" in his first collection, *The Same Door*. Although Updike was in his middle twenties when the first Maple tale appeared (and forty years old when *Museums and Women* was published), he must have foreseen what the distinctions between Tarbox and Olinger would mean for his fiction. For if Olinger is the place of the lost and lamented past, Tarbox is the residence of the sad and guilty present. The distance between William Young's snow at Olinger High School and the evening in the Village when the snow swirls by the window is much greater than that between Greenwich Village and the latest phone call from a lover in Tarbox.

Updike prepares the transitions well. Recall that in "Snowing in Greenwich Village," the Maples' marriage is not yet two years old and that they have no children. Apparently much in love with Joan, Richard nevertheless makes his first tentative move toward an adulterous affair when he escorts their female guest home in the snow. That he is the target of irony, a young husband befuddled by the woman's gestures, does not diminish the significance of his yearning. Years later, the Maples have moved to Tarbox, but it is still snowing in "The Taste of Metal." Although they now have four children,

Dick sends Joan to fetch the police following his minor car wreck in the snow. His decision to stay behind with the slightly injured Eleanor shows that the years have not changed him that much: "Moving from the hips up with surprising strength, Eleanor turned and embraced him. Her cheeks were wet; her lipstick tasted manufactured. Searching for her waist, for the smallness of her breasts, he fumbled through thicknesses of cloth. They were still in each other's arms when the whirling blue light of the police car broke upon them" (241).

A sense of loss defines this story. Richard's car will never again be new, Eleanor will never again kick her long legs so high, and Joan's marriage will never again be secure. It is not as if Joan is dull or unattractive. Everyone, including Richard, thinks her beautiful. But she realizes that marriage has taken its toll. Note her frustrated retort to Dick's accusation: "I have no lover! I let Mack kiss me because he's lonely and drunk! Stop trying to make me more interesting than I am! All I am is a beat-up housewife who wants to go play tennis with some other tired ladies!" (250). Significantly, we know that Mack is Eleanor's estranged husband. Joan's outburst of truth recalls the narrator's sensitive observation in "Wife-wooing": "Seven years have worn this woman." Nevertheless, Joan is still "smack-warm."

Reading the story of the Maples, one is reminded of William Dean Howells' description of his fifty-year marriage. "Marriage begins in love and ends in friendship." The Maples should hope for so much. The rounds of betrayal, accusation, and guilt, the pain and shame, the sheer agony of trying to hold on all suggest that the Maples will eventually lack even friendship, much less the possibility of a fifty-year marriage. And yet they survive. Despite all the red eyes and doubt, they continue to try. "Marching Through Boston" is a good example.

In this story, Updike places the Maples in the civil rights movement of the sixties. Joan is entirely committed, so much so that the night classes in non-violence and the courageous trek through Selma, Alabama, have a "salubrious" effect on this suburban mother of four. Richard is not convinced. In the other Maple stories, we learn that he admires President Johnson and supports the Viet Nam War. He is not against civil rights, nor is he pro-war, but he does distrust the false piety and jargon of organized protest. Thus when Joan reports that black men should march on the outside ranks of the women to protect their male self-esteem, or that black leaders counsel the marchers to face their "ego-gratificational motives," Dick, Updike, and the reader laugh. Dick despises the atmosphere of a fundamentalist revival meeting with the henchmen of Ralph Abernathy and Martin Luther King shouting, "Thass right. Say it, man," and he sees the hypocrisy as suburban audiences applaud when ridiculed by "dapper" young black speakers. Reading on, however, we realize that his distrust of the self-righteousness of organized protest mirrors his more fundamental frustration at the quality of his marriage. He punishes Joan because they are different; he resists her efforts to show him the necessity of giving; and he resents her newly found freedom. When he asks for attention by mocking black leaders or by overemphasizing his uncomfortable cold, Joan and the reader know that he is indeed a sick man.

For Joan blossoms during her involvement while Richard shrivels toward selfishness: "He had never known her like this. It seemed to Richard that her posture was improving, her figure filling out, her skin growing lustrous, her very hair gaining body and sheen. Though he had resigned himself, through twelve years of marriage, to a rhythm of apathy and renewal, he distrusted this raw burst of beauty" (222). The unexpected improvement in their sex life subtly wounds him when Joan rewards his promise to join the march by displaying renewed ardor.

The march is not what he expects. Popsicle vendors and peanut hawkers create a carnival atmosphere, and Martin Luther King grabs the spotlight. The day is cold and damp, and Dick carries the extra burden of a light fever. Most of all, his roving eye continues to seek out possible love affairs, this time a skimpy-bosomed teen-ager with braces. But Dick's depression is more than matched by Joan's joy. Back in the ranks of the marchers, she is "beautiful, like a poster, with far-seeing blue eyes and red lips parted in song" (231). Richard, unfortunately, is still associated with the King of Arabia who has eye trouble in "Giving Blood" (*The Music School*). Thus when they quarrel on the way home, Dick angry at being forced to listen to "boring stupid speeches," Joan defending the need to endure boredom in order to be witnesses, we know that his frustration is no match for her self-renewal. He mocks the incorrect English of the black speakers, and he uses his fever to cry for attention, but Joan is already on the telephone arranging, one assumes, the next meeting.

Updike characterizes Richard Maple as a weak man. Puzzled by Joan, Dick turns to Eleanor ("The Taste of Metal") who wears short skirts to show long thighs. Eleanor sits in the front seat of the car and crosses and recrosses her legs, but Joan occupies the back and warns Dick to watch the curves because of the snow. Her pun may not be deliberate, but it works. Since he sees Eleanor's curves but not the road's, the car hits a telephone pole and the marriage hits the skids. Those familiar with the Updike canon will note the cross reference to "Snowing in Greenwich Village." Caught again in the snow, Richard this time gives in to the siren. Perhaps remembering Rebecca's statement about being hot, he embraces Eleanor after turning on the heater. The policemen who pass by in pairs in the first story show up here to shine lights on the guilty couple.

Although Updike understandably writes primarily from the husband's point of view, he never implies that Dick deserves more sympathy than Joan. Indeed, the Maple stories work because Updike shows that designation of blame is not the issue. Guilt and the adulterous society replace love and the miracle of the Fifties, but the Maples continue to survive. How long depends largely upon Richard's ability to gain sight and insight. "Deeply cushioned in a cottony indifference," he prefers to ignore the shock that hitting the reality of the telephone pole creates. Like Eleanor, he views the pole not as a warning but as a nuisance. Ignoring rules diminishes life, suggests Updike, especially when the stakes are the social fabric itself.

Updike's balanced attitude toward this marriage, whose fluctuations reflect the changes in the quality of American domestic life, is illustrated in "Your Lover Just Called" and "Eros Rampant." In the former, Dick is confident that he is unjust when he accuses Joan of having lovers. Her reply that she is a worn-out housewife tired of being maneuvered into something she does not understand keeps our sympathy with her, especially since we know that Dick's accusation is hypocritical. Even his son asks him to "see," but by now his self-blindness seems permanent. Richard approaches the despicable in this story, for he takes pleasure in taunting Joan and Eleanor's estranged husband Mack for kissing. We do not know if Joan is having an affair, but her question exposes his hypocrisy: "Why are you so pleased?" But in "Eros Rampant," the first sentence—"The Maples' house is full of love"—becomes ironic when Joan confesses to a long series of lovers. Her charge, that Dick tells her she is beautiful but does not make her feel it, stuns him. Both partners contribute to the tension. Both are baffled by the results. Yet they stay together. In "Sublimating," now married eighteen years, they agree to give up sex since that is the primary sore point in their marriage. He buys a cabbage while she has the car washed. She makes the garden while he rejects her shy offer of sex in order to play golf: "love is merely the backswing." Neither, of course, is convinced that sublimation solves sadness.

Perusing these comments about a contemporary marriage crisis, the reader may well ask what makes these stories more than just another soap opera on the level of *True Confessions*. Part of the answer is the quality of the prose, something that is better experienced than analyzed. The rhythm of the sentences, the alliteration and allusions, the metaphors—all contribute to lift these tales beyond pulp fiction to short story art. Joan returns home from her job "flushed and quick-tongued, as if from sex" (255). A tipsy Dick experiences an accident that in "another incarnation he would regret" (238). Most of all, the stories about the Maples are valuable because of the insight Updike brings to them. He shows that he has been there, that he understands the "elemental constituents" of marriage: Woman, man, house.

The effects are rarely melodramatic. Readers used to the formulas of pop romance expect anger and display when the wife confesses her adulteries, but Updike knows better. Adultery can often enhance the value of used goods. Thus when Joan reveals her betrayals, Updike describes Dick so that his childish egotism is both unmistakable and perhaps an indication of at least one cause of their marital tension. Rather than huff and puff and slap Joan around, he is proud. He misses the irony of his situation. "Her head beside his shoulder, her grave polite pleasantries, the plump unrepentant cleft between her breasts, all seem newly treasurable and intrinsic to his own identity. As a cuckhold, he has grown taller, attenuated, more elegant and humane in his opinions, airier and more mobile" (264). At the same time, Updike knows that "love is pitiless." Dick torments Joan the way he has had his female cat and dog "fixed." Significantly, the children suspect the differences once the pets are deprived of natural passion. Although Joan's adultery urges Dick to make love with renewed ardor and exact from her a "new wantonness," he nevertheless pounds away until he has each detail in place: Dates, sites, motels, emotions. Details make the difference to him as he struggles to cover truth with the magic of fantasy. Details both incriminate and thrill. And always on the periphery are the children, the reality which warns the man in "Solitaire" and which shouts "no!" in Richard's dreams. Their drawings of houses, cats, and flowers tacked up around the kitchen, the children continue growing through awkwardness and knowledge much as their father thinks he grows, but they are unaware of the difficulties in the heart of the master bedroom. Surely Updike expects the reader to pick up the reference to the famous prophecy of disaster in Isaiah when Dick associates himself with a "watchman of the night." The humming sound which he hears in the telephone pole transformer at the end of "Eros Rampant" may be town gossip about the troubled Maples, but it may also suggest his need to listen to his troubled self.

Updike's various stories of love and marriage mirror the home life of middle-class America. Olinger becomes Tarbox, the fifties become the sixties and seventies, and innocence and pregnancy give way to compromise and betrayal. But the center does not fold, the marriage does not dissolve, and the nation does not collapse. His social fiction is a metaphor for America at mid-century. The last story, "Sublimating," takes the reader full circle to the first meditation in the book, "Museums and Women." The crises are all set up there. Richard and Joan Maple are now a prize exhibit in the gallery.

In 1976, Updike published a short story titled "Couples" in an edition limited to 250 signed copies (Cambridge, Massachusetts: Halty Ferguson). Although originally written in 1963, the story was rejected by the *New Yorker* and never published in journal or book form. Readers of the Updike canon will recognize from the title alone that the tale is a forerunner of the best-selling novel *Couples* (1968). As Updike admits in the introduction to the limited edition, the story is too crowded to be rendered successfully in short fiction; thus his abandonment of "Couples" in favor of *Couples*.

Yet some scraps were salvaged. Written at about the same time as "At a Bar in Charlotte Amalie" and "The Christian Roommates" (*The Music School*), an essay on Denis de Rougemont's theories of love (*Assorted Prose*), and the poem "Report of Health" (*Midpoint*), "Couples" provided a remark for "When Everyone Was Pregnant" ("You look just like a voluptuous big piece of wallpaper."), a simile for "Harv Is Plowing Now" (comparing breaking surf to a typewriter carriage), and many details for *Marry Me*. Despite what Updike defines as its "incidental faults of sentimentality and vagueness," the story clearly retains some significance for its author. The point here, however, is not the flaws of "Couples" or its echoes in later tales but its contribution to his continual observation of American domestic life.

"Couples" is important because it is among Updike's first attempts to write about suburban adultery, a subject, he explained in 1976, that, if "I have not exhausted it, has exhausted me. But I have persisted, as I earlier persisted in describing the drab normalities of a Pennsylvania boyhood, with the conviction that there was something good to say for it, some sad magic that, but for me, might go unobserved."[28] The magic is sad because time tarnishes the innocent glow, "the simple party pleasures," of the newly married. Updike's personal stake in these stories about loss of marital innocence is made clear in the introduction to "Couples": "The lofty and possibly unkind sociological tone of that novel [*Couples*], and the note of personal emotion struck in a number of short stories less clumsy than this one, are here still fused" (9). Personal short stories reflect social dilemmas. As we have seen, enchantment erodes to guilt around 1960.

Friendship inevitably degenerating to betrayal is at the heart of many of these short fictions. Living alone now, the narrator of "Couples" recalls a time when the other young marrieds of Tarbox "looked like safeguards, echoes, reinforcements of our happiness" (13). Parties are planned, sports are played, and maternity clothes are swapped together.[29] The narrator remembers: "In memory it seems we were playing at being adults, at being fathers and mothers and homeowners. We had all, it chanced, come to it new together, this incredible America where we managed, and controlled, and mattered" (15). The time is the late 1950s, and everyone is pregnant. But the safeguards slip away; the reinforcements shatter. Close proximity leads to physical desire; and adultery, secrecy, and pain are the results.

This story stresses what many others imply—that the puncturing of marital illusions coincides with the changing decade. Just as time's beat is inevitable, so is the betrayal of love and friendship. The final flowering of innocence—an appropriate metaphor here since Updike describes each couple in terms of a flower—occurs at a party which the narrator's wife gives him for his twenty-eighth birthday. Few readers want to insist upon the identification of the narrator and Updike, but in this case the possibility has merit if only because of Updike's statement in the introduction that "Couples" has a note of personal emotion. If the identification is acceptable, then the time of the birthday party may be 1960 (Updike was born in 1932). Never again will the idyl of the 1950s sustain them.[30] As the narrator admits, this party is the last of its kind: "The colors of the flowers were beginning to separate" (24). Adulterous love is not plotted, and no sense of conquest is felt, but partners are secretly switched while families disintegrate.

The lure of the unknown lingers as a false promise of renewal. A year following the birthday party, the narrator explains, "The shock of plunging into an affair quickly yielded to delicious sensations of freedom and elemental acceptance and new knowledge" (28). He decides to sacrifice his marriage, to play, however ironically, the role of the martyr in order to salvage these new possibilities for realigned couples. But at the end of the story he is alone, divorced from wife and not yet married to mistress, "without illusions, unless memories count" (40). Although he imagines marriage with the mistress, he is not eager to begin again the life of couples. The decade of the 1950s is a time of maternity clothes and joy; the next decade is a time of memory and loss. Significantly for those who have read this chapter or *Museums and Women*, the narrator's former wife now has a part-time job in a museum. Marriage is a relic.[31]

Notes to *Museums and Women*

1. Alice and Kenneth Hamilton disagree. *See* their essay on *Museums and Women* for an interpretation of the volume from a religious perspective which perhaps insists upon more theological nuances than the stories should be made to bear. "John Updike's 'Museums and Women and Other Stories,'" *Thought*, 49 (March 1974), 56–71.

2. Guy Davenport, "Temptations," *National Review*, 22 December 1972, pp. 1413-1414; Elmer F. Suderman, "Alas—Updike's Twice-Told Tales—Poor, Uric," *Carleton Miscellany*, 13(Spring-Summer 1973), 153-155; Dorothy Rabinowitz, "Books in Brief," *World*, 24 October 1972, pp. 52-53; Doris Grumbach, "Suburban Middle Age," *New Republic*, 21 October 1972, pp. 30-31. Davenport is blunt. Arguing that Updike is not effective with short stories, he says that *Museums and Women* has the "air of a retrospective show." He apparently lumps all of the stories together, for he suggests that the tales are no more than fragments of failed novels and thus have about them "a distinct air of the bottom of the barrel." Suderman agrees. Complaining that the collection is "the same old Updike," he insists that the themes with which Updike was once effective have worn out so that his

variations have become "more strained, more contrived." The once successful portrayals of mediocrity are now only mediocre. Similarly, Rabinowitz approaches *Museums and Women* with the attitude that it is the same old stuff. Updike offers little more than poignancy and wistfulness, and thus there is a "vacuity at the heart of these stories." Most of all, she dislikes Updike's tendency to make the inner vision the drama rather than the action of the protagonists. Rabinowitz reveals that she wants traditional short stories when she laments what she considers to be Updike's decision to emphasize his own sensibility over the potential for it in his characters.

3. Tony Tanner, "The Sorrow of Some Central Hollowness," New York *Times Book Review*, 22 October 1972, p. 5.

4. Robert Phillips does not like what he calls Updike's "pyrotechnical displays" in several sections of *Museums and Women*, but he recognizes that Updike is not merely repeating himself as the negative critics insist. Keith Mano concurs. Arguing that Updike's characters are "frankly less interesting" than the objects around them, Mano praises his insight in showing how men are known by their things, especially their houses. Like Grumbach, Mano questions Updike's style, suggesting that he is "so splendid" in the sentence and paragraph that the larger forms of the story and novel seem "perhaps secondary, an anti-climax." *See* Robert Phillips, "Museums and Women and Other Stories," *Commonweal*, 30 May 1973, pp. 92-94; and D. Keith Mano, "Every Inch an Updike," *Book Week*, 22 October 1972, p. 3.

5. Richard Todd, "Updike and Barthelme: Disengagement," *Atlantic*, 230 (December 1972), 130.

6. Peter T. Rohrbach, "Museums and Women and Other Stories," *America*, 16 December 1972, p. 536.

7. All would admit that the volume will hardly settle the debate between those who admire Updike as a preserver of language and those who insist that he writes beautifully about nothing, but Kanon extends his critical neck to declare that the stories in *Museums and Women* "are the work of perhaps the finest literary craftsman working in America today." Updike combines a pictorial sensibility with a tinker's fascination with things, and like Vermeer, one of his favorite painters, he can "light a small moment and fill it with importance." Those looking for post-war hysteria or intimations of apocalypse will be disappointed. Charles Deemer agrees that the apparent "smallness" of Updike's subject matter makes some critics misjudge him as minor: "The reason he is so often underrated, I would venture, is that he explores the private lives, the hopes and losses and despairs, of people about whom it has become fashionable to think nothing at all...." *See* Joseph Kanon, "Satire and Sensibility," *Saturday Review*, 30 September 1972, pp. 73, 78; Charles Deemer, "Exploring Suburbia," *The New Leader*, 22 January 1973, pp. 18-19; William H. Pritchard, "Long Novels and Short Stories," *Hudson Review*, 26(Spring 1973), especially pp. 239-240.

8. Some of the British reviewers share Pritchard's high regard for *Museums and Women*. The anonymous reviewer for the London *Times Literary Supplement*, for example, suggests that Updike is good enough to "eat half a dozen of his literary contemporaries for breakfast." *See* "At the Flashpoint," *Times Literary Supplement*, 4 May 1973, p. 488. Others are not as sure. *See* Richard Freeman, "More Couples," *The Observer Review*, 29 April 1973, p. 30; and Francis Hope, "Too Much," *New Statesman*, 27 April 1973, p. 626. It is interesting to note that in general the British reviewers try to outdo Updike's verbal cleverness with language tricks of their own. What seems to count in some of their reviews is not the perception of the insights but how wittily they are expressed.

9. Thomas Molyneux, "The Affirming Balance of Voice," *Shenandoah*, 25 (Winter 1974), 32.

10. For a linguistic approach to the language of "Museums and Women," see Alfred F. Rosa, "The Psycholinguistics of Updike's 'Museums and Women,'" *Modern Fiction Studies*, 20(Spring 1974), 107–111.

11. John Updike, *Museums and Women and Other Stories* (New York: Knopf, 1972), 5. Further references will be to this edition.

12. John Updike, *Picked-Up Pieces* (New York: Knopf, 1975), 167.

13. Frank Gado, "Interview with John Updike," *First Person: Conversations on Writers and Writing* (Schenectady, New York: Union College Press, 1973), 89.

14. John Updike, *Rabbit, Run* (New York: Knopf, 1960), 225.

15. Alice and Kenneth Hamilton, "John Updike's 'Museums and Women and Other Stories,'" 67.

16. Phillips, 93.

17. Updike, *Picked-Up Pieces*, 518.

18. John Updike, *Assorted Prose* (New York: Knopf, 1965), 146.

19. Updike, *Rabbit, Run*, 133–134.

20. For another story on the metaphysical implications of golf, see "Intercession," *The Same Door* (New York: Knopf, 1959).

21. Updike, *Picked-Up Pieces*, 95.

22. Updike, *Picked-Up Pieces*, 102.

23. Updike, *Picked-Up Pieces*, 499.

24. Quoted in Eric Rhode, "Grabbing Dilemmas," *Vogue*, 1 February 1971, p. 184.

25. Phillips, 93.

26. Charles Thomas Samuels, "John Updike," *American Writers: A Collection of Literary Biographies*, ed. Leonard Ungar (New York: Scribners, 1974), 226.

27. "View from the Catacombs," *Time*, 26 April 1968, p. 74.

28. John Updike, "Couples," (Cambridge, Massachusetts: Halty Ferguson, 1976), 9. Further references will be to this edition.

29. In the more recent story "Atlantises," Updike writes, "people never tired of parties. There were beach parties, lawn parties, housewarming parties, office parties, birthday parties, post-party parties, all with 'something of the barbaric....'" *New Yorker*, 13 November 1978, p. 44.
30. In *The Coup*, Updike writes, "It turns out the Fifties were when all the fun was, though nobody knew it at the time." John Updike, *The Coup* (New York: Knopf, 1978).
31. In March 1979, Updike published the collected Maples' Stories as *Too Far To Go* (New York: Fawcett, 1979).

PROSE:
Assorted Prose (1965)
Picked-Up Pieces (1975)

Assorted Prose

"Better to praise and share than blame
and ban."

—Picked-Up Pieces

The disappointment which greeted *Assorted Prose* (1965) was based not so much upon material in the collection but upon expectations by the critics.[1] Where, the general question ran, is the major work by the young author of poems, short stories, and especially *Rabbit, Run* and *The Centaur?* Not, answered many reviewers, in the pages of *Assorted Prose.*

Walter Sullivan's response is typical. Praising Updike as the American who writes the best conversation, the best description, and the best "working prose" of all his contemporaries, Sullivan dismisses most of the collection as leftovers from the desk and wastebasket. Although he appreciates the book reviews, he finds the selections from the "Talk of the Town" section of the *New Yorker* egotistical, the parodies silly, the report on Ted Williams pretentious, and the autobiographical pieces disappointing. He sides with those who expect *Moby-Dick* from the author of *Rabbit, Run:* "Skillfully written as these are, they appear to go nowhere; they tell us nothing. This is to me the paradox of Updike's major work: he writes so remarkably well and achieves so little."[2] The anonymous reviewer for *Newsweek* feels the same way. Noting that at only age thirty-three, Updike has already published three novels and "reams" of short stories, the critic condescendingly points out that Updike "continues to be the most promising young writer around."[3] He calls on Updike to write a "really meaningful" novel, not just another polished gem but "the bench mark of an oeuvre." *Assorted Prose* too much resembles nibbling before a banquet despite the astonishing twists and turns of Updike's syntax.[4]

Not everyone agrees with these censures. If Walter Sullivan dismisses the long essay on Ted Williams as pretentious, D.M. Davis describes it as "the cream of the book."[5] He calls attention to recent efforts to make non-fiction the art form it used to be, and he appreciates Updike's miscellaneous work as a major factor in the renaissance of the occasional essay.[6]

Reading through the negative comments about *Assorted Prose*, one wonders if the critics are judging Updike not on what he offers but on what he avoids. The persistent call from reviewers to our contemporary authors that they all publish masterpieces or the "bench mark of an oeuvre" reflects the *Moby-Dick* syndrome in American letters. That is, no author can be said to have arrived until he takes his turn at the Great American Novel, and a long one at that. Updike expressed his opinion on this issue as long ago as "An Ode" in *The Carpentered Hen* (1958). It is not that the questions raised by critics are insignificant but that many of the comments miss the point. To ask if Updike takes chances with his fiction and thus helps to keep the novel alive, or if he communicates a sense of commitment, or if he offers more than the sterile spectaculars of style is to raise legitimate inquiries. But to judge him a disappointment only because he has not written a book the equal of *Moby-Dick* or *The Golden Bowl* or *Absalom, Absalom!* is to undervalue a considerable achievement by a remarkably versatile writer. From today's perspective, it is ironic that these three masterpieces were attacked by the critics of the day. The choice is not to publish something great or be a failure but to write with intelligence and grace. A contemporary reviewer's definition of greatness is nearly worthless in the final analysis of an author's work when placed beside the all-demanding criteria of time, scholarly analysis, and the luck of public opinion.

Updike understands these problems. He reviews all sorts of authors, from Paul Tillich to J.D. Salinger with intelligence, high standards, and most of all sympathy for the struggling writer, and he always asks not for the great American novel but for the best the author can do at the moment. A case in point is his review of Salinger's *Franny and Zooey*. Updike believes that Salinger can do better than the long stories about the Glass family, and he does not shrink from pointing out what he considers to be flaws. Surely many fans of both Updike and Salinger will agree that "Salinger loves the Glasses more than God loves them. He loves them too exclusively. Their invention has become a hermitage to him. He loves them to the detriment of artistic moderation. 'Zooey' is just too long; there are too many cigarettes, too many goddamns, too much verbal ado about not quite enough" (237). But to criticize is not always to condemn. Updike offers encouragement as well as censure: "When all reservations have been entered, in the correctly unctuous and apprehensive tone, about the direction he has taken, it remains to acknowledge that it is a direction, and that the refusal to rest content, the willingness to risk excess on behalf of one's obsessions, is what distinguishes artists from entertainers, and what makes some artists adventurers on behalf of us all" (238–239).

Of all the reviews of *Assorted Prose*, only Granville Hicks's illustrates these demanding qualities of criticism and tolerance. Even his title is instructive: "They Also Serve Who Write Well." This is not to say that Hicks judges *Assorted Prose* a masterpiece but to applaud his appreciation of serious writing well done. He does not like everything in the collection. Calling Updike "precocious and prolific," he names some of the material "apprentice" work, says that the parodies "scarcely seem worth republication," and notes that Updike does not pretend to be a great critic. Yet if Updike the reviewer is not a great critic, he is always an interesting commentator, and he always has something to say. The collection as a whole shows versatility of subject matter and mastery of language. Hicks is aware of the debate which the publication of *Assorted Prose* generated about Updike's writing to that point, so he asks rhetorical questions as a lead to serious answers: "But, some people ask, isn't he spreading himself too thin? Has he written anything that is worthy of his talents? Isn't it time he wrote a Great Book?" Hicks's questions read like an unintentional parody of some of the reviewers discussed above, and his answers are to the point: "In the same way, it might be a good thing for critics to contemplate what Updike has accomplished in a decade — two excellent novels and many first-rate stories—and not to spend so much time worrying about the books he hasn't yet even attempted."[7]

Some of the worry apparently eased in the decade between *Assorted Prose* and Updike's second miscellaneous volume *Picked-Up Pieces* (1975). Perhaps one reason is that in the intervening ten years he wrote so much that he was no longer judged the promising young writer both prolific and precious but rather the major author of a considerable canon. Between *Assorted Prose* and *Picked-Up Pieces* he published four novels, the unified cycle of tales *Bech: A Book*, two volumes of short stories, one book of poems, and one play. Some reviewers abandoned the question of where is his *Moby-Dick* to ponder the thornier query of the significance of his achievement. The comments on *Picked-Up Pieces* reflect this change in attitude.

Rather than advise Updike to abandon essays and reviews in order to concentrate on the pursuit of the Great American Novel, Lawrence Graver urges him to continue the fruitful, although doubtlessly frustrating, balance of journalism and fiction. He describes *Picked-Up Pieces* as "a splendidly cluttered Italian museum where profane and sacred treasures, monuments and miniatures, make dizzying claims on our attention," and he is impressed enough with Updike's wit to note that "even the footnotes sparkle."[8] More important, perhaps, for those who continue to doubt the value of these miscellaneous pieces is Graver's observation that similar concerns enliven both essays and novels: Sentences which blend Updike's self-effacement and self-regard, description which shows his respect for mundane circumstances, and themes which illustrate his passion for human connectedness.

Calvin Bedient is a bit more critical. Noting Updike's cheery intelligence, knack for lightness, and persuasive reviews, he points out what he considers to be special pleas in Updike's criticism which tend to make it lurch to one side. In general, he is disturbed not by Updike's sidetrack to the occasional essay, a direction which bothers many commentators on *Assorted Prose,* but by his tendency to urge mimesis in fiction as if reality were agreed upon and thus defined. Although Updike sees a "reverent submission to reality" as the essential ingredient for lasting art, Bedient suggests that this prescription is "too sweet, already archaic" when set against the achievements of many modern authors.[9]

The jacket blurb for *Assorted Prose* echoes with Updike's own rhythms. The miscellany is described as a "motley but not unshapely collection" in which the author searches "for touchstones, for the clarifying pinch of magic." Whether that pinch is found is a matter of individual judgment, but the motley assortment is certainly well shaped. Updike arranges *Assorted Prose* into "Parodies," "First Person Plural" (*New Yorker* editorial comments), "Hub Fans Bid Kid Adieu," "First Person Singular" (autobiographical sketches), and "Reviews," and he introduces it all with a Foreword.

Although Thomas B. Morgan dismisses the Foreword as "a diffi-
dent, hasty preface, disappointingly brief and depressingly irrelevant," I find it humble in tone and apologetic in manner.[10] Morgan
wants Updike to use the Foreword to develop the implications about
fiction in the reviews, but one should read it as no more than a
comment on why and how certain pieces were written. Here we
learn, for example, that except for a few requests to place some
comments in a more lasting form, most notably "Hub Fans Bid Kid
Adieu," Updike selected most of the material on his own initiative,
"as one more attempt to freeze the flux of life into the icy permanence of print" (vii). The parodies were written between 1956 and
1961 when he was "young at heart" and hoped to emulate his first
literary idols, Thurber and Benchley. The editorial "we" of "First
Person Plural" is the voice of a collection of "dazzled farmboys" as
the rural-bred Updike toured the urban sidewalks of New York from
1955 to 1957 to write for the "Talk of the Town" section of the *New
Yorker.* A major part of the "First Person Singular" section, "The
Dogwood Tree: A Boyhood," was first published in Martin Levin's
Five Boyhoods and is now judged by Updike to have "the under-
cooked quality of prose written to order, under insufficient personal
pressure" (ix). The two pieces on uncles have their current form because they failed as short stories, and "The Lucid Eye in Silver Town"
was rejected in 1956 only to be revised and published in 1964 in
the *Saturday Evening Post* and, says Updike, *Pravda* (June 21, 1964).
Finally, he explains that of the books reviewed he was asked to write
about some (those by Sillitoe, Aiken, Agee, and Hughes) and that he
asked to comment on others (those by Salinger, Spark, and Nabokov). Other pertinent information may be found in the Foreword,
but a more interesting point may be that Updike's own deprecatory
tone seems to have persuaded some reviewers to treat the collection
too harshly. Demanding a masterpiece, they read an assortment
which the author himself describes as motley.

Updike's judgment seems fair. *Assorted Prose* does not have the
intellectual weight of *Picked-Up Pieces,* but it is fun to read. The
parodies are a case in point. If they deserve this rescue, this freezing
of "the flux of life into the icy permanence of print," it is only because they serve as examples of Updike's apprentice work. Many of
them were written in 1956 and 1957 before the publication of his
first book, and thus they hold a place in his canon relative to the
position of, say, *New Orleans Sketches* in William Faulkner's. The

difference, however, is interesting. By reprinting them himself, Updike may have parodied his parodies and gotten the jump on the literary scholar who specializes in digging up apprentice material which some readers might prefer to stay hidden. It is not that the parodies lack skill but that, except perhaps for the parody of Harry Truman with its unintentional comparison with Richard Nixon's self-serving memoirs, they seem little more than amusing efforts to try one's hand at a demanding genre. Their relationship to some of Updike's light verse, especially in *The Carpentered Hen*, is obvious—delightful to read but hardly memorable.

Updike's burlesques are designed not so much to ridicule as to entertain. His style is never barbed or antagonistic, and his targets are not selected so as to have an impact on contemporary affairs in the manner of political parodies of earlier centuries. These burlesques are organized more to illustrate his wit than to criticize his subject. "The American Man: What of *Him*?" is an example. Written, like much of his light verse, as an occasional piece prompted by a sign or a statement in a magazine, in this case *Life*, this short parody of the journal editorial contains many of the effects found in the other examples of light prose. The tone, for instance, is mock-seriousness expressed by the use of understatement ("Lord Baltimore...was a man. So was Wyatt Earp."). Illustrations are made ridiculous by lists of incongruous names (Lord Baltimore, Wyatt Earp, and Calvin Coolidge). Silly poeticisms are included to show the implied author's command of good English (the Pilgrims and their "water-weathered ships"). Ridiculous examples of cause and effect illustrate the author's knowledge of history and logic (too many trees scarred the American male's mental make-up and thus led to a high suicide rate). Language is turned in on itself in the form of clichés which hit a target ("Free Way of Life") and sexual puns which bring a smile (in his home, the American male "cunningly gets his way"). Finally, the qualities of fairness and seriousness are suggested when he admits that men have some "insidious shortcomings" (which he does not have time to list) and when he quotes a few lines from Robert Frost's "The Gift Outright" to throw the careless reader off the track. Updike follows this general format in many of the parodies.

No doubt all of this is clever, but many readers will wonder if the end product is worth the effort. Perhaps a fair way to answer is to inquire if the reader enjoys parody. If he does, then he may appreciate a few of Updike's burlesques. One problem with the parodies in *Assorted Prose* is that some seem dated or even silly today. "Anywhere Is Where You Hang Your Hat" makes fun of the Post Office campaign of several decades ago to convince the public of the advantage of including postal-zone numbers on the addresses of envelopes. These numbers have now become the even more obnoxious zip-codes, and the Post Office itself is a national joke. The point is that Updike's parody of the 1950s does not transcend its time and hardly touches the ridiculousness of the Post Office in the 1970s and 1980s. More on target and more humorous is "Postal Complaints" of the "First Person Plural" section. There Updike expresses his appreciation for the old, individualized local post offices, each with its "wanted" posters for "Dillinger and Aaron Burr," and he despairs of the new buildings built in the name of sterility and functionalism (66). Similarly, the parody of intellectual essays, "What Is a Rhyme?," is an amusing illustration of the circumlocutions, parenthetical asides, esoteric references which baffle even intellectuals, and sprinkling of quotations in foreign languages which are all found in T.S. Eliot's prose. The piece is clever but hardly worth repeated readings.

Like many readers I turn to parodies if I am interested in the target being hit. In these instances, the burlesque is more than just an example of the genre; it offers a particular point of view on a subject which may obsess, infuriate, or even bore the reader. Pleasure, not instruction, is the point in these cases. The reader laughs at himself as well as with the author. For those who know of Updike's skill in describing athletic contests and his appreciation of sports, especially golf, "Drinking from a Cup Made Cinchy" is an interesting entertainment. Explaining that he wrote the parody after reading too many books on how to play golf, he captures the exasperating and often apparently contradictory instructions which these books, usually copiously illustrated, impose upon the week-end duffer longing to break 80. Updike has done better with his golf stories, notably Rabbit's round with Eccles in *Rabbit, Run*, "The Pro" (*Museums and Women*), and the cleverly titled "Is There Life After Golf?" (*Picked-Up Pieces*), but nowhere else does he show better the sheer difficulty of learning this most frustrating sport. As a golfer since youth who is struggling mightily and failing miserably to keep his handicap at three or lower, I can testify to the accuracy of Updike's understated despair at two crucial "helpful hints" which all golf manuals include: (1) "Don't be tense." (2) "Don't be 'loose.'" The parallel with learning to drink coffee in social situations without spilling is unusual and accurate. Making fun of America's delight with How–To manuals seems more to the point than scoring off easy targets like Jack Kerouac's *On the Road* in "On the Sidewalk."

In general, Updike's fun at the expense of the literary establishment is entertaining because he often laughs at himself. As a prolific reviewer and commentator on all sorts of books written by all kinds of people, he knows to avoid a format and style which degenerate into formula. His parody "Why Robert Frost Should Receive the Nobel Prize" takes a deserved swipe at unsympathetic critics who attack many authors under the guise of praise. The essay is not so much a criticism of Frost's poetry as it is an exposure of the clichés attached to him in his later years and a rebuke of those who would place Frost against his more obviously experimental peers as if the reader had to make a choice for the sake of "healthy sanity in literature and in life" (30). His comment in *Picked-Up Pieces* is to the point: "Better to praise and share than blame and ban." As for the difficulties of book reviewing itself, or even of keeping up with the necessary reading, one need only examine "The Unread Book Route" to watch Updike smile at himself. The smile is honest. Later on he provides what may be taken as an acceptable generalization about the value of these pieces of burlesque. In the review section of *Assorted Prose*, he discusses Dwight Macdonald's edition of *Parodies: An Anthology from Chaucer to Beerbohm—and After*, and he writes, "If great parodists are not great writers, great writers, conversely, are not great parodists" (246). If Updike is finally ranked as great, a pointless debate which one assumes would amuse him, the judgment will not be based on his parodies.

The "First Person Plural" section, comprised of notes and comments written for the *New Yorker*, is not as ephemeral, for it serves as a kind of middlebrow version of American history and interests between 1956 and 1965. The unhappy progression from the relative stasis of President Eisenhower's second term to the cataclysm of President Kennedy's death and beyond gives form to this section and tone to the essays. The change from a description of Central Park to comments on what Updike calls "The Assassination" is telling.

The visit to Central Park as described for the *New Yorker* is now worthless by itself, but for the Updike reader it has its pleasures. Published in 1956, three years before his first novel *The Poorhouse Fair*, the description is an early example of several traits in Updike's prose which he would later develop to high praise: The eye for simile (great rocks emerging from snow drifts and "glistening like the backs of resurrected brontosaurs"; the "resurrected" is appropriate because the time is the first day of spring); the interest in unusual and usually little known places, animals, and things ("tahr," "aoudad," and "Coati"); and most of all the love affair with the quotidian, with things as they are (men playing checkers, boys throwing snowballs, a woman dropping her camera). Developed in his contributions to the "Talk of the Town" section of the *New Yorker*, these characteristics in his early prose became the hallmarks of his later novels and short stories. Updike's penchant for mimesis and the realistic novel has its germ in these occasional pieces of description. Although he discusses his preference for realism in the Reviews section of *Assorted Prose*, he illustrates it here. The essay on pigeons, for example, may be amusing, but it is also a carefully researched paper on bird lore full of reliable information. The same is true of the report on Antarctica. Updike cites facts, describes things, and shows his awareness of relevant history. In each case, however, his humor nullifies the possibility of soporific scholarship. After discussing the mythical, historical, and religious backgrounds of pigeons, he informs us with a straight face that while fifty thousand pigeons live in Manhattan, they cannot vote. Besides, only five are listed in the telephone book—"two Edwins, two Georges, and one Pete" (57). The fascinating history of Antarctica ends the same way. Learning that the snow precipitation does not keep up with the ice lost off the continent in the form of bergs, he comments that were Antarctica to melt completely, "strange viruses and bacteria could be unleashed on the world." Worse, he implies, New York City would be covered with three hundred feet of water. He ends with a deadpan "This is not likely to happen in our time" (64). The careful notation of facts (*see also*, "Old and Precious") and the skill with surface description join the eye for simile and the understated humor to make the prose of these sketches a forerunner of the novels on which Updike's reputation currently rests.

Few readers of "First Person Plural" will fail to be impressed by the astonishing range of subjects covered in these short paragraphs. Updike writes knowledgeably of dinosaur eggs, the parks of New York, and John P. Marquand. The cross references to his more substantial pieces of writing are obvious to those who wish to pursue them. "Crush vs. Whip," for example, looks toward the widely read "Hub Fans Bid Kid Adieu" in showing off Updike's knowledge of baseball with its special world of statistics and records. The reports of art shows and the musings on the inheritors of Cubism remind the reader of his days as an art student in England and also provide a frame for the later stories "Still Life" (*Pigeon Feathers*) and the title story of *Museums and Women*. And the obituary for Grandma Moses contains a quotation which illustrates how graciously he connects his report for the day with his view of the world: "Little is said nowadays about the wisdom of age. Perhaps such wisdom is dreaded, for there is melancholy in it" (102). All of these selections are well written. But if "First Person Plural" is to retain any significance beyond the relative value present in the apprentice work of an important author, it will be found in the sketches which, when read together, detail by way of both metaphor and fact another of America's falls from innocence.

Updike's occasional pieces for the *New Yorker* chronicle this decline during the unhappy decade between 1955 and 1965. His wisdom is indeed melancholy. The place to begin is with "Spatial Remarks," four pages written between November 1957 and August 1964. In November 1957, Updike recalls a third-grade teacher debunking the deity of the moon by telling him that the mysterious sphere is no more than "a mammoth stone." The catalyst for this memory is the Russian threat to win the space race by using a satellite to splash red paint across the lunar craters. Yet for the moment Updike retains his innocent view of the moon. Nearly two years later, however, in September 1959, he regrets that the mystery and thrill of expectation which should accompany any exploration, especially of something as unknown as space, have been diminished by television comedians and backs of cereal boxes which have made "this whole awesome business too familiar to all of us" (72). His observation is true, one which both laments the lack of poetry in our technological advances and looks forward to Norman Mailer's discussion of what was missing when Neil Armstrong left a footprint on the moon (*Of a Fire on the Moon*). Worse, says Updike in March 1963, the magnificent space probes which assure us that no life exists on the planets not only diminish the imagination but increase man's sense of cosmic loneliness.

The point of these comments is not a debunking of science but a questioning of results. Updike is no anti-intellectual. The extraordinary range of his book reviews attests to his inquisitive and open mind. Accepting what has been gained in the space experiments, he also asks what has been lost. Never directly stated in any one sketch, but present in a series of them when read together is the implication that the United States around 1960 gave up once again its innocence, naiveté, and youth; abstract values, perhaps, but nevertheless qualities which contribute to the greatness of the country. Something is wrong when the heroics of space exploration become boring in only two years because of exploitation by television comedians and cereal makers.

Updike also suggests that America experienced a decline in morality in the late 1950s. In "Morality Play," written in October 1959 as an editorial on the television quiz show scandals, he notes, "The mysterious and awful thing about the television quiz scandals is not that the jaded souls who ran the show were hoaxers but that dozens, and perhaps hundreds, of contestants, almost all of whom must have applied in the simplicity of good faith, were successfully enrolled in the hoax" (86). From a post–Watergate perspective, Updike's opinion might seem naive, but at the time it was expressed, Americans had not been even further disillusioned by the assassinations of the 1960s, the debacle of the Viet Nam War, and the corruption of Richard Nixon's Presidency. As Updike points out, the dishonesty of the television scandals did not touch politicians but fouled instead the "faces you saw in a walk around the block." The challenge was moral, and the challenge was not met. What happened, he asks, to that "simplicity of good faith"? Walt Kelly's famous line would have applied to these cheaters: "We have met the enemy, and he is us." At the end of an imagined interview between an about-to-be corrupted contestant and a cynical television producer, Updike writes, "They embrace, and, as the Curtain Falls, the West Declines noticeably" (90).

The loss Updike discusses in these editorials is not nostalgia for the Pennsylvania boyhood or the time when everyone was pregnant but rather astonishment at what is happening to the country as a whole. His sense of decline is exacerbated by the televised reports of the 1960 Democratic Convention which he discusses in "Obfuscating Coverage" (July 1960). He deplores the "shoulders, smirks, rudeness, and cynicism" of the network reporters, and he wonders what will happen to the democratic process of nominating and electing a leader when the rational discussion of issues is neglected because reporters who hope to be television stars goad the candidates into loss of composure, anger, platitudes, and lies in front of a population addicted to the tube. What happens, he wonders, when the men with cameras and microphones are presumably exempt "from mundane considerations like courtesy"(91)?

Heroes are still to be found among those who do not cheat on quiz shows or cover political conventions, but as Updike notes in "Two Heroes" (December 1960), we scarcely recognize them anymore. The nation's agony during the Civil Rights movement is another sign of decline. Twelve years after publishing this sketch in the *New Yorker*, Updike wrote of the Civil Rights campaign in "Marching Through Boston" (*Museums and Women*) in which his character Richard Maple sees, among other considerations, the self-righteousness of the black leaders and the masochism of the white marchers. In "Two Heroes," however, Updike looks for heroes among those faces on the block, and he finds amid all the loss of innocence two parents who brave the obscenities of "segregationist banshees" to escort their white daughters to a newly integrated New Orleans elementary school. Of all the thousands of parents who might have done the same, he finds only two—hardly enough to count for more than a symbolic act. But being an artist, Updike knows that symbols matter: "Out of two thousand, two. Strangely, it seems enough" (97). So does an Eisenhower. In "Eisenhower's Eloquence" (May 1962), a title which at first glance might seem ironic because of the President's normally gray sentences, Updike amusingly discusses the value of live Presidents no longer in office. The point of the editorial is praise of Eisenhower's observation that "Only Americans can hurt America." The state of the country has been the primary topic of Updike's "First Person Plural" opinions all along. He looks about in order to comment, but the depressing scene reflects a nation which once believed in its own morality now declining to make room for a jaded successor.

Even the architecture advertises the loss. "What we miss, perhaps, is hopefulness. These new skyscrapers do not aspire to scrape the sky; at the point of exhaustion, where the old skyscrapers used to taper, gather their dwindling energy, and lunge upward with a heart-stopping spire, these glass boxes suffer the architectural embarrassment of having to house the air-conditioning apparatus, and slatted veiling snuffs out their ascent" (109, "Mostly Glass," October 1962). Updike's discouragement reflects his disappointment with the space program: A nation diminishes when it exchanges aspiration for functionalism. The greatest loss of all, because it meant the destruction of both fact and symbol, was the assassination of President Kennedy. With that death, America lost the leader who aspired to guide the country out of the cultural doldrums of the late 1950s. In "The Assassination" (November, December 1963), Updike views the murder as a symbol of our "deep unease" and an omen we must heed: "Christmas this year has the air of a birthday party carried on despite a death in the family" (119). One is reminded of the pathetic comment in *Couples* that the party must go on despite the assassination because the Scotch has already been purchased and the invitations mailed. What does it mean, he asks, to discover that although we no longer smile, we are still human? When he describes a Mass celebrated several weeks after the President's death, he implies the necessity of a reacquaintance with religious sureties, a suggestion which comes as no surprise to his readers and which is then supported by his obituary for T.S. Eliot (January 1965).

The deaths of President Kennedy and Eliot symbolize for Updike the startling destruction of political, cultural, and religious presence necessary to the moral welfare of a nation. Updike's opinion–writing in "First Person Plural" shows how unhappily keen he was while reporting the national scene during the bleak decade from 1955 to 1965. These editorials do not grow stale because they have a touch of prophecy. Looking at a declining America in the late 1950s, he foresaw the disillusioned America of the 1960s.

Disappointment with part of the world he sees as an adult may be one of the reasons why Updike returns so often to the world he remembers as a boy. Preoccupation with his own childhood and adolescent years is a hallmark of his early fiction and poetry. As he writes in "The Dogwood Tree: A Boyhood," "The difference between a childhood and a boyhood must be this: our boyhood is what any boy in our environment would have had" (165). This sense of specialness, as if growing up in Shillington, Pennsylvania, all but automatically guaranteed him the rewards of stability and permanence, pervades his writing from the beginning, encouraging the tone of nostalgia and supporting the theme of continuity through change. Returning to his own past as he does in his early work, Updike manages to give it the permanence of art and simultaneously to express the secure sense of place he felt while living in Shillington. Yet in most of his writing about the small town, the sense of belonging to a special place does not neutralize his awareness of being alone. Reading through Updike's fictional and non–fictional accounts of his childhood, one notes the loneliness, the quality of isolation within even his family of five. Lines from the autobiographical poem "Leaving Church Early" (*Tossing and Turning*) are appropriate here: "We were/diseased, unneighborly, five times alone, and quick." The individuality of each life, the demands of memory, and the necessity for nostalgia are at the heart of the six autobiographical essays which comprise the "First Person Singular" section of *Assorted Prose*.

These sketches constitute for now the available biographical materials on John Updike. The extent of the blend of fact and fiction is anyone's guess. But if the essays are not to be used as unquestionably reliable accounts of his life, they may be read as revealing insights into a particular past as the author remembers it. The most important is "The Dogwood Tree: A Boyhood." He now describes the essay disparagingly (ix). "The Dogwood Tree" may not be Updike at his best, but it is a fascinating account of the boy one meets in much of his fiction and of the settings for the stories themselves.

Characterizing the essay is the notation of loss. Friends grow up or move, buildings are demolished, and death enforces change. Yet the dogwood tree, planted at Updike's birth, still stands as a still-point amid the permanence of mutability. The symbol is appropriate: "It has taken me the shocks of many returnings, more and more widely spaced now, to learn, what seems simple enough, that change is the order of things. The immutability, the steadfastness, of the site of my boyhood was an exceptional effect, purchased for me at unimaginable cost by the paralyzing calamity of the Depression and the heroic external effort of the Second World War" (165). The significance of this statement for his short stories is unmistakable, for it reads like a gloss of his writing. Readers of Updike who are unaware of the unusually close relationship between his life and his fiction will find "The Dogwood Tree" revealing. Note, for example, the affinities of tone and subject matter between the passage just quoted and the ending of "The Persistence of Desire" (*Pigeon Feathers*): "In this armor he stepped into the familiar street. The maples, macadam, shadows, houses, cement, were to his violated eyes as brilliant as a scene remembered; he became a child again in this town, where life was a distant adventure, a rumor, an always imminent joy." The detail of "violated" eyes may expose Clyde's faulty vision of the present becoming the past, but Updike's understanding of the urge is clear. Unlike Clyde, he longs not to be a child again but to hold on to the stability which a sense of place can provide: "My father's job paid him poorly but me well; it gave me a sense of, not prestige, but *place*. As a schoolteacher's son, I was assigned a role; people knew me. When I walked down the street to school, the houses called, 'Chonny.' I had a place to be" (166).

Again and again, Updike's fiction and autobiographical essays proclaim his upbringing as a child of the small town where the ground is always cracked pavement and the playing fields packed dirt. To read "The Dogwood Tree" is to enter the world as remembered and described in *Telephone Poles*: "The town was fringed with things that appeared awesome and ominous and fantastic to a boy" (156). One of the delights of Updike's work is that these things are just as awesome and fantastic to the man. His art focuses on a world of middleness where things are to be observed and cherished, where packed dirt itself is a joy. The daily routine of the average and the thereness of telephone poles and tires are the ingredients for the permanence of place. These things seem so stable, so common that many of us never see them. But Updike looks, and with remarkable clarity. Of all contemporary American writers, he is our artist of the everyday:

Is the true marvel of Sunday skaters the pattern of their pirouettes or the fact that they are silently upheld? Blankness is not emptiness; we may skate upon an intense radiance we do not see because we see nothing else. And in fact there is a color, a quiet but tireless goodness that things at rest, like a brick wall or a small stone, seem to affirm. A wordless reassurance these things are pressing to give. An hallucination? To transcribe middleness with all its grits, bumps, and anonymities, in its fullness of satisfaction and mystery: is it possible or, in view of the suffering that violently colors the periphery and that at all moments threatens to move into the center, worth doing? Possibly not; but the horse-chestnut trees, the telephone poles, the porches, the green hedges recede to a calm point that in my subjective geography is still the center of the world. (185-186)

Keith Mano apparently questions Updike's love affair with the middle ground when he wonders why Updike does not take liberties with his material and when he names him "a middle class realist."[11] Reading Mano's mild censure, one assumes that he does not accept the above quotation which is among the most important of Updike's non-fiction statements. The need to write about middleness is not a refusal to take chances but an affirmation of life. His childhood in the shadow of the dogwood tree is still so much a part of his present that to abandon it would be to deny self: "The center of my boyhood held a calm collection of kind places that are almost impossible to describe, because they are so fundamental to me, they enclosed so many of my hours, that they have the neutral color of my own soul" (170). Updike might be the first to agree that the colors of the periphery threaten the neutrality of the middle, but he would be the last to dismiss the calm center of his subjective geography.

Those who claim that he writes beautifully but has nothing to say may have missed the point. As a chronicler of mundane things still awesome and fantastic, he keeps us in touch with the items of this world. Other people begin elsewhere and thus have their own sense of place, but for him the focal point is always Shillington or the farm. His ideas of hedges and dogwood trees are forever measured by what he experienced there: "For all of them—for all four of my adult guardians—Shillington was a snag, a halt in a journey that had begun elsewhere. Only I belonged to the town" (155).

One way to read the biographical essays in "First Person Singular" is as a collection of sources for themes, descriptions, and events in the fiction and poetry. Those who place "The Dogwood Tree" against the rest of the canon will surely note the allusions. Few will miss, for example, the connection between the following quotation and "Leaving Church Early": "I was an only child. A great many only children were born in 1932; I make no apologies. I do not remember ever feeling the space for a competitor within the house. The five of us already there locked into a star that would have shattered like crystal at the admission of a sixth" (154). For those who know only the novels, the description of Mrs. Updike cutting the grass and the memories of the County Home and Shillington high school will recall *Of the Farm*, *The Poorhouse Fair*, and *The Centaur*. Readers of the short stories will recognize allusions to adolescent love in "Flight" and "A Sense of Shelter" (*Pigeon Feathers*). The comment on religion looks forward to "The Deacon" in *Museums and Women*. The point is that the biographical essays supply this kind of information for those who wish to pursue it. Much more important, in my opinion, is what "First Person Singular" reveals about Updike himself and his need to write.

More than anything else, "The Dogwood Tree" confirms the influence of his formative years in a small Pennsylvania town. Although the stasis which brought security resulted from the disaster of the Depression, Updike is grateful for the stability: "My environment was a straight street about three city blocks long" (165). Secure as an only child in a family of grandparents and parents, and wanting no siblings, he nevertheless literally aches with the need to belong. A slap in the face from a popular third-grade girl is received not as a rebuke but as a joyous sign of initiation; a defeat in a fight with other boys is not a moment of shame but an indication of involvement with the "circumambient humanity that so often seemed evasive" (176).

It does not seem too strong to say that his return to this focal point in personal essays, fiction, and poems is an exorcism of the past. For all of the specialness of his small-town youth, Updike calls attention to his need to escape. Shillington may be the center, but the world lies beyond. Recall Joey Robinson's effort to leave the farm by reading science fiction (*Of the Farm*). Similarly, Updike remembers his first infatuation with art as "a method of riding a thin pencil line out of Shillington" (185). As he describes the last of summer in 1945, the sense of ending is clear. President Roosevelt is dead; World War Two is over; and the Updikes move, appropriately on Halloween night, from the big white house to the Plowville farm. The moment is, as he writes, the end of his boyhood. And yet as he steps toward the future, he glances back over his shoulder to look once more at the dogwood tree: "Against the broad blank part where I used to bat a tennis ball for hours at a time, the silhouette of the dogwood tree stood confused with the shapes of the other bushes in our side yard, but taller. I turned away before it would have disappeared from sight; and so it is that my shadow has always remained in one place" (187). Escaping in space, he remains behind in time. With this final look at the dogwood tree, he secures forever his past for the purposes of art.

Twenty-nine years after that move on Halloween night, and nine years following the original appearance of "The Dogwood Tree," Updike published *Buchanan Dying* as a "final homage" to his native state. The decision to turn from his special sense of place may or may not be final, but the other five essays in "First Person Singular" show him making the necessary passage from boyhood toward the horizon. None of the sketches is as significant as "The Dogwood Tree." Originally published in the *Saturday Evening Post*, "The Lucid Eye in Silver Town" is more a portrait of the father than an autobiography of the son, and thus it has particular interest for fans of *The Centaur*. Always agreeing with everyone to the point of unintentionally infuriating his listeners, the father is described as passive, self-effacing, committed, and wise. The essay is a snapshot of George Caldwell. "My Uncle's Death" is another fond memoir of an adult relative in which Updike mentions the "mystery called 'family,'" the main topic of much of his short fiction. "Outing: A Family Anecdote" is an early hint of the tension, which he later fictionalizes in tales and novels, between himself as an adult about to be married and his parents. The mother's comment to his fiancée that Updike men lean on their women might have come directly from the pages of *Of the Farm*. Similarly, the description of the father driving the four of them on a frustrating and doubtlessly symbolic trip to Pennington, New Jersey, recalls the story "Home" (*Pigeon Feathers*). Neither these nor the short "Mea Culpa: A Travel Note" and "Eclipse" have the charm or biographical importance of "The Dogwood Tree," but when read as a unit, "First Person Singular" offers the best information currently available on the background of Updike's fictional world.

The final section of *Assorted Prose* is a collection of seventeen reviews totaling nearly one third of the book. Some of the reviews might be better defined as critical essays, for they are learned discussions on such subjects as the history of parody ("Beerbohm and Others"), rhyme ("Rhyming Max"), and contemporary theology ("Faith in Search of Understanding"). In the absence of formal prefaces in which he discusses his own writing, or of a series of essays on the art of fiction itself, the reviews collected in *Assorted Prose* provide as of 1965 the most informative indication of the qualities Updike admires in literature. This is not to say that he is using the reviews to establish himself as a critic. Most of them were written not for academic audiences but for mass-market magazines. Yet the essays testify to his curiosity, intelligence, and ability always to have something interesting to say. Reviewing is a sideline for him: "I think it good for an author, baffled by obtuse reviews of himself, to discover what a recalcitrant art reviewing is, how hard it is to keep the plot straight in summary, let alone to sort out one's honest responses. But reviewing should not become a habit."[12]

Framing his comments is a general assessment of American literature in the late 1950s and early 1960s. Updike is not pleased. In a reference to James Agee, he defines what he calls a "very sick literary situation":

A fever of self-importance is upon American writing. Popular expectations of what literature should provide have risen so high that failure is the only possible success, and pained incapacity the only acceptable proof of sincerity. When ever in prose has slovenliness been so esteemed, ineptitude so cherished? In the present apocalyptic atmosphere, the loudest sinner is most likely to be saved; Fitzgerald's crack-up is his ticket to Heaven, Salinger's silence his claim on our devotion. The study of literature threatens to become a kind of paleontology of failure, and criticism a supercilious psychoanalysis of authors. (264)

His disapproval of an apocalyptic atmosphere in literature parallels his sense of a national decline in culture as expressed in the editorials of "First Person Plural." Updike's point is that authors must be honored only for their writing. The adventures or life style of the writer should be of little or no consequence. Judgments of art are clouded when cults of personality interfere. Although Updike mentions no names, he may have in mind the glorification of the Beat writers in the late 1950s. His dismay at the tendency to esteem slovenly prose just because the author is deemed important echoes his parody of Jack Kerouac in "On the Sidewalk," and his disgust at the unrealistically high expectations which the public has of literature suggests that the *Moby-Dick* syndrome affects readers as well as authors and critics.

The literary situation is not good. In his review of *The Gates of Horn*, Harry Levin's study of French realists, Updike touches on a popular topic, the death of the novel. Students of literature know that the rise of the English novel in the eighteenth century was linked to the demands of realism and the tastes of the middle class. Today, two and a half centuries later, many theorists still argue that given its origins the novel must be by definition realistic. If that prescription is so, says Updike, then perhaps the novel must go the way of the epic: "If the novel is in essence realistic, and if 'the realistic movement and the bourgeois lifestyle' are linked in a necessary 'cohabitation,' then indeed the novel may be as dead as the epic and the romance, for at least in the West social entropy has melted away the aristocrat and the peasant whose flanking contrast gave the term *bourgeois* pungency and shape" (272). But Updike himself is not ready to assign fiction to the tombstone. His appreciation of the anti-realistic novel indicates that the "very sick literary situation" is more the result of popular expectation than artistic decline. "Prose narrative needs to refresh itself at the springs of myth and dream. Is this to be deplored? The contemporary attempts to shake off the heavy spell of realism, however seemingly formless and irresponsible, are a worthy phase of man's attempt to educate himself through literature" (272). These comments were first published in 1963. One can almost see John Barth, John Hawkes, and Thomas Pynchon, anti-realistic novelists whose reputations rose in the 1960s, standing behind Updike's declaration that the novel must periodically renew itself.

This spirit of constructive criticism, reflecting both hope for and disappointment in the current literary scene, informs the general tone of the reviews. As Updike explains in *Picked-Up Pieces*, it is better to praise than blame. Unlike many commentators on litera-ture, he tries not to evaluate a novel according to preconceptions of what fiction should be. A case in point is the review of Muriel Spark which praises her writing while simultaneously defining for the American audience some distinctions between American and British fiction. Note his appreciation for the proximity of literature and national culture:

The use by a serious author of fun-house plots, full of trapdoors, abrupt apparitions, and smartly clicking secret panels, may strike American readers as incongruous. We are accustomed to honest autobiographical shapelessness. Ishmael and Huck Finn are alike adrift on vessels whose course they cannot control, through waters whose depths are revealed with a shudder. We remain somewhat aghast at a world that has never been tamed, by either a consecrated social order or an exhaustive natural theology. Our novels tend to be about education rather than products of it; they are soul-searching rather than worldly-wise. English fiction, for all the social and philosophical earthquakes since Chaucer, continues to aspire, with the serenity of a treatise, to a certain dispassionate elevation above the human scene. Hence its greater gaiety and ease of contrivance." (305-306)

Although clearly written for an audience different from Richard Chase's, these comments may be read as an addition to the discus-sion of the distinctions between British and American fiction which Chase expresses in his seminal study *The American Novel and Its Tradition*. Updike's remarks were published in 1961 before the gen-eral acceptance of authors like Barth, Hawkes, and Pynchon, and thus his opinions may seem dated today. But at the time he was praising Muriel Spark, American writers had not yet made commonplace a novel which has as its subject the intricate business of writing a novel. In 1961 audiences may have indeed labeled fun-house plots contrived by serious authors as incongruous, but only seven years later Barth published the respected *Lost in the Funhouse* with its maze of smartly clicking trapdoors. The point is not that Updike was wrong about American fiction and its audience but that his prediction that the novel would have to refresh itself at the spring of anti-realism was farsighted. American literature is generally, as he says, a "scraggly association of hermits, cranks, and exiles" (319).

Updike's sympathy with the struggling author, no matter how scraggly, is a hallmark of his reviews. He knows, for example, the difficulty of developing one's own voice: "One puts down *A Christmas Garland* wondering why the man who wrote it [Max Beerbohm] did not, in his own voice, write great things" (244). Or, discussing the failures of James Agee, he suggests that Agee's genius was "for spontaneous, gregarious commentary rather than patient, eremitical invention" (267). Similarly, he understands the trials of even beginning to write: "The lack of connection between the experiences, usually accumulated by the age of twenty, that seem worth telling about, and the sophistication needed to render them in writing, is the Unmentionable at the root of the mysterious Fall of so many auspicious beginners" (230).

These essays reveal a knowledgeable, patient, and understanding reviewer, qualities he admires in other literary commentators. Yet a sympathetic reader is not synonymous with an indiscriminating critic. Updike is never afraid to evaluate. In addition to sympathy, the reviews illustrate his ability to dissect a shortcoming in a sentence or two: Conrad Aiken "evokes comparison with the very best; and then suffers from the comparison. Just as his poems, compared with, say, Wallace Stevens', seem formless and wan, his short stories, compared with Hemingway's, seem stylistically indecisive, and, compared with Faulkner's, insufficiently material and grasping" (231). Updike also willingly criticizes while hoping for the best. To his credit, he never goes for the knockout. He laments bad writing, especially by authors he admires, but he also tries to remind the reader of the writer's better work: "The appearance, in the yellow dust jacket that has become traditional, of one more collection of pieces by the late James Thurber is a happy event, even for the reviewer obliged to report that the bulk of the pieces are from his last years and as such tend to be cranky, formless, and lame" (239). Updike's intelligence guides him from essay to essay. Again and again he makes discriminations based upon knowledge and taste. Challenging Dwight Macdonald's label of the "Oxen of the Sun" episode from *Ulysses* as parody, Updike defines the difference between a parodist like Max Beerbohm and a novelist like James Joyce: "*A Christmas Garland* is a program of flawless impersonations by an actor whose own personality is invisible. The 'Oxen of the Sun' episode is a boisterous 'turn' taken in an antic succession of loosely fitting costumes; behind the bobbing masks we easily recognize the vaudevillian himself, Shem the Penman, the old flabbergaster" (246-247). His evaluation of Macdonald's anthology of parody is much more than a review. He knows so much and writes so well that the essay transcends the expected limits to assume the weight of a critical discussion on the history and art of parody. Reading the essay, a college student, for example, would find a useful introduction to the definitions and distinctions of a specialized art form. Updike even links the decline of parody to the decline in humor as a genre, a questionable but nevertheless interesting idea:

Laughter is but one of many potential human responses; to isolate humor as a separate literary strain is as unnatural as to extract a genre of pathos or of nobility from the mixed stuff of human existence. Insofar as 'serious' literature is indeed exclusively serious, then humor, as in the Victorian age, has a duty, in the Parliament of Man, to act as the loyal opposition. But when, as in this century, the absurd, the comic, the low, the dry, and the witty are reinstated in the imaginative masterworks, then humor as such runs the risk of becoming merely trivial, merely recreational, merely distracting. A skull constantly grins, and in the constant humorist there is a detachment and dandyism of the spirit whose temporary abeyance in this country need not be cause for unmitigated lamenting. (255-256)

One may disagree and still admire Updike's ability to turn a review for a popular magazine into an essay for literary specialists. And yet he is never serious to the point of being dull. Humor is often the key to an Updike review, even if it becomes an essay. In his long analysis of Denis de Rougemont's theories of love, for example, Updike paraphrases and comments with a grin on how the famous sword between Tristan and Iseult becomes a threat to international peace. The sword foreshadows "the equally artificial devices of the countless playwrights, novelists, and scenarists who so wearilessly have obstructed the natural union of lovers and whose pathetic inventions continue to propagate, all unwittingly, a heresy inimicable to marriage, social stability, and international peace" (285). What can we do but smile?

In general, the qualities Updike admires in others are characteristics of his own writing. The intelligence, humor, and stamina which he finds in Alan Sillitoe are surely present in his fiction. His admiration of Conrad Aiken's easy movement in the "swimming minds of women willing to fall in love" reflects his novels of suburban adultery and the difficulties of marriage (233). His appreciation of Salinger's "wry but persistent hopefulness" is significant because it matches what Updike believes to be the shape of contemporary American life. His praise of Muriel Spark as one of the few writers with the resources and daring to alter as well as feed "the fiction machine" recalls his unspectacular but nevertheless notable efforts to refresh fiction by writing about the little things of this world. Finally, his observation that Mrs. Spark writes the "prose of a poet who has decided that prose is something else again" reminds us that Updike's genius with language and style receives praise from even those who claim he has nothing to say.

In short, the reviews collected in *Assorted Prose* amount to a repository of ideas about literature. They should be read not as a formal statement of theory but as an informal collection of thoughts. Written directly to express Updike's judgment of the book in question, the reviews indirectly reveal a good deal about his own art. His instinct to collect them seems to me correct. Many of the books discussed and some of Updike's opinions of them will eventually lose significance, but the ideas about literature gleaned from the collection as a whole will remain a valuable introduction to his achievement.

If there is one piece in *Assorted Prose* likely to gain in reputation and join Updike's best short stories as supreme examples of his art, it is "Hub Fans Bid Kid Adieu." Written as a report of Ted Williams' last game (September 28, 1960), the essay rivals the sportswriting of masters like Roger Angell and Herbert Warren Wind in its combination of well-written prose and knowledge of a particular sport. Updike wrote "Hub Fans" not because he had to but because he cared. His love affair with the world of baseball and its microcosm in Fenway Park is indirectly expressed on page after page.

As is usual with adults who care about sports, Updike began his interest in baseball while a boy. The nostalgia associated with his early short stories, the long–ago event so clearly remembered and so poetically expressed, is present here. This is no mere report of a significant day in baseball but an expression of emotion, a gesture of gratitude. A hero retires. An era ends. Were it not for the documentation of facts and statistics, the essay could be read as another Updike short story in which he laments the loss of a moment and yet preserves it in art. The key to this piece is not Updike the adult joining 10,453 other fans to witness a last hurrah but that boy in Pennsylvania who first knew of Ted Williams from the box scores: "I remember listening over the radio to the All-Star Game of 1946" (133). This final farewell to the aging slugger is Updike's homage to his own youth.

Boy becomes adult, and baseball takes on that special meaning which baffles its detractors. Considered by many to be the only sport with the perfect blend of offense and defense, lull and drama, baseball is, as Updike writes, "a game of the long season, of relentless and gradual averaging-out" (133). Averages are the heart of its history, the stuff which makes the myths. Showing the mark of the true fan, Updike expresses his love affair with baseball statistics when he recounts, among other pieces of esoteric knowledge, Williams' minor-league days. Such things matter in baseball, as, for example, this note on the 1941 season when Williams hit an incredible and since unequaled .406: "The sweet saga of this beautiful decimal must be sung once more. Williams, after hitting above .400 all season, had cooled to .39955 with one doubleheader left to play" (131). Only a man with baseball fever could write of statistics in such words as "saga" and "beautiful."

Updike is a fan who knows how to write. Some of his finest descriptions are tucked away in this essay. At the emotion-filled moment when Williams finally circles the bases after performing the extraordinary feat of hitting a home run in his last at bat, the day is appropriately gloomy. The atmosphere, both literally and figuratively, suggests an end of something. Updike writes, "The afternoon grew so glowering that in the sixth inning the arc lights were turned on—always a wan sight in the daytime, like the burning headlights of a funeral procession" (145). A groundskeeper retrieving batting-practice home runs from the screen on the left-field wall walks "like a mushroom gatherer seen in Wordsworthian perspective on the verge of a cliff" (127). And then there is the description of Fenway Park which expresses the special charm of that venerable stadium: "Fenway Park, in Boston, is a lyric little bandbox of a ballpark. Everything is painted green and seems in curiously sharp focus, like the inside of an old-fashioned peeping-type Easter egg. It was built in 1912 and rebuilt in 1934, and offers, as do most Boston artifacts, a compromise between Man's Euclidean determinations and Nature's beguiling irregularities" (127). The park is, in short, a reproduction of the regularities and quirks of baseball itself. The specialness of Fenway Park captures the uniqueness of baseball of which Ted Williams was a reflection. A hero to millions, he was a loner. A graceful athlete, he spit at fans. Disliked by some newsmen, he made news for twenty years:

But of all team sports, baseball, with its graceful intermittences of action, its immense and tranquil field sparsely settled with poised men in white, its dispassionate mathematics, seems to me best suited to accommodate, and be ornamented by, a loner. It is an essentially lonely game. No other player visible to my generation concentrated within himself so much of the sport's poignance, so assiduously refined his natural skills, so constantly brought to the plate that intensity of competence that crowds the throat with joy. (134)

One wants to pay a similar compliment to Updike. What other contemporary American author could have brought to a description of a baseball game such knowledge, observation, and style? He so successfully renders the atmosphere of that day that the allusions to mythic heroes are not ridiculous but appropriate. The names of Jason, Achilles, Nestor, Hamlet, and Leonardo mingle with the names of more earthbound giants like Ruth, Dimaggio, Musial, Mantle, and Cobb. Updike understands the ambiguity surrounding men who aspire to myth, and he knows that Williams is no exception: "Greatness necessarily attracts debunkers, but in Williams' case the hostility has been systematic and unappeasable. His basic offense against the fans has been to wish that they weren't there" (130).

But Updike was there, and in a sense he still is. In "Hub Fans," he first recalls Williams' career in baseball, which amounts to a short course in the history of the sport since 1939, and he then describes the memorable last game: "From my angle, behind third base, the ball seemed less an object in flight than the tip of a towering, motionless construct, like the Eiffel Tower or the Tappan Zee Bridge. It was in the books while it was still in the sky" (146). This essay is an elegy to an era. Men played not for pension plans but for pride. Updike makes the aging god come alive. Williams' head is held at a "self-deprecating and evasive tilt." He slouches as if he were a "six-foot-three inch man under a six-foot ceiling." He stands on third base "swinging his arms with a sort of prancing nervousness." And yet this fallible middle-aged man also touches the gods. After he circles the bases following the home run, the fans, Updike included in the "we," scream, weep, and yell for Ted. But he does not reappear from the dugout. He does not tip his cap: "Our noise for some seconds passed beyond excitement into a kind of immense open anguish, a wailing, a cry to be saved. But immortality is non-transferable" (146).

Updike is aware, of course, of hyperbole. A touch of irony here and there grounds the essay in the world of the mundane where some men do strike out. He notes, for example, that when Williams told the assembled multitudes before the game that they were the sport's greatest fans, "we applauded ourselves lustily." And yet that day *was* special to him. Seventeen years after "Hub Fans" was published in the *New Yorker*, and twelve years after its appearance in *Assorted Prose*, Lord John Press printed a limited edition of three hundred signed copies for which Updike wrote a short introduction. There we learn that Williams liked the piece as much as Updike's public, and that he indirectly asked Updike to write his biography. Updike refused, but he acknowledges that the myth has grown greater. Nearly four decades have passed since that .406 season, and no one in those years has hit .400. More important, perhaps, is that the essay on Williams' last game still remains Updike's link to his boyhood. The elegy is as much for his lost youth as for his lost hero. Nostalgia and history merge, and the result is art. Still, Updike insists on the puncturing edge of irony: "But among my literary fantasies, along with being the American Proust and the male George Eliot, is one of being Angell's harbinger; I made *The New Yorker* safe for baseball."[13] After irony is considered, style appreciated, and knowledge of baseball admired, "Hub Fans Bid Kid Adieu" is finally a testament of love. As Updike writes in the introduction to the limited edition, "Love shows." Indeed it does—for heroes, for baseball, for childhood, and, most of all, for art.

Notes to *Assorted Prose*

1. John Updike, *Assorted Prose* (New York: Knopf, 1965). Further references will be to this edition.

2. Walter Sullivan, "Updike, Spark and Others," *Sewanee Review*, 74 (July–September, 1966), 712.

3. "The Gymnast," *Newsweek*, 17 May 1965, p. 108.

4. Thomas B. Morgan also praises the style while questioning the content. Admitting that the author writes "beautiful sentences," he suggests that at least in the book reviews collected in *Assorted Prose* Updike disciplines his lyric power with a conviction which is missing from his fiction. *See* Thomas B. Morgan, "A Casual Collection," New York *Times Book Review*, 13 June 1965, p. 10.

5. D.M. Davis, "An Updike Reader: From Obituaries to Pigeon Prose, The Touch Is Sure, Pictures Clear," *National Observer*, 21 June 1965, p. 19.

6. Two essays in British journals also judge *Assorted Prose* as more than scrapings from the study-room floor. Although the British edition unfortunately lacks, among other selections, the essay on Williams (perhaps because baseball is too strange for non-American readers), David D. Galloway praises Updike's prose in terms which argue that the style supports content after all: "Certainly the most striking prose is to be found in the fragmentary autobiographical sketches, where Updike's ability to crystallise the apparent irrelevant images of contemporary life, to force us to see quotidian detail with fresh insight, is generously exercised." Similarly, Richard Mayne describes *Assorted Prose* as a kind of write-it-yourself magazine full of "well-tailored" nostalgia, reviews of high quality, and the delicate intentness of craftsmanship, but he believes the book to be not quite equal to the "formidable" talent exhibited in *Rabbit, Run*. *See* David D. Galloway, "Belfast Blues," *Spectator*, 4 February 1966, p. 142; and Richard Mayne, "Epicures etc.," *New Statesman*, 4 February 1966, p. 169.

7. Granville Hicks, "They Also Serve Who Write Well," *Saturday Review*, 15 May 1965, pp. 25-26.

8. Lawrence Graver, "Picked-Up Pieces," New York *Times Book Review*, 30 November 1975, p. 39.

9. Calvin Bedient, "Picked-Up Pieces by John Updike," *New Republic*, 27 December 1975, p. 29. Like Bedient, the British reviewers generally approve of Updike's miscellaneous prose. John Russell, for example, noting that even the index is funny, does not quarrel with Updike's ideas about reality and fiction. Focusing not on the literary theorist but on the successful author who has managed to remain interested in many things, he praises Updike's ability to write excellent essays despite his reputation as a best-selling novelist:

Big-selling novelists do not always appear to advantage in their occasional writings. Some turn grouchy and competitive; others, pseudo-Olympian. Sometimes the differences of length, pace and tone quite unman them; sometimes we glimpse shortcomings of character which the author in question contrived to keep out of his fictions. Altogether it's a touchy business. But it is a business from which John Updike emerges very well.

The keys to Updike's success are sympathy, curiosity, interest, and intelligence. It is significant that Updike claims to write not for New York but for a spot just east of Kansas where a teen-aged country boy will one day find his books. This imaginary boy may even be a replica of the young Updike stuck out there on the Pennsylvania farm, lacking for the moment the author's verbal versatility and adventuresome mind, but perhaps gaining them, like Updike, from books opened to escape the spaces and the quiet. Similarly, Martin Amis sees in Updike an "alert and ironic layman unanxiously detached from the world of literary commerce.... As a literary journalist, John Updike has that single inestimable virtue: having read him once, you admit to yourself, almost with a sigh, that you will have to read everything he writes." In a word, he is never dull. Although Amis challenges Updike's sympathy with translated novels and his insistence on realistic fiction, he never advises him to give up the sidelight of literary journalism to assume the title of full-time novelist. *See* John Russell, "John Updike: Picked-Up Pieces," London *Times Literary Supplement*, 19 March 1976, p. 309; and Martin Amis, "Life Class," *New Statesman*, 19 March 1976, p. 368.

10. Morgan, "A Casual Collection," 10.
11. D. Keith Mano, "Doughy Middleness," *National Review*, 30 August 1974, p. 987.
12. Charles Thomas Samuels, "John Updike: The Art of Fiction XLIII," *Paris Review*, 12(Winter 1968), 95.
13. John Updike, *Hub Fans Bid Kid Adieu* (Northridge, California: Lord John Press, 1977), xi.

Picked-Up Pieces

"What we want from fiction, and what
fiction is increasingly loath to give
us, is vicarious experience."

—*Picked-Up Pieces*

Updike's concern for the art of the novel is the primary focus of *Picked-Up Pieces* (1975).[1] A miscellany of substantial length and density of thought, the book sparkles from a combination of intellect and wit as illustrated by the formal index which includes entries for *Rabbit, Run* and rabbit manure. Although a decade separates *Assorted Prose* and *Picked-Up Pieces*, several topics and expressions link the two. The young man in awe of James Thurber becomes the mature man who finally meets him. Notions of deity are then comically reinforced: "He sat, talking and drinking tea until I wondered why his bladder didn't burst" (4). A note of self-irony humanizes both books: "Let us hope, for the sakes of artistic purity and paper conservation, that ten years from now the pieces to be picked up will make a smaller heap" (xix). In both miscellanies, Updike appreciates the dilemma of writing about dozens of living authors while hoping to avoid the demands of big-city literary circles. He laughs at himself while smiling at others: "I must be one of the few Americans with a bachelor-of-arts degree who has never met either Robert Lowell or Norman Mailer" (5). His accounts of encounters with John O'Hara and Joyce Cary reveal a similarly humorous self-appraisal.

Reading *Picked-Up Pieces*, one better understands why Ted Williams is a hero of *Assorted Prose*. Updike's definition of creativity applies to baseball players as well as novelists: "Any activity becomes creative when the doer cares about doing it right, or better" (xx). Williams cared and thus made the last home run a work of art in the world of sports. Other links with *Assorted Prose* depend upon similarity of subject matter. The long "Letter from Anguilla," written originally for the *New Yorker*, recalls the research work performed for the essay on Antarctica. Updike's praise of David Levine's caricatures extends his earlier homage to Max Beerbohm and to the art of parody in drawing and prose. The introduction to *Soundings in Satanism* is another meditation on God, theology, and Karl Barth. This short piece also indirectly comments on Updike's fiction, for he risks receiving yet another charge of sentimentality to express his general air of hope. Finally, the long reviews of Kierkegaard's journals resemble, as do many of the essays in *Assorted Prose*, beautifully written seminar papers in an advanced course for laymen. Updike knows not only Kierkegaard's biography but the history of modern theology. He speaks of Christianity as "my curious hobby," and he laughs at the time when, for a while, he was in danger of becoming a kind of Religion Editor for the *New Yorker*. His essays on theologians are so well informed that one reads them not to learn about Updike but simply to learn.

In spite of these connections with the earlier miscellany, *Picked-Up Pieces* is very much its own book. It is more somber in tone, more intellectual in content, more eclectic in taste, and less personal in subject matter. Reading the section of reviews which comprises eighty percent of the book is like confronting a long collection of well-written, wittily expressed critical essays. Updike's reviews may be studied as well as enjoyed. Cross references abound. Favorite topics emerge. Pet theories begin to take shape. And always in the background is his concern that the reader be prepared. The following quotation perhaps suggests why he takes such care with his reviews: "For a book to be great in a reader's life it is not enough for the book to be great; the reader must be ready" (162). Updike discusses books by other authors not to show off erudition but to educate. Commenting on Vladimir Nabokov's post-*Lolita* novels, fictions which often seem more the playthings of a magician than the pronouncements of a seer, Updike urges the reader to greater effort: "The failing may be ours; we are not ready, we are too dull of ear, too slow of eye, too much in love with the stubborn muteness of the earth to read the meaning behind his magic" (215). Still, the author controls the affair: "When a book fails to agree with a reader, it is either because the author has failed to realize his intentions or because his intentions are disagreeable" (199).

Updike's intentions in *Picked-Up Pieces* are agreeable. He does not overestimate his opinions. Calling his journalism a "stunt," he doubts that reviewing is good for him, but he admits that he can "muster" an opinion about anything written in or translated into English. Even the charge of being esoteric is parried when he explains that he was assigned the books imported from Europe as a means to avoid the temptation to take pot shots at his American peers. Especially important in the Foreword to *Picked-Up Pieces* is the explanation of his code for reviewing. These guidelines range from not blaming the author for failing to achieve what he does not attempt, through providing enough direct quotation, to citing a successful example of the author's work if the book in question seems deficient. The golden rule, "Review the book, not the reputation," recalls his argument in *Assorted Prose* that an author must be judged solely by his achievement. In most of the essays in *Picked-Up Pieces*, Updike follows his own code. More important than the rules themselves is the attitude they express. Showing extraordinary sympathy for the author, he always hopes for the best when he takes up a book to review.

Readers uninterested in the abstractions of critical theory may nevertheless examine *Picked-Up Pieces* with pleasure. Thumbnail descriptions of famous authors are everywhere, some pungent, others clever, but always amusingly to the point. T.S. Eliot lecturing at Harvard, for example, is "a gem of composure within a crater of applause" (3). Andrei Voznesensky's photograph in the New York *Times* makes the Russian author's face look "faintly bloated, like a nun's squeezed in her wimple" (9). The fictions of Henry Miller are "not novels, they are acts of intercourse strung alternately with segments of personal harangue" (21). Finally for the moment, Hemingway's *Across the River and into the Trees* "drained magic from *all* of Hemingway's headwaiters and undermined forever the consolations of café stoicism" (129). These mini-descriptions are as fine an indication of Updike's debt to Thurber and Beerbohm as the poems in *The Carpentered Hen*. One would welcome Updike captions for David Levine's caricatures of the literary lights of the Western world.

He brings these same traits of precision, intelligence, and wit to most of his better essays. A few were originally speeches which reveal Updike in the role of the reluctant but increasingly more agreeable public man. Preferring the relative anonymity of a magazine's pages to the public exposure of an appreciative crowd, he admits that he dislikes answering letters from college students even though he will now and then fly to Korea to give a talk on "Humor in Fiction." The locales for these speeches are as widespread and exotic as the titles of the books he reviews: Anguilla, London, Seoul, and Adelaide, South Australia. Again and again he accepts the opportunity to discuss the art of fiction. He describes writing as "an act of willful play." He compares storytelling to music because it shares with music "the medium of time, and perhaps its genius, its most central transformation, has to do with time, with rhythm and echo and the sense of time not frozen as in a painting but channelled and harnessed as in a symphony" (36). What makes this opinion interesting is that it follows a description of his own writing as pictorial, a method, he says, which he does not recommend and which may be a "perversion of the primal narrative urge."

Readers of the short stories know that some of his best pictures are of adolescence and young adulthood. A few of the essays in *Picked-Up Pieces* communicate the nostalgia, the memory of better times when innocence was in flower and everything smelled clean. In the midst of an article on living in London, which ends with a poem in praise of America, he recalls the beauty of our casual restaurants and vacant lots. In an essay on cemeteries he remembers the burial grounds of Pennsylvania and asks, "Why is it that everyone else lacks the sanguine, corporeal, anguished reality of these farmers, these people of red sandstone?" (61). True to his need to capture his past in art, he turns the discourse on cemeteries from a description of graveyards to a memory of a visit to his mother and an emotional acceptance of the continuity of change. Catching his own shadow in the image of his son, he recalls teaching the boy to ride a bike by taking him to the traffic-free avenues of the local cemetery. The metaphor is all too clear. It does not, says Updike, "bear thinking about."

For all of the nostalgia, witty descriptions, and rules of reviewing, however, most of the material in *Picked-Up Pieces* is concerned with the state of the novel and the achievement of novelists. Updike "musters" something to say about nearly everyone: Giants like Dostoevsky, T.S. Eliot, Auden, Camus, Knut Hamsen, Joyce, Proust, Nabokov, and Borges; and relative newcomers like Barry Hannah, Walter Abish, Michael Ayrton, and Jerzy Kosinski. His reviews of other writers in other centuries are just as current as his comments on yesterday's big book, for Updike evaluates individual novels within the context of fiction as a genre. To his credit, he rarely lapses into the pontifical pose of the insider preaching to the ignorant masses. A smattering of self-irony steadies the perspective. As he explains in the essay on Dostoevsky's *The Gambler*, "Self-humiliation is one of the writer's most useful aids; it puts him in touch with the basal humanity that dignity, honors, flattery, and prosperity would estrange him from" (139). Famous in Ipswich, Updike remembers Shillington. He is so familiar with the canons of literary heavyweights that he can compare several in one essay. The review of Proust is a case in point. Quoting one of his favorite passages, he writes, "Hemingway would have rendered this action in twenty words; Balzac, in a hundred and made us feel the chemist's shop, and hear the ring of francs on the counter. Proust's tendrilous sentences seek out an essence so fine the search itself is an act of faith" (163). Of his favorite Nabokov, he suggests, "Rich, healthy, brilliant, physically successful, he lacks the neurasthenic infirmities that gave the modernism of Proust, Joyce, Kafka, and Mann its tender underside" (204).

Updike's evaluations and judgments are more than clever observations wittily phrased. The reader may be grateful that they do not coalesce into, for want of a better phrase, a theory of fiction, but when read as a whole, the opinions do suggest some of his general ideas about the novel. Taking a cue from Dr. Johnson who once defined "novel" as "a small tale, generally of love," Updike joins those who find an element of romance at the heart of most traditional fiction. The novel, as it has been known for centuries, is sentimental. This opinion might be an indirect defense of his own fiction against those who level charges of sentimentality as if the word were a poison dart. Updike has a point. In an age of capitalism and machines, huge cities and television, man may need romance in novels to assure him that his emotions are "substantial and significant": "Erotic love then becomes a symbol, a kind of code for all the nebulous, perishable sensations which we persist in thinking of as *living*" (20). The welfare of the novel affects the stability of the culture. Salvation is at stake, because the successful novelist has social as well as artistic impact:

The bourgeois novel is inherently erotic, just as the basic unit of bourgeois order—the family unit built upon the marriage contract—is erotic. Who loves whom? Once this question seems less than urgent, new kinds of novels must be written, or none at all. If domestic stability and personal salvation are at issue, acts of sexual conquest and surrender are important. If the issue is an economic reordering, and social control of the means of production, then sexual attachments are as they are in Mao's China—irrelevant, and the fewer the better. (402)

Updike does not want the question of who loves whom to become less than urgent. Yet neither does he approve of ignoring reality as the romantic element in fiction lunges toward wish fulfillment of the kind found in daydreams. Updike is clear. The novelist is properly concerned with "the strict small circumstance, the quizzical but verifiable fact" (20).

No wonder he questions the direction of contemporary fiction. With traditional obstructions to love and to descriptions of sex now removed, the novel as we know it will be altered. Updike fears the change: "The subversive burden will shift, I fear, from sex to violence, and the threat of society, and the problem for censorship, lies not, in my opinion, with the description of sexual acts but with fantasies of violence and torture" (21-22). Novels like *Last Exit to Brooklyn* and *The Painted Bird* illustrate this unhappy direction with their long passages of unrelieved brutality. It is not that Updike advocates ignoring violence. Dire events occur everyday. Yet "the obligation of the artist, when dealing with them, as with sex, is to be, not inexplicit, but accurately alive to their complicated human context.... A fanatic and dazed narrowing of comprehension seems to be in progress. The sour riots of the Sixties are not likely to call forth the ebullient rapture of a Kerouac, let alone the refined anguish of a Huysmans" (22). These remarks come from a speech Updike delivered in February 1969 titled "The Future of the Novel," and they show that not squeamishness but mimesis is at issue. The key phrase is "accurately alive." Updike is no prude about the depiction of brutal events, but he wants fiction to do justice to the human complexities which originally create the violence. To write acceptable novels requires a widening of comprehension, not a narrowing into political proclamations or indulgent fantasies. Anti-realist novelists who are "accurately alive" to human complexities can fly from formal conventions to what Updike calls a "wonderful freedom."

He explains this point in a speech entitled "Why Write?" given in Adelaide, South Australia, in March 1974. Defining his motivation as a writer, he argues that the improvement of social conditions and the betterment of mankind are not basic concerns. Accuracy is. Nobility of purpose should not be substituted for authenticity in execution. To do so, says Updike, would "certainly be to forfeit whatever social usefulness I do have" (32). He consistently reiterates the venerable notion that fiction is mimesis. "We must write where we stand; wherever we do stand, there is life; and an imitation of the life we know, however narrow, is our only ground" (32). Mimesis is all; it demands, as he says, "no displacement." The world may confound the novelist by being everything from balky to humiliating, but in the act of mimesis the novelist may confront the world by adjusting, even purifying it.

Perhaps the unspoken hero of many of Updike's reviews and essays in *Picked-Up Pieces* is Erich Auerbach, author of *Mimesis*. Although his name is mentioned only twice, his celebration of fiction as imitation is a rallying cry throughout the book. In a short two-page speech, for example, originally given in March 1964 on the occasion of receiving the National Book Award for *The Centaur*, Updike expresses his support for mimesis in novels. Some of the phrases read like definitions:

"... a virtue seldom extolled these days, that of *accuracy*, or *lifelikeness*."

"... modern fiction does seem, more than its antecedents, the work of eccentrics."

"Fiction is a tissue of literal lies that refreshes and informs our sense of actuality."

"Reality is—chemically, atomically, biologically—a fabric of microscopic accuracies."

"Language approximates phenomena through a series of hesitations and qualifications; I miss, in much contemporary writing, this sense of self-qualification, the kind of timid reverence toward what exists that Cézanne shows when he grapples for the shape and shade of a fruit through a mist of delicate stabs. The intensity of the grapple is the surest pleasure a writer receives." (16–17)

I have isolated these quotations only to emphasize Updike's concern about the future of fiction. He is not developing an esthetic theory, but he is urging a habit of honesty. He asks not for a return to the traditional realistic novel as it was practiced in the nineteenth century but for accuracy of portrayal by the author who is the perceiver. The writer may discover, or he may invent, but his "verbal texture" should correspond to the "tone of life as it arrives on his nerves."

There is, he believes, a "thinness" in current fiction, an inability or an unwillingness to show how the world operates, and, thus, a rejection of what Updike argues is a minimal obligation to the reader: To write a book that is factually right. "Good works of art direct us back outward to reality again; they illustrate, rather than ask, imitation."[2] This belief explains why he shows in such rich detail and lyrical prose the way a janitor sweeps a school hallway or a minister conducts a Sunday School class.

Given Updike's reservations about the ability of contemporary authors to grapple with the shapes and shades of reality, one wishes for more reviews of current American writers. How, one wonders, would he evaluate John Barth's *Lost in the Funhouse* or John Hawkes's *Second Skin*? The reader of *Picked-Up Pieces* must be satisfied with the thoughtful essays on Jorge Luis Borges and Vladimir Nabokov, two of many contemporary authors Updike does admire. In praising Borges, he indirectly expresses his opinion of some current American fiction: Trash. Honoring Borges' "gravely considered oddity," he wonders if it can serve as a clue to the way out of the trashiness and narcissism of American novels. As his appreciation of the Argentine writer shows, Updike does not dismiss artifice. Yet the way to revitalize the tired traditional novel is to learn not from Kerouac or the Salinger of the Glass stories but from the Borges of *Ficciones* and the Nabokov of *Lolita*. Borges may be ironic, his messages hidden, and his verbal texture more created than discovered, but his stories "answer to a deep need in contemporary fiction—the need to confess the fact of artifice" (188). Still, Updike questions the extent of the value of artifice. An implied query echoes through many of these essays: How far may creativity be pushed before it violates mimesis? Most readers of Updike's prose know of his appreciation of Nabokov's novels, especially of those before *Ada*. The author of *Lolita* renews language and observes life. He shows us ourselves. But, muses Updike, is art always a game? An author like Nabokov may stake his career on the certainty that art is a game, but his most daring tricks are often his most disturbing traits. Perhaps the game goes too far when, in *Ada*, nature itself is artifice: "If Nature is an artifact, however, there must be, if not an Artist, at least a kind of raw reality beneath or behind it, and the most daring and distressing quality of his novels is their attempt to rub themselves bare, to display their own vestments of artifice and then to remove them" (210). Thus while Updike praises Nabokov's vision, his deft ability to coin the arresting phrase, and his skill at setting up combinations as if he were a chess master, he disapproves of his creating the planet Antiterra in *Ada* because it slips into semi-reality. Updike admits that his prejudice is for earthbound fiction. Decency may dictate that the names of small towns be faked, but metropolises and nations are unique enough to demand their own names.

Updike recognizes the countercharges. Asking himself the rhetorical question, what is reality, he answers, that which exists. He is aware that many readers may accuse him of elevating the realism of a dreary Zola above the anti-realism of a delightful Nabokov, and he admits that most of Nabokov's risks are calculated. But, he wonders, does Nabokov mean to write dialogue which is little more than "quibble and prank" or to create a hero who is nothing more than a brute? Updike does not deny the pleasures of the imagination, but he does insist that they adhere to reality. His definition of art reemphasizes his celebration of mimesis: "Art is part game, part grim erotic tussle with Things As They Are; the boxes must have holes where reality can look out and readers can look in" (208).

At times, he explains the shift from mimesis as part of the tendency in contemporary fiction to thrive on disillusionment. Disillusionment causes separateness which in turn may encourage fragmentation in plot and character. Arguing that the twentieth century assumes too easily the inability of one person to touch another's heart, he writes, "Such solipsism renders obsolete the interconnectedness of action that comprises 'plot' and the trust in communication that gives a narration voice and pulse. Formless tales blankly told may be the end result" (289). His insistence on mimesis thus joins his desire for an element of romance in the novel. Too much ingenuity closes the window through which the reader looks at reality. In his essay on Gunter Grass's *From the Diary of a Snail*, he criticizes Grass for overworking an image. The complaint is not against ingenuity in general but against its random use which results in distortion. "What we want from our great imaginers is not fuel but fire, not patterns but an action, not fragmented and interlaced accounts but a story" (301). He expresses similar reservations about Witold Gombrowicz's *Ferdydurke*, noting that it has the form but not the substance of greatness. Energetic surface covers static event.

One does not always agree with Updike's general prescriptions, for one wonders if his urging of action instead of pattern and of story instead of interlaced accounts results in a kind of false dilemma whereby the reader must choose one kind of novel over another if he hopes to see fiction survive. Surely many readers respond by noting that honest perception accurately portrayed may lead to novels of pattern and formal pyrotechnics if the author views reality as fragmented. The writer who sees the world as fractured cannot always create novels with recognizable settings, logical transitions, and plots built around a beginning, a middle, and an end. After reading *Picked-Up Pieces*, the reader wants to ask if Updike reserves the compliment of "integrated work" only for successful conventional novels.

Yet it is to his credit that while he questions the strategies of new fiction, he rarely dismisses them. Writing clearly and knowledgeably, he shows, even in short reviews, that he has read enough to grant him the authority to discuss the state of the art as he sees it. One of his most pressing arguments is that the novel cannot use the techniques of cinema and painting to a significant extent. Robbe-Grillet's effort, for example, to substitute description for movement is false, just as his desire to describe the thereness of things by using verbal montages fails to take into account the different kinds of audience participation encouraged for a man reading a book and a man watching a film. If a picture is worth a thousand words, a motion picture is worth a million. The novel cannot compete on that level. Updike's opinion of Robbe-Grillet's experiments applies to any number of untraditional, anti-realistic novels: "They instead seem mannered devices intended to give unsubstantial materials an interesting surface" (358). The result is not the permanence of art but the ephemera of chic.

Two-thirds of the way through *Picked-Up Pieces*, Updike defines the novel: "...if by novel we understand an imitation of reality rather than a spurning of it" (362). He does not mean old-fashioned fiction; he means mimesis. Motion is often the key. Joyce and Kafka established the limits for the avant-garde novel more than six decades ago, but, says Updike, few experimental authors have gone beyond them. Too often in modern literature, movement gives way to prolongation. Novels conclude but lack development toward an ending. They are, in a word, motionless: "What we want from fiction, and what fiction is increasingly loath to give us, is vicarious experience" (386). Surrealism is fine, and literary experiments are praiseworthy, but only when unusual vision and extraordinary technique result from the extremity of the author's "ardor for reality." Only then do literary games reward the player. Thus Updike rarely divides good novelists and bad along the lines of realism and anti-realism, as his scathing review of realist James Gould Cozzens' *Morning Noon and Night* shows: "Beginning, forty years ago, with a style of sober purity, James Gould Cozzens has purposely evolved a prose unique in its mannered ugliness, a monstrous mix of Sir Thomas Browne, legalese, and Best-Remembered Quotations" (416).

All this is not to imply that Updike is correct in every essay in *Picked-Up Pieces*. Some evaluations are questionable. His praise of Erica Jong's *Fear of Flying*, for example, seems based more on his appreciation of a woman writing sassy prose and four-letter words than on appraisal of artistic merit. Unlike the superb analyses of Proust, Kierkegaard, Joyce, Nabokov, and Borges, this review combines overwriting and hyperbole. Similarly, one asks how he can mention Sylvia Plath in the same sentence with Yeats and Roethke. But for knowledge of subject, variety of taste, sympathy with other authors' interest in technique, and willingness to take a stand, Updike's essays in *Picked-Up Pieces* are the most informed body of literary criticism by an American novelist writing today.

Notes to *Picked-Up Pieces*

1. John Updike, *Picked-Up Pieces* (New York: Knopf, 1975). Further references will be to this edition.
2. Charles Thomas Samuels, "John Updike: The Art of Fiction XLIII," *Paris Review* 12(Winter 1968), 107, 114.

PLAY

Buchanan Dying (1974)

Buchanan Dying

"I do not believe there is an
honest man in Pennsylvania."

—Kate Thompson to Mary Ann Cobb
(January 1861)

Buchanan Dying (1974)[1] is surely not among Updike's popular successes, yet it is the most unexpected volume in his canon to this date. A closet drama in three acts totaling one hundred–eighty–pages plus an eighty–page Afterword, the book is described on the jacket cover as "a play meant to be read." Those who do read it will encounter Updike's version of the life and dying of James Buchanan, fifteenth President of the nation and, as the jacket reminds us, one of America's "lesser known, and least appreciated" leaders. Updike explains that his purpose "insofar as it is historical, is not to bury the immortal Lincoln, but to revive the forgotten Buchanan." He also claims that the play is "my favorite among my books."[2] If Buchanan is unknown and unloved, he remains in some quarters denigrated and even despised. One question still raised by historians and those who care is how much should he be appreciated? Perhaps it is hardly necessary to explain that James Buchanan was President from 1857 to 1861 and thus has been blamed since then for failing to devise a policy to eliminate the causes of the Civil War.

Although present at the first signs of impending battle, Buchanan was not around to lead the nation through the war. Many people contend that he could not lead the country anywhere. Why, then, is this President of the 1850s a fit subject for a play written by an author in the 1970s? In the opinion of some commentators, he is not a fit subject for anything. As Irvin Ehrenpreis argues, "Even an expert playwright would be daunted by the task of wringing a coherent drama from the story of James Buchanan."[3] Yet Updike pulls it off, at least most of it. Writing from a complex of motives to be discussed below, he places Buchanan on his deathbed reviewing in hallucination and reverie the highlights of his life, and he suggests that in the long act of dying the maligned President successfully counters most of those who would fault him. An instructive way to approach Updike's "play meant to be read" is to examine the comments of those who know both *Buchanan Dying* and Buchanan's Presidency.

A sympathetic reader of Updike's fiction, Professor Ehrenpreis supplies a precise overview of James Buchanan's life and then criticizes Updike for manipulating facts and improvising motive. As Ehrenpreis points out, Buchanan was a competent man of ordinary wisdom unable to resolve a crisis of extraordinary dimension. He was ill with dysentery when elected President in his late sixties, and the one term of office did little to alter his reputation as a politician hesitant to challenge Congress or to interpret the Constitution.

Perhaps the relative failure of Buchanan's Presidency resulted from developments in his formative years. Updike suggests as much. Born into a large Scotch-Irish family in southern Pennsylvania near Updike's own birthplace, Buchanan learned early to welcome work and to worship God. Educated to be a lawyer, he soon accepted the political necessities of trimming opinions to fit party doctrine and of pretending indifference to hide ambition. This sense of hesitancy, this willingness to tread a narrow road of the safe and true, shaped not only his political life but also his social affairs. He never married, a fact Updike attributes to Buchanan's mishandling of the young heiress Anne Coleman and her subsequent death following the break-up. The tragedy gave him the excuse he needed to avoid marriage until all problems were settled, a state of perfection which never arrived, of course.

Updike, however, goes a bit further. With artistic license which Ehrenpreis apparently disapproves of in this instance, Updike implies that Miss Coleman's mysterious death so quick on the heels of the broken engagement was suicide and that her death made Buchanan forever wary of the irrational elements always present in affairs of the heart. Ehrenpreis knows that information about Anne Coleman's tragedy is sketchy, unreliable, and thus open to all sorts of speculation, but he does not accept Updike's characterization of her as veering toward anti–establishment intellectualism (she quotes Byron) and anti–Victorian sexuality (she shows her breasts). With splendid humor, Ehrenpreis doubts Anne Coleman's spiritual relationship with Jill of *Rabbit Redux*. So do I. Yet if Miss Coleman were indeed just a bit liberal for her day in matters of head and heart, Updike's portrayal of the association between the adventuresome young woman and the careful young man could hold possibilities for drama.

Ehrenpreis also questions Updike's dramatization of Buchanan's theology. He points out, for example, that all readers of American history know that information about Buchanan's religious beliefs is much more reliable than speculations about his love affairs, and thus he criticizes Updike's implication that Buchanan could not accept the reality of human evil. Buchanan's lifelong acceptance of Calvinism, even of a "softened" variety, would be enough to acquaint him with expressions of iniquity. Updike may be correct, says Ehrenpreis, when he links Buchanan's fear of the irrational with sexual impotence and legalistic politics, but the author falters when he has his character confess that his most serious problem is not the specter of irrationality but the divergence of self and action.

Finally, Ehrenpreis wonders about dialogue and technique. The speeches sound too much alike and thus do not act as revelations of character. With the exception of the autobiography of Andrew Jackson in Act II, the language sounds anachronistic or false to those who know the period. Similarly, many readers will be puzzled by leaps in time which seem arbitrary, mixtures of real and illusory characters which seem confusing, and changes in tone from ironical to sympathetic which seem inexplicable. Why, wonders Ehrenpreis, does Updike remain so neutral about Buchanan's flaws and virtues?

The point of all this is that questions of variations in historical accounts often determine a reader's reaction to *Buchanan Dying* more than matters of structure, style, and dramatic content. Ehrenpreis argues that if the closet drama held the reader's attention the "unhistorical features" might be overlooked. But Updike bewilders those unfamiliar with the history of Buchanan's life because he blends internal musings with external reality to the point where fiction and fact become indistinguishable. Those who need help should consult the long Afterword in which Updike discusses motive and materials.

Arthur Schlesinger, Jr., calls the Afterword "cocky and discursive" in his essay which focuses on the relationship between history and fiction. In "The Historical Mind and the Literary Imagination," he discusses Updike's recreation of a President judged by a historian as eminent as Henry Steele Commager to be the worst chief executive in the history of the country.[4] With wit and intelligence, Professor Schlesinger describes *Buchanan Dying* as more ambitious and mysterious than Gore Vidal's *Burr* because it is easier to "rehabilitate a villain than a bore." Yet Schlesinger wonders what could have possibly led the "Twentieth-century magician of language" to resurrect the nineteenth-century failure in politics.

For all of Updike's association with Pennsylvania, Buchanan's home state, the answer to Schlesinger's question is found in the epigraph from Kierkegaard which Updike quotes: "I wanted to write a novel in which the chief character was to have been a man who had a pair of spectacles with one lens that reduced as powerfully as oxy-gas-microscope and the other that magnified equally powerfully; in his interpretation everything was very relative." Not everyone knows that James Buchanan was literally nearsighted in one eye and farsighted in the other. More important than this historical fact is the portrait Updike constructs from Kierkegaard's potentially powerful metaphor, for Buchanan's relativity in a time of dire crises all demanding absolute decisions had national as well as personal consequences. The union dissolved shortly after he left the Presidency, and his reputation was forever ruined in American history.

Arthur Schlesinger knows as much about nineteenth-century American history as anyone, but he does not take Updike to task for sifting the historical facts through the literary imagination. Noting that few historians will be convinced by this "glittering case" for Buchanan as tragic hero, Schlesinger argues, correctly I think, that such imaginative reconstructions are nevertheless useful. Updike himself may describe *Buchanan Dying* as a "strangely shaped, radically imperfect book," but it is also creative because it reminds historians that the past is populated, not by stereotypes rendered lifeless by repetitious historical pronouncements, but by human beings. Facts may be rearranged, and professional judgments may not be altered, but the literary imagination applied to historical affairs of great magnitude can often persuade careful readers to make a fresh examination of the stereotype.

The stereotype of James Buchanan which Updike challenges is that of Old Public Functionary, the staid legalistic executive who froze into inaction when the moment demanded leadership because he saw the crises of the South out of one eye and the problems of the North out of the other. In *Buchanan Dying*, Updike exchanges the Old Public Functionary for a new tragic hero. The book may be historical revisionism, but it is also fascinating speculation: James Buchanan not as the great equivocator but as the selfless sacrificer. Rather than an indecisive bungler who walked out of the White House and left Abraham Lincoln with an intolerable catastrophe, Updike proposes a President who personified the national dilemma itself. For example, the man who pronounced secession unconstitutional also argued that neither the President nor Congress had the constitutional force to coerce recalcitrant states into submission.

Professor Schlesinger is especially good at pointing out the contrasts between historical fact and literary reconstruction. Noting that Buchanan committed himself to a "drastic doctrine of executive impotence," he argues that the President was wrong to deny the power of the federal government to confront secession, and he shows that Buchanan supported the South in the most crucial matter of all, the perpetuation of slavery. It is not that Buchanan applauded slavery but that he could not see human bondage as the overwhelming moral issue of his age. Thus Updike's characterization may be dismissed by those who read with only the historical eye because, by minimizing the concessions the President was willing to make to the South, Updike suggests that Buchanan was an honorable man caught tragically in the middle. In his Afterword, he speaks of Buchanan's restraint as "wise instinct," but many historians believe that the President's intent was not to gain time to build a righteous cause and a superior army but to live by the Constitution as he defined it and to hope, surely unreasonably, that the nation would somehow devise constitutional guarantees for slavery and thereby avoid war.

Still, for all his praise of Updike's drama as reverie, Professor Schlesinger joins Irvin Ehrenpreis in questioning the use of language in *Buchanan Dying*. He admits that Updike is usually a magician with words, but he wonders if in the play the author writes "speeches so stilted as to be unspeakable" despite the effort to blend actual utterance as recorded in memoirs and letters with imagined discourse. These possible flaws are balanced by such exceptional passages as the reconstruction of the last letter from Anne Coleman to Buchanan breaking their engagement, and the portrait of Andrew Jackson which Ehrenpreis also praises. For those who do not have the time to read Philip S. Klein's *President James Buchanan* (1962), a reliable history book which Updike also consulted, Schlesinger's essay will supply some of the historian's interpretations perhaps needed to temper the artist's creations.

Other pertinent commentary is not so historically oriented. D. Keith Mano, for example, calls attention to Updike's statement in the Afterword that he wrote *Buchanan Dying* as his "final volume of homage to my native state," and he exclaims in mock surprise that "only a magnificent eccentric could run up debts to Pennsylvania."[5] More to the point, says Mano, is the confession that Updike wrote the closet drama as "an act of penance for a commercially successful novel set in New England." Mano adds a telling although perhaps exaggerated comment to this revelation in the Afterword, for he claims that Updike was "mortified by *Couples'* success" to the point of believing that he had "committed a gross abuse of the artistic will. He wouldn't look at the royalty statements. They accused him."[6] Thus Updike, often the eccentric but always the gentleman, published a book about America's worst president designed to "repel vulgar royalties." Calling the play "trite in form," and praising the Afterword as far more entertaining, Mano celebrates Updike's fairness in recreating a president who had as much decisiveness as Rabbit Angstrom.[7]

Considering the disagreement generated by *the* curio in Updike's impressive achievement, one should begin reading *Buchanan Dying* not with Act I but with the oft-praised Afterword. There Updike explains that his original plan was to write a novel about Pennsylvania's only president, and that he was "balked" in part by the novelistic touches in Philip Klein's *President James Buchanan*: "With such an intimate reconstruction already in print, there seemed little the fictionist could do but seek another form for the re-ordering of circumstance" (185). This re-ordering of circumstance disturbs Professor Ehrenpreis and delights Professor Schlesinger, and it is a characteristic of *Buchanan Dying* with which all readers must come to terms. For Updike all but says that he is writing not history but fiction based upon history. Although he may be faithful to the facts of Buchanan's life as revealed by historians such as Klein, he will also be loyal to the demands of his imagination as it suggests motives and thoughts not literally known. He describes himself, after all, not as a historian but as a "fictionist." What could be clearer: *Buchanan Dying* is a re-ordering of circumstances in light of the creative impulse.

Similarly, I fail to see how the charge of "pedantic" is appropriate to the Afterword. Although Updike cites sources in the manner of the professional scholar, especially the work by Klein and George Ticknor Curtis, he does so only to specify the historical framework and to encourage those so inclined to consult the data themselves. It seems to me that these references to the facts exonerate Updike from the charges of pedanticism and misrepresentation of history, for they indicate how little is known beyond the specifics of names, dates, and places. The scarcity of information invites the fictionist to fill in the gaps. A case in point is the matter of Anne Coleman and James Buchanan.

Updike cites what little is known about her mysterious and sudden death shortly following the dissolution of her engagement to the future President, especially the accounts by Judge Thomas Kittera, Blanche Nevin, and George Ticknor Curtis. He even quotes the obituary for Anne Coleman which appeared in the Lancaster (Pa.) *Journal* of December 11, 1819, and which may or may not have been written by Buchanan himself. Further, he explains the discrepancy between his spelling of Anne and those in contemporary documents which omit the final "e." The only certain facts are that Miss Coleman and Buchanan were engaged, that they quarreled over something perhaps incidental but at least momentarily serious, and that Miss Coleman broke the engagement and fled sixty miles to Philadelphia where she suddenly died. As Updike notes, "The affair fueled gossip and yellow journalism for the rest of Buchanan's life" (189). Would the papers about Anne Coleman which Buchanan preserved for fifty years but which were destroyed unopened at his death have explained the mystery? Did Miss Coleman commit suicide? Did her death result from medical treatment she was then receiving for a severe cold? If the affair produced ill feelings, gossip, and rumor among those closest to the tragedy in 1819, surely it could justifiably excite the creative imagination of a fictionist in 1974. Updike examines the sources, chooses the version hinting at suicide written by Leonora Clayton to Mary Ann Cobb, and goes on from there to construct his tale.

The result is that Buchanan's apparent inability to love Miss Coleman becomes one of the prominent metaphors in the play. For just as his bungling of that affair ended in tragedy, death, and endless speculation about Buchanan the man, so his mishandling of the Southern states, which he also said he loved, resulted in secession, war, and endless theorizing about Buchanan the President. Updike's Buchanan speaks of the South as "her," describes it as "our wife," and admits "I loved the South...but I gulled her." Although one may be hard pressed to prove that the President literally deserted the South as he apparently did Anne Coleman, the possibility that such an unconscious duplication prompted him is fascinating.

Violations of historical probability are surely acceptable in versions created by the artist's imagination. Updike's Buchanan reveals that he is cursed with a "sense of impotent detachment and cool fatality," an unfortunate trait which accounts as much for his impotence as his legalism and which, in the play, illustrates his helplessness while Miss Coleman plunges to suicide and the union stumbles toward war. Kierkegaard's metaphor plagues him to the end. Seeing a long way out of one eye, but a short distance out of the other, he becomes immobile in the grip of relativity. Updike hints that Anne Coleman knew as much. In one reverie, Buchanan is confronted with the imagined last letter from her which accuses him more bitterly than any subsequent historian: "My warmth accosts in you a deceptive coolness as unalterable as the mask of death" (138). Indeed, Updike's title suggests that Buchanan's entire life was an unalterable act of dying. The deathbed scene which frames the entire play and determines the substance of the reveries about the President's life illustrates for Updike the incapacitating impotence of a tragic man.

One question is whether Anne Coleman's death is a strong enough metaphor to determine the merger of internal reverie and external event which comprises the action while Buchanan is dying. In order to hint at the relationship between dream and reality, Updike creates a number of cross references, repetitions, and echoes. An event in present time will strike a chord in the dying President's memory and thus send him back to a moment in the past which is then acted out as a way of suggesting motive for or cause of his opinions and decisions. Every reader recognizes, for example, that the bells heard all through the play echo the bell Buchanan's mother hangs around his neck so that as a boy he will not become lost in the forest. If the forest represents the mysterious unknown and the lure to explore darkness and deepness, the bell may be the warning which calls one back to the safety of the clearing and the sanity of rationality. The reader may even go further and wonder if the mother is thus a primary cause of Buchanan's hesitancy to plunge into the tangles of catastrophic national crises and promising love affairs. This device is not innovative. Updike uses cross references and repetitions to bind reality and reverie in *The Centaur* and in many of his short stories. The question is not one of technique but of effect. The demands Updike places upon the metaphor of Anne Coleman's love and death may be too great. That a dying President, especially a President at the time of the Civil War, would experience hallucination and self-doubt is one thing, but it may be quite another to suggest that Miss Coleman's tragedy links nearly every event and feeling in Buchanan's life from the guilt he now suffers because his sister Mary dies the year he is born to the subconscious depths of impotence and indecisiveness. Most of the female characters in the play have some parallel with the fated young woman. Even in the discussion of Kate Thompson in the Afterword, we read of Anne Coleman's ghost "moving, somehow, taking its revenge" (241). Updike's Afterword indicates how he arrived at the esthetic decision to place Buchanan's failure with Miss Coleman at the center of all of the President's problems.

Of equal interest in the Afterword is the rationale for presenting Buchanan as Hamlet instead of Polonius. Updike reveals, for example, Professor Klein's worry that he might publish yet another character assassination of the much maligned President, and he offers his book as an indication of "how far my intentions were from any denigration of our hero" (193). Presumably irony is not a factor here. Although Updike discusses and quotes from such nineteenth-century defenses of Buchanan as Curtis' *Life of James Buchanan* (1883) and the standard laudatory campaign biography, *The Life and Public Service of James Buchanan* by R.G. Horton (1856), he finds most of the historical imperative for a defense in Allan Nevins' *The Emergence of Lincoln* (1950).

Nevins by no means apologizes for Buchanan, but he does flesh out the man beyond the stereotype of Old Public Functionary. If Scotch-Irish Buchanan showed none of the mettle of Scotch-Irish Jackson, Calhoun, and Polk, he nevertheless had more civil experience and ability than Taylor, Fillmore, and Pierce. This opinion may have been the opening Updike needed, for his subsequent quotations from Nevins in the Afterword show how he arrived at his sympathetic portrayal of Buchanan in the play. What many historians define as indecisiveness and fear when confronted with the recalcitrance of South Carolina, Nevins describes as sane policy. "My point," says Updike, "is that time was on the side of the North, and that by buying time Buchanan did all that the Union could ask."[8] Buchanan's program of "peace, conciliation, and delay" is thus viewed as the decision of a statesman hoping to preserve the Union without carnage. Rather than act against the South, he worked for peace and waited. Updike goes beyond Nevins (who lists Buchanan's blunders) and argues that the President's refusal to fire the first shot of what would surely be a Civil War was not timidity, as it is so often judged, but "wise instinct." Recall Schlesinger's opinion that the President failed to see slavery as the moral question of his age. Updike's Buchanan refuses to confront the South because he knows that the North will be rallied to the Union cause only if it appears to be righteous. Looming always behind this troubled man at this catastrophic moment is the specter of Anne Coleman. Failure in love, failure in politics—little wonder that Updike looks at James Buchanan and sees Hamlet.

One of Updike's most telling comments which explains his revisionist portrayal of the President occurs near the end of the survey of sources in the Afterword. Explaining that he does not find in the history books confirmation that Buchanan was America's worst chief executive, he calls attention to the man's competence in foreign affairs, and then he writes, "Elected amid rising sectionalism to keep the peace for four more years, he performed the job for which he was hired" (210). Readers of *Buchanan Dying* may ask if Presidents should do a bit more, if the position is more than a "job."

Finally, the Afterword offers some insight into Updike's attitude toward his play. Calling *Buchanan Dying* a "radically imperfect book," he nevertheless gives the impression of affection for it as if the drama were the naughty child of a steadily expanding brood. It may not be polished, proportioned, or graceful, but the effort to shape its existence is a labor of love. Guilt over the commercial success of *Couples* may indeed have been a motivating factor in the research which led to the composition of *Buchanan Dying*, but the nostalgia associated with the short stories is also present in Updike's accounts of how he came to write his "imperfect" play. Buchanan reminds him of home in Pennsylvania, and Pennsylvania recalls for him grandparents and uncles who were in touch with an older and perhaps more innocent time. Describing his Uncle John, Updike writes, "His kindly, eerie wheeze of a voice, sighing 'Johnny' with a caressing tone of lament, arose from a green world where men would not breathe again, a Pennsylvania dying about us, though its buildings like bones remained. I wanted to dive into that lost green, and set a novel there" (256). Those familiar with the Updike canon cannot help but think of stories like "In Football Season" and "When Everyone Was Pregnant" while reading these words, for his sensitive ability to reach out and gently touch his heritage is one of the glories of his achievement. A point about *Buchanan Dying* is that he reaches beyond the imaginary Olinger to grasp Pennsylvania and a past moment in America itself. For all the penance involved in his effort to write a play, one also recognizes his affection for a lost President, a lost family, and a lost time. That he simultaneously accumulated research materials on Buchanan, turned forty, and buried his father suggests the extraordinary close affiliation Updike feels between his personal heritage and his native region. *Buchanan Dying* is a summation of and a farewell to a tone and subject matter which have directed his writing for fifteen years: "Here is Buchanan, I am rid of him, and this book, a mosaic with more tesserae than matrix, constitutes, I trust, my final volume of homage to my native state, whose mild misty doughy middleness, between immoderate norths and souths, remains for me, being my first taste of life, the authentic taste" (259). The connection between middle-of-the road James Buchanan and the middleness of Pennsylvania need hardly be emphasized.

The novel that he planned never materialized, of course, developing from research materials, to chapters and ideas later abandoned, to a closet drama. Updike indicates that his original impetus was not Buchanan but Kierkegaard's description in his *Journals* (December 10, 1837) of the man with relative vision. Beginning with the story of a wicked high-school principal, he moved to the idea of a "novel with a stationary hero, a man in bed dying" (251). His third idea was to write a tetralogy "of which the first novel would be set in the future, the second in the present, the third in the remembered past, and the fourth in the historical past" (252). The first three became *The Poorhouse Fair, Rabbit, Run*, and *The Centaur*, but the fourth never took shape until he discarded the novel format to compose the "radically imperfect" play. Significantly, then, *Buchanan Dying* is a kind of substitute for an aborted fiction Updike never finished because he could not get into his subject's life. Leaving the problem of surfaces to set designers and the interpretation of psychology to the actors, he found that a play was possible wherein speech could be all.

The sounds of various voices begin with the series of five epigraphs which Updike describes as symmetrical. Arranged chronologically, the epigraphs move from Kierkegaard's 1837 notation for a novel, to

John Quincy Adams' description of Buchanan as "the sneaking scrivener" (1841), to James K. Polk's left-handed compliment about an able man but an old maid (1848), to Henry Adams' predicting the impeachment of Buchanan (1861), to Joseph Holt's praise of the embattled leader as "eminently a conscientious man" (1884). Placing the epigraphs in this manner, Updike suggests that contemporary and posthumous commentaries on Buchanan are just as relative as Kierkegaard's potential hero and the President's decision-making skills. Evaluations of character depend upon angles of vision, and angles of vision depend upon priorities of circumstances. Buchanan himself recognizes this truth when he quotes Bishop Berkeley to Anne Coleman: "Yet are we not...creatures all of one another's eyes?" (38). For a man hoping to hold a middle course on a rocky road, variations in opinions of his navigational prowess are likely to be the rule. Were it not for matters of symmetry, Updike might have added a sixth epigraph, this one from Kate Thompson's January 1861 letter to Mary Ann Cobb: "I do not believe there is an honest man in Pennsylvania." At any rate, these quotations illustrate the many voices of history which echo around the reader before he begins to read the play.

A key to Updike's method may be found early in Act One when the sick Buchanan tells his nurse that facts are overestimated and that "we live down here among shadows, shadows among shadows" (5). During the course of the three acts, the central fact is Buchanan's dying and the central scene is his bedroom at Wheatlands in Lancaster, Pennsylvania, where he retired following Lincoln's inauguration. Yet Updike enlivens this potentially dreary scene with the shades of people long since dead and the shadows of events long since settled. The result is a merger of reverie and history. As Buchanan reviews his life with the stimulus of both hallucination and consciousness, the dry evidence of chronology and facts gives way to an interesting blend of suppositions and possibilities. Just as the important people in Buchanan's life tend to merge into one another during his deathbed reveries, so Updike constructs the drama around actors who must play more than one role in order to illustrate the resemblances the dying man now sees among his many acquaintances. Facts as determined by later historians do not count as much in this play as interpretations rendered by the former officeholder.

Buchanan himself supplies an image to illustrate the sorry spectacle of a President dying in a country which now maligns his term of office. He likens his position in a dream to the paradox of being as majestic as a pinioned eagle on the lawn. Now caught in the grip of an impending death, the literal act of dying seems to him the purpose of his entire life. Updike links the deaths of Buchanan's sister Mary, Anne Coleman, the Union in war, and the President to suggest how, despite the trappings of prestige and power, Buchanan's one unalterable action has been a long life of dying.

The old man believes as much. Perhaps his most telling comment in Act One is his equation of death with dancing and diplomacy: "Dying, I discover, is rather like dancing, and not unlike diplomacy; legerity and tact are paramount. I was a fair country dancer in my time" (8). He implies his hope that the same may be said of his diplomatic prowess, but the rest of the play raises questions about his political tact. Because of the equation, Buchanan's prayer to be "worthy" of his dying suggests the severity of his doubts about his administration. Can it be, he wonders, that the stench of death permeated his four years in the White House and finally fouled the entire land with the first shot of the Civil War? Are the qualities of legerity and tact enough to guarantee a successful President or even a graceful dancer? Did he step, finally, too nimbly between North and South only to stumble embarrassed to the floor? President James Polk, a chief executive who enjoys a more substantial posthumous reputation than Bucahanan, implies a similar connection between death and his life in diplomacy: "Well, what is life for any of us, but a busy dying?" (96). Seen in this light, the present tense of the title takes on graver implications than just the specific moments of the President's death. Buchanan, for example, comments as secession grows imminent: "*Mr.* James Buchanan, as a seeker of his own interest, is dead. There remains only the President of the United States" (119-120). Yet by the time South Carolina severs its ties with the Union, his own advisers declare him a corpse.

Why? The answer lies in his tendency toward relativity. Although Updike clearly characterizes the President as a man who stands firmly upon his belief in the Constitution, he also dramatizes his tendency to waver between opposing actions in spite of his definition of government as "either organized benevolence or organized madness" (15). Kierkegaard's metaphor sets the tone. Despite Buchanan's pride in not needing eyeglasses, he nevertheless has one nearsighted and one farsighted eye. He tells one of his advisers that "all the factors were relative." Note, for example, his comment about slavery:

"I never claimed, slavery was no evil; I merely claimed for it the constitutional protection the framers unambiguously specified" (20). Slavery by this definition is not a moral issue at all but a question of property rights. With legalism nullifying morality, Buchanan may hesitate in taking decisive action against South Carolina because federal property has not yet been attacked. Updike hints that the President finds the crisis ambiguous because the Supreme Court has declared slaves as property. Given Buchanan's devotion to the Constitution, he can hardly do otherwise.

Yet for all the skill of Updike's defense, one has to wonder about the perspicacity of a lifetime politician who can declare that there are "no enemies in politics, only potential allies" (21). While the entire country, both North and South, clamors for decisiveness, Updike's Buchanan chooses the action of inaction in the belief that inaction is the nation's last hope, firm action the abyss. Relativity all but becomes policy when, in his December 3, 1860, speech to Congress, he denies the power of the federal government to force a state to its definition of right and just action: "Apart from the execution of the laws, so far as this may be practicable, the Executive has no authority to decide what shall be the relations between the federal government and South Carolina. He has been invested with no such discretion.... The question fairly stated is: Has the Constitution delegated to Congress the power to coerce a State into submission? After much serious reflection, I have arrived at the conclusion that no such power has been delegated to Congress or to any other department of the federal government" (113). Updike shows that this penchant for relativity soon becomes a director of presidential policy when Buchanan neither reinforces Major Anderson at Fort Sumter nor withdraws him. Hired to keep the peace for four years, he does the job. Yet even he now wonders if he could have done more.

Nowhere are Buchanan's tendencies toward relativity and inaction more poignant than in his association with the wealthy Anne Coleman. Although they have pledged their affection, Buchanan cannot bring himself formally to propose marriage. The reasons are many. He shies from her father's disapproval. He dislikes the charge of fortune hunting. He fears the privileges of passion. Even when Anne declares her love, a brave confession in light of the Victorian conventions which govern their courtship, even when she bares her breasts to show her humanity, Buchanan sees both goddess and cow. The dichotomy paralyzes him. Astonishingly, he says that the beauty of her breasts brings him closer to death. Equating the mystery of sexuality with the lure of the abyss, he fails to respond to her physical invitation or to pursue her when she flees to Philadelphia to die, choosing instead to remain in Lancaster to work on a legal matter. For all of the charges against Buchanan from politicians on both sides of the Mason-Dixon line, Updike suggests that Miss Coleman's accusation is the most penetrating: "Because, ungoaded, you stand stock still, like a horse before his stall, though it brims with green hay. What holds you back? Marry me" (44). He does not move. Unable to respond to her appeal to "laugh, rage, assault me," he meets her invitations to marriage and sex with a speech which later echoes in his political addresses and policies: "You urge decision in a delicately balanced world. Let us force no event that gradual causes will in time render inevitable" (46). While talking with her, he hears the bell which protects him as a child from becoming lost in the forest and all it represents. He fears the lure of everything that lingers beyond the clearing. Updike implies not only the connection between Buchanan's failure with Anne and his difficulties in the White House but also that the aborted love affair is more tragic in the President's life than the Civil War.

Miss Coleman's accusations of immobility and coldness suggest both physical and psychological impotence even though Updike understands Buchanan's tactics with South Carolina, Fort Sumter, and Lincoln to be the strategy of statesmanship. Others accuse him in more angry terms. George Coleman denigrates Buchanan's honor. John Forney claims he is an ingrate who misleads others into doing his dirty work. John Slidell says that the President hides his opinions. Lest his advisers and some readers argue that he hasn't any, Buchanan defends his Presidency as the trial of a man who managed unaided in the midst of a maelstrom: "In this perilous center, for a space of months, I ruled alone. The South and the North beat upon me as two raging oceans, and I held" (25). Determination to hold, says Updike, is cause enough for our gratitude. And yet his Buchanan also believes that "all action... partakes of the nature of sin" (46). When Anne Coleman accuses him of accepting the stringencies of life while spurning the bounties, the President counters that she embraces the freedoms of life while rejecting the terror. In scenes such as these, he seems to have stepped from the pages of Kierkegaard's journal.

One eye detects practical manipulation, the other moral concern. For example, Buchanan's design to expand the country into Cuba and Mexico may have been a genuine effort to extend United States land mass, but it may also have been a plan to placate Southerners who demanded additional areas for slavery. An unfortunate implication is that he does not bother to please New England in these matters because the Northeast corner does not support him in the election. Where does manipulation leave off and morality begin? The scene between James Buchanan and Andrew Jackson provides a partial answer.

Although ambiguous, the meeting does suggest distinctions between two men destined to be President which may, inadvertently perhaps, place the younger man Buchanan in the wrong. Jackson's response to Buchanan's cautious queries about the post of Secretary of State may smack of righteous indignation, but it also speaks of principle. Outlining a personal history of action, both violent and direct, Updike's Jackson discerns a truth about Buchanan as early as 1824: "I've been there, Mr. Buchanan, and out the other side. You're still this side, and that makes a man gingerly" (83). The scene is powerfully developed, perhaps the best in the play, for it hints that Buchanan will be as uneasy about firm action in politics as he is with Anne Coleman. Jackson gives him the advice of a confident man: "…when ye've put the fear of the worst behind ye, ye'll know where the power lies in God's own country: it lies in the passions of the people. With the people in yer guts, ye can do no wrong" (84). Unfortunately for Buchanan, and maybe for the country, he never is on such close terms with the people. Whether or not this potential shortcoming means that he cannot act from principle with conviction and decisiveness is a question which remains ambiguous. President Polk warns, "Agile vacillation is no route to the Presidency: a firm course, rather, maintained with an inspired disregard of secondary effects" (95). Buchanan apparently sees more than just secondary effects.

Yet Updike believes that in not directly acting to meet the South Carolina crisis, Buchanan indeed responds with principle. The verdict of history may disagree, but the play argues that the President at least keeps the peace until Lincoln assumes the job. Perhaps he takes heart from Polk's comment in 1848: "To be President of the United States, sir, is to act as advocate for a blind, venomous, and ungrateful client" (94). How far this comment is from Andrew Jackson's faith in the people. Updike reminds us that Buchanan's clients are still ungrateful.

At the end, dying and given to the reveries which comprise the drama, the President asserts that "Posterity will do me justice" (179). That may one day be so, but for the moment posterity needs this nudge from Updike's imagination. Creating a character to whose vision God presents riddles, Updike abandons his own novel to write Kierkegaard's in the form of a play.

Notes to *Buchanan Dying*

1. John Updike, *Buchanan Dying* (New York: Knopf, 1974). Further references will be to this edition.
2. John Updike, "One Big Interview," *Picked-Up Pieces* (New York: Knopf, 1975), 513. James Atlas, "John Updike Breaks Out of Suburbia," New York *Times Magazine*, 10 December 1978, p. 72.
3. Irvin Ehrenpreis, "Buchanan Redux," *New York Review of Books*, 8 August 1974, p. 6.
4. Arthur Schlesinger, Jr., "The Historical Mind and the Literary Imagination," *Atlantic Monthly*, 233 (June 1974), 54-59.
5. D. Keith Mano, "Doughy Middleness," *National Review*, 30 August 1974, pp. 987-988.
6. Mano, 987.
7. Stanley Weintraub also comments upon Updike's need for penance, and he terms the book "only an indulgence for which Updike must be forgiven." It is not that Weintraub dismisses *Buchanan Dying* as a total failure but only that he judges it minor. Calling it "an absorbing piece of writing by a contemporary master," he criticizes many of the speeches, applauds the evocation of Andrew Jackson, and admires Updike's speculation that Buchanan's indecisiveness may have resulted from his fatal hesitation to marry the voluptuous Anne Coleman. The negative commentators are not as forgiving as Weintraub. Peter S. Prescott describes *Buchanan Dying* as "two-thirds closet drama and one-third lumpy essay." Acknowledging Updike's sympathy and intelligence, he insists that the book does not offer enough to redeem a "wordy, ungainly," and ill-advised effort. Peter Straub is even more upset. He confesses that he cares deeply about Updike's work, but he finds *Buchanan Dying* a "full-scale literary disaster, phony and dull as sliced white bread." Finally, Michael Putney accuses Updike of leaning on pedantry the way a sportswriter falls back on statistics. Wondering why Updike casts Buchanan as Hamlet when nearly everyone else sees him as Polonius, Putney so despairs of the book that he asks if *Buchanan Dying* is Updike's spoof, his *Pale Fire*. See Stanley Weintraub, "Closet Drama," *New Republic*,

22 June 1974, p. 26; Peter S. Prescott, "Immobile President," *Newsweek*, 24 June 1974, pp. 82, 85-86; Peter Straub, "Wise Women," *New Statesman*, 10 January 1975, p. 50; and Michael Putney, "Historian Updike Looks at... James Buchanan??," *National Observer*, 6 July 1974, p. 17.

8. Updike, "One Big Interview," 513.

A Concluding Note

One should not draw final conclusions about an author as adept at so many different genres as John Updike. To provide a summary statement at this stage of his career is presumptuous; to offer a prediction about his future is risky. Updike delights because he surprises. One never knows what the next book will be. Alastair Reid's description of the multiple qualities of *The Coup*, Updike's latest novel at this writing, is to the point: "Call *The Coup* a caper, an indulgence, a tract, a chronicle, a fable—and it is all these things at different times—the fact is that Updike's sentences can be read with the pleasure that poetry can, and the fingers are more than enough to count the novelists of whom such a thing can be said,"[1] Whether imagining the presidency of a historical personage like James Buchanan, or creating the history of an imaginary country like Kush, Updike's sentences shine.

Yet many readers believe that the style outshines the substance. The catch phrases of the negative evaluations mentioned in the preceding chapters continue to echo around this impressive canon: "All wind-up and no delivery"; "writes like an angel but has nothing to say"; "great issues aren't at issue in his work." What can one do except to shake his head and ask the reviewers to reread. Updike's reaction to this kind of carping is generally true: that many critics treat his books as disappointing versions of the ones they might have written if they had had the same material. But they do not have his material, and they do not have his style. Still, as he himself notes, there is no way a writer can please every reader. Author of more than twenty volumes, Updike has pleased millions.

To call attention to more than half of his books has been the purpose of this study. This is not to say that the novels are a lesser accomplishment but only to argue that the poems, stories, prose, and play warrant examination. It may well be that Updike is creating an achievement which will be judged by future readers as second to none in his time. The canon is already of superior quality. But his achievement cannot be properly appreciated without an evaluation of the other John Updike, the one the literate public does not know as well.

Although there is no way to determine reader awareness with certainty, *Buchanan Dying* is probably the least known of Updike's books. Whether one accepts Keith Mano's insistence that Updike was "mortified" by the commercial success of *Couples* to the extent that he refused to look at the royalty statements, and the implication that the play was written to lose money and thus even out the balance sheet, is beside the point.[2] Yet Updike admits in the Afterword to *Buchanan Dying* that he wrote the closet drama as "an act of penance for a commercially successful novel set in New England." He must have received absolution, for the book was neither widely reviewed nor widely read. Those who know Updike primarily as the author of *Couples* and *Rabbit, Run* are not likely to be familiar with *Buchanan Dying*. Yet the play is of enormous interest to those who wish to examine his devotion to the historical roots of his part of Pennsylvania. Although it is fiction and thus not to be read as pure history, *Buchanan Dying* adds to the concrete basis of the myth which Updike is creating about Olinger and the surrounding vicinity much the same way William Faulkner used the Civil War as a foundation for his Yoknapatawpha myth. Posterity would have it that James Buchanan joins Flick Webb, Ace Anderson, and perhaps even William Young as a Pennsylvanian of great ability who failed to meet his promise, but Updike argues otherwise. The degeneration from Buchanan's politics to Flick's gasoline pumps may one day be seen as a significant part of Updike's myth of America.

The poetry has a bit wider audience than the play if only because many of the poems were first published in the *New Yorker*. Not many readers, however, know about his collections of poetry. Even Updike admits that *Midpoint* is his least reviewed book. The problem is that Updike the poet is defined, if that phase of his writing is examined at all, as an author of light verse. For some readers this designation means that the poetry should be dismissed. To identify him with light verse is not a complete error, for he is especially adept with rhyme, puns, and witty turns of phrase. Updike takes light verse seriously as his essay about Max Beerbohm shows. Fun with language keeps language alive. But to limit his achievement to comic poems is to ignore the majority of his poetry. Evidently, the misnomer of light versifier was applied to the author of *The Carpentered Hen*, and it has stuck through succeeding collections which are largely made up of serious poems. Updike's more conventional poetry adds to the reader's appreciation of how he handles small details while celebrating the quotidian magic of common lives and everyday events. It is difficult to label him a light-verse poet when reading "Bath After Sailing" or "Seven Stanzas at Easter." More important, perhaps, is the summarizing revelation in "Midpoint" which pulls together his past before turning him toward the future. The autobiographical poem leads to *Tossing and Turning* and the truly fine lyrics in which a relatively young man contemplates death. Many readers of an author mistakenly judged to be primarily a novelist generally consider his poetry to be a sidelight, but such is not the case with John Updike and especially with the poems after *The Carpentered Hen*.

Those who want to know some of Updike's ideas about poetry should turn to the appropriate essays in *Assorted Prose* and *Picked-Up Pieces*. As readers of the *New Yorker* realize, he reviews all kinds of books with regularity and perspicacity. The range of subjects and authors is astonishing. In many of the essays, he discusses his own theories of poetry, fiction, philosophy, and religion to create a framework for the analysis of the book at hand. Some of these prose pieces, especially "Hub Fans Bid Kid Adieu," have earned high reputations as contemporary examples of the essayist's art. But when read together, the essays have a different and perhaps more substantial impact. Instead of occasional pieces of review and commentary scattered in various magazines and published at various times of the year, the essays when studied as collections define a body of ideas essential to an overview of Updike's art. Carefully perusing *Assorted Prose* and *Picked-Up Pieces*, one notices a parallel with the poetry from *The Carpentered Hen* through *Midpoint* to *Tossing and Turning*: He begins largely with comedy and commentary, and he moves toward seriousness and analysis. Two general topics concern Updike throughout his gatherings of essays—the troubled state of the nation and its culture, and the changing art of the novel and its goals. This conclusion is not the place to review the points made in the preceding chapter on Updike's prose, but it should be pointed out that his continuing insistence upon the necessity for mimesis and realism is bound to be disputed in an age which is witnessing a general break with the conventions of traditional fiction.

Of all the writing by the other John Updike, the short stories are the best known and probably will remain so. Poetry and essays are not widely appreciated in the United States, and a play not meant to be acted is not likely to be read. Such is not the case with the tales. "Lifeguard" and "A & P" are often anthologized in textbooks, and "Pigeon Feathers" and "A Sense of Shelter" are frequently debated in quarterlies. These four stories are part of *Pigeon Feathers*, his second and most popular collection. From the vantage point of hindsight, one can see how *Pigeon Feathers* began the transition to the later collections and the resulting debate about the quality of his short fiction. Although his interest in persistent desire and enticing memory upsets some readers, the form of the stories apparently disturbs many more. In some of the tales, Updike writes what may be called lyrical meditations rather than conventional short fictions. Character and dramatic action give way to prose rhythms and mood, and the story takes a step toward the essay. "Wife-wooing," among others in *Pigeon Feathers*, looks forward to "The Music School" and "When Everyone Was Pregnant." Those who insist upon evaluating short stories by traditional standards may have trouble accepting as fiction these tales in which the quality of the prose shapes the predicament of the character. Lyrical or poetic prose encourages the tone of nostalgia and the mood of reverie. Many of the stories, especially those about the Maples, are written in a standard format as the action rises and falls toward resolution, but Updike's primary contribution to the art of short fiction is to be found in stories like those mentioned above including "Leaves" and "Harv Is Plowing Now." There is a delicacy which rewards the patient reader.

This study is not meant to suggest that every piece of Updike's writing is successful. I doubt if even he would claim as much. His canon is so large and so varied, covering so many genres and so many years, that it is bound to contain sections which he would like to rewrite. But if an author has the right to be judged by his best work— and he does—then the achievement of John Updike is impressive indeed.

Notes to Conclusion

1. Alastair Reid, "Updike Country," *New Yorker*, 25 December 1978, p. 69.
2. D. Keith Mano, "Doughy Middleness," *National Review*, 30 August 1974, p. 987.

Selected Checklist of
the Other John Updike

Updike, John. *The Carpentered Hen and Other Tame Creatures*. New York: Harper and Brothers, 1958.
   The Same Door: Short Stories. New York: Knopf, 1959.
   Pigeon Feathers and Other Stories. New York: Knopf, 1962.
   Telephone Poles and Other Poems. New York: Knopf, 1963.
   Olinger Stories: A Selection. New York: Vintage, 1964.
   Assorted Prose. New York: Knopf, 1965.
   The Music School: Short Stories. New York: Knopf, 1966.
   Midpoint and Other Poems. New York: Knopf, 1969.
   Museums and Women and Other Stories. New York: Knopf, 1972.
   Buchanan Dying: A Play. New York: Knopf, 1974.
   Picked-Up Pieces. New York: Knopf, 1975.
   Tossing and Turning: Poems. New York: Knopf, 1977.

The primary bibliography of John Updike is still expanding. Three helpful sources are C. Clarke Taylor, *John Updike: A Bibliography* (Kent, Ohio: Kent State University Press, 1968) and Michael A. Olivas, *An Annotated Bibliography of John Updike Criticism 1967–1973, and A Checklist of His Works* (New York: Garland, 1975), and Ray A. Roberts, "John Updike: A Bibliographical Checklist," *American Book Collector*, 1, Nos. 1 and 2, new series (Jan.-Feb., March-April, 1980), pp. 5-12, 40-44; 39-47. The following checklist notes insofar as I have been able to determine with the help of Taylor, Olivas, and Roberts the dates and places of first publication of Updike's poems, short stories, and essays which he has collected. Some of the poems, stories, and essays were originally published in the collections. At this writing many of Updike's poems, tales, and essays are uncollected. I acknowledge with gratitude the help of my graduate assistants Michael Adams and Caroline Bokinsky in compiling the following checklist. Jane Thesing, Assistant Reference Librarian at Cooper Library, University of South Carolina, also helped me track down some of the fugitive pieces.

THE CARPENTERED HEN

"The Population of Argentina." *Harvard Lampoon*, 142 (February 1953), 17.

"Mountain Impasse." *Harvard Lampoon*, 142 (April 1953), 11.

"Poetess." *Harvard Lampoon*, 142 (September 1953), 4.

"Footnotes to the Future." *Harvard Lampoon*, 142 (October 1953), 14. (As "Why the Telephone Wires Dip and the Poles are Cracked and Crooked.")

"Duet, with Muffled Brake Drums." *New Yorker*, 14 August 1954, p. 74.

"Dilemma in the Delta." *Harvard Lampoon*, 143 (September 1954), 22.

"Player Piano." *New Yorker*, 4 December 1954, p. 169.

"The Clan." *New Yorker*, 18 December 1954, p. 119.

"Song of the Open Fireplace." *New Yorker*, 8 January 1955, p. 31.

"Shipboard." *New Yorker*, 15 January 1955, p. 93. (As "Shipbored.")

"Recitative for Punished Products." *Punch*, 9 February 1955, p. 194.

"March: A Birthday Poem." *New Yorker*, 12 February 1955, p. 38.

"Youth's Progress." *New Yorker*, 26 February 1955, p. 28.

"V.B. Nimble, V.B. Quick." *New Yorker*, 2 April 1955, p. 36.

"Lament, for Cocoa." *New Yorker*, 14 May 1955, p. 163.

"Humanities Course." *New Yorker*, 4 June 1955, p. 100.

"Sunglasses." *New Yorker*, 16 July 1955, p. 65.

"An Imaginable Conference." *New Yorker*, 6 August 1955, p. 24.

"Sunflower." *New Yorker*, 10 September 1955, p. 136.

"Pooem." *New Yorker*, 1 October 1955, p. 34.

"An Ode: Fired Into Being by *Life's* 48 Star Editorial, 'Wanted: An American Novel.'" *New Yorker*, 15 October 1955, p. 47. (As "An Ode.")

"The Story of My Life." *New Yorker*, 5 November 1955, p. 212.

"Superman." *New Yorker*, 12 November 1955, p. 56.

"The Newlyweds." *New Yorker*, 19 November 1955, p. 157.

"To an Usherette." *New Yorker*, 10 December 1955, p. 190.

"A Bitter Life." *New Yorker*, 7 January 1956, p. 26.

"Tsokadze o altitudo." *New Yorker*, 25 February 1956, p. 115.

"Publius Vergilius Maro, the Madison Avenue Hick." *New Yorker*, 31 March 1956, p. 32.

"Mr. High-Mind." *New Yorker*, 28 April 1956, p. 44.

"Little Poems." *New Yorker*, 21 July 1956, p. 73.

"Tao in the Yankee Stadium Bleachers." *New Yorker*, 18 August 1956, p. 28.

"Old Faces of '56." *New Yorker*, 27 October 1956, p. 36. (As "Popular Revivals, 1956.")

"Due Respect." *New Yorker*, 17 November 1956, p. 50.

"A Wooden Darning Egg." *Harper's*, 213 (December 1956), 34.

"Capacity." *New Yorker*, 5 January 1957, p. 29.

"The Sensualist." *New Yorker*, 16 February 1957, p. 30.

"Scenic." *New Yorker*, 9 March 1957, p. 97.

"A Rack of Paperbacks." *New Yorker*, 23 March 1957, p. 124.

"Song in American Type." *New Yorker*, 30 March 1957, p. 30. (As "Tune, in American Type.")

"The One-Year Old." *Ladies Home Journal*, 74 (March 1957), 172.

"Philological." *New Yorker*, 6 April 1957, p. 109.

"Glasses." *New Yorker*, 20 April 1957, p. 139.

"A Modest Mound of Bones." *Commonweal*, 26 April 1957, p. 92.

"Planting a Mailbox." *New Yorker*, 11 May 1957, p. 103.

"Ode III.ii: Horace." *Commonweal*, 7 June 1957, p. 254.

"Ex-Basketball Player." *New Yorker*, 6 July 1957, p. 62.

"Even Egrets Err." *New Yorker*, 7 September 1957, p. 74.

"Rm. 28, National Portrait Gallery, London." *New Yorker*, 2 November 1957, p. 40.

THE SAME DOOR

"Friends from Philadelphia." *New Yorker*, 30 October 1954, pp. 29-32.

"Ace in the Hole." *New Yorker*, 9 April 1955, pp. 92-99.

"Tomorrow, and Tomorrow, Etc." *New Yorker*, 30 April 1955, pp. 80-91. (As "Tomorrow and Tomorrow and So Forth.")

"Dentistry and Doubt." *New Yorker*, 29 October 1955, pp. 28-30.

"The Kid's Whistling." *New Yorker*, 3 December 1955, pp. 127-134.

"Snowing in Greenwich Village." *New Yorker*, 21 January 1956, pp. 30-33.

"Toward Evening." *New Yorker*, 11 February 1956, pp. 28-30.

"Who Made Yellow Roses Yellow?" *New Yorker*, 7 April 1956, pp. 28-34.

"His Finest Hour." *New Yorker*, 23 June 1956, pp. 26-31.

"Sunday Teasing." *New Yorker*, 13 October 1956, pp. 46-48.

"A Trillion Feet of Gas." *New Yorker*, 8 December 1956, pp. 51-56.

"Incest." *New Yorker*, 29 June 1957, pp. 22-27.

"The Alligators." *New Yorker*, 22 March 1958, pp. 28-31. (Reprinted in *Parents Magazine*, 40 [September 1965], 62-63.)

"A Gift from the City." *New Yorker*, 12 April 1958, pp. 45-64.

"Intercession." *New Yorker*, 30 August 1958, pp. 24-27.

"The Happiest I've Been." *New Yorker*, 3 January 1959, pp. 24-31.

PIGEON FEATHERS

"Still Life." *New Yorker*, 24 January 1959, pp. 35-41.

"Vergil Moss." *New Yorker*, 11 April 1959, pp. 99-105. (As "Walter Briggs.")

"Should Wizard Hit Mommy?" *New Yorker*, 13 June 1959, pp. 38–40.

"The Persistence of Desire." *New Yorker*, 11 July 1959, pp. 22–26.

"Flight." *New Yorker*, 22 August 1959, pp. 30–37.

"Dear Alexandros." *New Yorker*, 31 October 1959, pp. 40–41.

"A Sense of Shelter." *New Yorker*, 16 January 1960, pp. 28–34.

"Wife-Wooing." *New Yorker*, 12 March 1960, pp. 49–51.

"You'll Never Know, Dear, How Much I Love You." *New Yorker*, 18 June 1960, pp. 39–40.

"Home." *New Yorker*, 9 July 1960, pp. 26–31.

"Archangel." *Big Table*, 2, v (1960), 78–79.

"The Doctor's Wife." *New Yorker*, 11 February 1961, pp. 35–38.

"The Crow in the Woods." *Transatlantic Review*, no. 8 (Winter 1961), 47–50.

"The Astronomer." *New Yorker*, 1 April 1961, pp. 28–30.

"Lifeguard." *New Yorker*, 17 June 1961, pp. 28–31.

"A & P." *New Yorker*, 22 July 1961, pp. 22–24.

"Pigeon Feathers." *New Yorker*, 19 August 1961, pp. 25–34.

"Packed Dirt, Churchgoing, A Dying Cat, A Traded Car." *New Yorker*, 16 December 1961, pp. 59–92.

"The Blessed Man of Boston, My Grandmother's Thimble, and Fanning Island." *New Yorker*, 13 January 1962, pp. 28–33.

TELEPHONE POLES

"Bendix." *New Yorker*, 15 February 1958, p. 30.

"The Menagerie at Versailles in 1775." *Harper's*, 216 (May 1958), 78.

"Reel." *New Yorker*, 3 May 1958, p. 133.

"Caligula's Dream." *Commonweal*, 17 June 1958, p. 327.

"Kenneths." *New Yorker*, 5 July 1958, p. 59.

"Upon Learning That a Bird Exists Called the Turnstone." *New Yorker*, 4 October 1958, p. 39.

"Toothache Man." *New Yorker*, 15 November 1958, p. 58.

"3 a.m." *New Yorker*, 29 November 1958, p. 168.

"Party Knee." *New Yorker*, 13 December 1958, p. 46.

"The Moderate." *New Yorker*, 10 January 1959, p. 103.

"Deities and Beasts." *New Republic*, 30 March 1959, p. 17.

"Suburban Madrigal." *New Yorker*, 25 April 1959, p. 100.

"In Praise of ($C_{10}H_9O_5$)." *New Yorker*, 16 May 1959, p. 44.

"Sonic Boom." *New Yorker*, 8 August 1959, p. 89.

"Tome-Thoughts, from the Times." *New Republic*, 10 August 1959, p. 20.

"The Fritillary." *New Yorker*, 15 August 1959, p. 28.

"Thoughts While Driving Home." *New Yorker*, 26 September 1959, p. 180.

"Idyll." *New Yorker*, 10 October 1959, p. 50.

"How to Be Uncle Sam." *Syracuse 10*, 2, No. 1 (October 1959), 32–33.

"Trees Eat Sunshine." *Syracuse 10*, 2, No. 1 (October 1959), 31.

"Mobile of Birds." *New Yorker*, 19 December 1959, p. 32.

"Winter Ocean." *New Yorker*, 20 February 1960, p. 139.

"A Song of Paternal Care." *New Yorker*, 19 March 1960, p. 169.

"Modigliani's Death Mask." *New Yorker*, 26 March 1960, p. 34.

"Tropical Beetles." *New Yorker*, 9 April 1960, p. 154.

"B.W.I." *New Yorker*, 30 April 1960, p. 98.

"Mosquito." *New Yorker*, 11 June 1960, p. 32.

"Meditation on a News Item." *New Yorker*, 16 July 1960, p. 38.

"Summer: West Side." *New Yorker*, 30 July 1960, p. 26.

"Agatha Christie and Beatrix Potter." *New Yorker*, 26 November 1960, p. 52.

"Wash." *New Yorker*, 3 December 1960, p. 161.

"Cosmic Gall." *New Yorker*, 17 December 1960, p. 36.

"Telephone Poles." *New Yorker*, 21 January 1961, p. 36.

"February 22." *New Yorker*, 18 February 1961, p. 40.

"Seven Stanzas at Easter." *Christian Century*, 22 February 1961, p. 236.

"Comp. Religion." *New Yorker*, 8 April 1961, p. 51.

"Upon Learning That a Town Exists in Virginia Called Upperville." *New Yorker*, 20 May 1961, p. 135.

"Maples in a Spruce Forest." *Commonweal*, 2 June 1961, p. 252.

"The Descent of Mr. Aldez." *New Yorker*, 3 June 1961, p. 132.

"Recital." *New Yorker*, 10 June 1961, p. 29.

"Vermont." *Harper's*, 223 (July 1961), 67.

"I Missed His Book, But I Read His Name." *New Yorker*, 4 November 1961, p. 142.

"Old–Fashioned Lightning Rod." *New Yorker*, 18 November 1961, p. 171.

"Les Saints Nouveaux." *Harper's*, 224 (January 1962), 71.

"The Stunt Flier." *New Yorker*, 6 January 1962, p. 59.

"Marriage Counsel." *New Yorker*, 20 January 1962, p. 103.

"The High–Hearts." *New Yorker*, 24 February 1962, p. 30.

"The Short Days." *New Yorker*, 10 March 1962, p. 126.

"Earthworm." *New Yorker*, 12 May 1962, p. 145.

"Die Neuen Heiliger." *Harper's*, 225 (August 1962), 44. (As "Die Neuen Heiligen.")

"Seagulls." *New Yorker*, 25 August 1962, p. 28.

"Calendar." *American Scholar*, 31 (Autumn 1962), 550.

"White Dwarf." *New Yorker*, 1 September 1962, p. 67.

"The Great Scarf of Birds." *New Yorker*, 27 October 1962, p. 52.

"Flirt." *Commonweal*, 30 November 1962, p. 253.

"Bestiary." *New Yorker*, 1 December 1962, p. 228.

"Exposure." *New Yorker*, 8 December 1962, p. 49.

"Vibration." *New Yorker*, 23 February 1963, p. 30.

"Hoeing." *New Yorker*, 27 April 1963, p. 142.

"Erotic Epigrams." *Commonweal*, 14 June 1963, p. 327.

"Pop Smash, Out of Echo Chamber." *What's New.*

OLINGER STORIES

"Friends from Philadelphia." *New Yorker*, 30 October 1954, pp. 29–32. (From *The Same Door.*)

"The Alligators." *New Yorker*, 22 March 1958, pp. 28–31. (From *The Same Door.*)

"The Happiest I've Been." *New Yorker*, 3 January 1959, pp. 24–31. (From *The Same Door.*)

"The Persistence of Desire." *New Yorker*, 11 July 1959, pp. 22–26. (From *Pigeon Feathers.*)

"Flight." *New Yorker*, 22 August 1959, pp. 30–37. (From *Pigeon Feathers.*)

"A Sense of Shelter." *New Yorker*, 16 January 1960, pp. 28–34. (From *Pigeon Feathers.*)

"You'll Never Know, Dear, How Much I Love You." *New Yorker*, 18 June 1960, pp. 39–40. (From *Pigeon Feathers.*)

"Pigeon Feathers." *New Yorker*, 19 August 1961, pp. 25–34. (From *Pigeon Feathers.*)

"Packed Dirt, Churchgoing, A Dying Cat, A Traded Car." *New Yorker*, 16 December 1961, pp. 59–92. (From *Pigeon Feathers.*)

"The Blessed Man of Boston, My Grandmother's Thimble, and Fanning Island," *New Yorker*, 13 January 1962, pp. 28–33. (From *Pigeon Feathers.*)

"In Football Season." *New Yorker*, 10 November 1962, pp. 48–49. (Later in *The Music School.*)

ASSORTED PROSE

"No Dodo." *New Yorker*, 26 November 1955, pp. 43–45.

"Notes and Comment." *New Yorker*, 31 March 1956, p. 23. (As "Central Park.")

"Our Own Baedeker." *New Yorker*, 31 March 1956, pp. 25–26.

"Voices in the Biltmore." *New Yorker*, 14 April 1956, pp. 32–33. (As half of "Postal Complaints.")

"The American Man: What of Him?" *New Yorker*, 12 January 1957, p. 22.

"Old and Precious." *New Yorker*, 30 March 1957, pp. 26–27.

"Anywhere is Where You Hang Your Hat." *New Yorker*, 8 June 1957, pp. 97–101.

"Notes and Comment." *New Yorker*, 16 November 1957, p. 41. (As part of "Spatial Remarks.")

"Notes and Comment." *New Yorker*, 15 March 1958, p. 31. (As half of "Postal Complaints.")

"Dinosaur Egg." *New Yorker*, 19 April 1958, pp. 31–32.

"Notes and Comment." *New Yorker*, 10 May 1958, p. 29. (As "Upright Carpentry.")

"Outing." *New Yorker*, 14 June 1958, pp. 28–29. (As "Outing: A Family Anecdote.")

"Notes and Comment." *New Yorker*, 21 June 1958, p. 21. (As "Crush vs. Whip.")

"Gate." *New Yorker*, 24 January 1959, p. 29. (As "Metro Gate.")

"On the Sidewalk." *New Yorker*, 21 February 1959, p. 32.

"Drinking from a Cup Made Cinchy." *New Yorker*, 21 March 1959, pp. 41–42.

"Cancelled." *New Yorker*, 25 July 1959, pp. 21-23.

"Notes and Comment." *New Yorker*, 26 September 1959, p. 33. (As part of "Spatial Remarks.")

"Notes and Comment." *New Yorker*, 24 October 1959, pp. 33–34. (As "Morality Play.")

"What is a Rhyme?" *Contact*, 2 (1959), 57–60.

"Confessions of a Wild Bore." *New Yorker*, 6 February 1960, pp. 34–35.

"Voices from Downtroddendom." *New Republic*, 9 May 1960, pp. 11–12.

"Why Robert Frost Should Receive the Nobel Prize." *Audience*, 7 (Summer 1960), 45–46.

"Notes and Comment." *New Yorker*, 16 July 1960, pp. 23-24. (As "Bryant Park.")

"Notes and Comment." *New Yorker*, 30 July 1960, p. 15. (As "Obfuscating Coverage.")

"Notes and Comment." *New Yorker*, 6 August 1960, p. 19. (As "John Marquand.")

"Hub Fans Bid Kid Adieu." *New Yorker*, 22 October 1960, pp. 109-131.

"Snow from a Dead Sky." *New Republic*, 28 November 1960, pp. 26-27.

"Notes and Comment." *New Yorker*, 10 December 1960, p. 43. (As "Two Heroes.")

"The Unread Book Route." *New Yorker*, 4 March 1961, pp. 28-29.

"Alphonse Peintre." *New Yorker*, 18 March 1961, pp. 159-161.

"Mr. Ex-Resident." *New Yorker*, 5 August 1961, p. 27.

"Beerbohm and Others." *New Yorker*, 16 September 1961, pp. 163-176.

"Anxious Days for the Glass Family." New York *Times Book Review*, 17 September 1961, pp. 1, 52. (As "Franny and Zooey.")

"Creatures of the Air." *New Yorker*, 30 September 1961, pp. 161-167.

"Notes and Comment." *New Yorker*, 23 December 1961, p. 17. (As "Grandma Moses.")

"John Updike (1940s)." In *Five Boyhoods: Howard Lindsay, Harry Golden, Walt Disney, William K. Zinsser and John Updike*, ed. Martin Levin. New York: Doubleday, 1962, pp. 155-198. (As "The Dogwood Tree: A Boyhood.")

"Foreword." In *The Young King and Other Fairy Tales* by Oscar Wilde. New York: Macmillan, 1962, pp. iii-v. (As "A Foreword for Young Readers.")

"Briefly Noted." *New Yorker*, 24 March 1962, p. 176. (As "Stuffed Fox.")

"Spring Rain." *New Yorker*, 21 April 1962, pp. 31-32.

"Notes and Comment." *New Yorker*, 19 May 1962, p. 31. (As "Eisenhower's Eloquence.")

"Notes and Comment." *New Yorker*, 11 August 1962, p. 15. (As half of "Doomsday, Mass.")

"No Use Talking." *New Republic*, 13 August 1962, pp. 23-24.

"Notes and Comment." *New Yorker*, 13 October 1962, p. 41. (As "Mostly Glass.")

"Indignations of a Senior Citizen." New York *Times Book Review*, 25 November 1962, p. 5. (As "Credos and Curios.")

"My Uncle's Death." *Saturday Evening Post*, 2 March 1963, pp. 48-50.

"Notes and Comment." *New Yorker*, 9 March 1963, pp. 31-32. (As part of "Spatial Remarks.")

"Notes and Comment." *New Yorker*, 1 June 1963, pp. 23-24. (As "Three Documents.")

"More Love in the Western World." *New Yorker*, 24 August 1963, pp. 90-104.

"Between a Wedding and a Funeral." *New Yorker*, 14 September 1963, pp. 192-194.

"The Classics of Realism." *American Scholar*, 32 (Autumn 1963), 660-664. (As "Honest Horn.")

"Faith in Search of Understanding." *New Yorker*, 12 October 1963, pp. 203-210.

"Notes and Comment." *New Yorker*, 19 October 1963, p. 43. (As "Free Bee-hours.")

"Eclipse." *Saturday Evening Post*, 16 November 1963, p. 92.

"Mea Culpa." *New Yorker*, 16 November 1963, pp. 137-140.

"Notes and Comment." *New Yorker*, 7 December 1963, p. 45. (As half of "The Assassination.")

"Notes and Comment." *New Yorker*, 21 December 1963, pp. 21-22. (As half of "The Assassination.")

"Notes and Comment." *New Yorker*, 18 January 1964, p. 23. (As "Beer Can.")

"Briefly Noted." *New Yorker*, 1 February 1964, pp. 97-98. (As "Tillich.")

"Rhyming Max." *New Yorker*, 7 March 1964, pp. 176-181.

"Modern Art." *New Yorker*, 11 April 1964, pp. 31-32.

"The Lucid Eye in Silver Town." *Saturday Evening Post*, 23 May 1964, pp. 54-61.

"Notes and Comment." *New Yorker*, 22 August 1964, p. 23. (As part of "Spatial Remarks.")

"Grandmaster Nabokov." *New Republic*, 26 September 1964, pp. 15-18.

"How How It Is Was." *New Yorker*, 19 December 1964, pp. 165-166.

"Notes and Comment." *New Yorker*, 16 January 1965, p. 25. (As "T.S. Eliot.")

THE MUSIC SCHOOL

"In Football Season." *New Yorker*, 10 November 1962, pp. 48-49.

"A Madman." *New Yorker*, 22 December 1962, pp. 34-38.

"Giving Blood." *New Yorker*, 6 April 1963, pp. 36-41.

"The Indian." *New Yorker*, 17 August 1963, pp. 24-26.

"At a Bar in Charlotte Amalie." *New Yorker*, 11 January 1964, pp. 26-32.

"Twin Beds in Rome." *New Yorker*, 8 February 1964, pp. 32-35.

"The Christian Roommates." *New Yorker*, 4 April 1964, pp. 44-74.

"The Morning." *New Yorker*, 18 July 1964, pp. 24-26.

"The Dark." *New Yorker*, 31 October 1964, pp. 61-62.

"Leaves." *New Yorker*, 14 November 1964, pp. 52-53.

"The Music School." *New Yorker*, 12 December 1964, pp. 50-52.

"The Rescue." *New Yorker*, 2 January 1965, pp. 28-31.

"The Hermit." *New Yorker*, 20 February 1965, pp. 38-46.

"The Bulgarian Poetess." *New Yorker*, 13 March 1965, pp. 44-51. (Also in *Bech: A Book*.)

"The Stare." *New Yorker*, 3 April 1965, pp. 41-43.

"My Lover Has Dirty Fingernails." *New Yorker*, 17 July 1965, pp. 28-31.

"Four Sides of One Story." *New Yorker*, 9 October 1965, pp. 48-52.

"Avec La Bébé-Sitter." *New Yorker*, 1 January 1966, pp. 24-27.

"Harv Is Plowing Now." *New Yorker*, 23 April 1966, pp. 46-48.

MIDPOINT

"Farewell to the Shopping District of Antibes." *New Yorker*, 20 April 1963, p. 50.

"Expose." *New Yorker*, 25 May 1963, p. 40.

"My Children at the Dump at Ipswich." *Transatlantic Review*, no. 14 (Autumn 1963), 70. (As "My Children at the Dump.")

"Some Frenchmen." *New Yorker*, 9 November 1963, p. 54.

"Azores." *Harper's*, 228 (January 1964), 37.

"Lamplight," *New Republic*, 29 February 1964, p. 22.

"Sea Knell." *New Yorker*, 28 March 1964, p. 44.

"Vow." *New Yorker*, 23 May 1964, p. 48.

"Fireworks." *New Yorker*, 4 July 1964, p. 28.

"Roman Portrait Busts." *New Republic*, 6 February 1965, p. 21.

"Poem For a Far Land." *New Republic*, 13 March 1965, p. 17.

"Sunshine on Sandstone." *New Republic*, 17 April 1965, p. 26.

"Postcards from Soviet Cities: Moscow, Kiev, Leningrad, Yerevan." *New Yorker*, 29 May 1965, p. 34.

"Decor." *American Scholar*, 34 (Summer 1965), 412.

"Home Movies." *New Republic*, 8 January 1966, p. 23.

"The Amoeba." *New Republic*, 25 June 1966, p. 23. (As "Amoeba.")

"Seal in Nature." *New Republic*, 15 October 1966, p. 16.

"The Amish." *Saturday Review*, 22 October 1966, p. 4.

"Air Show." *New Republic*, 17 December 1966, p. 25.

"Antigua." *New Yorker*, 11 February 1967, p. 46.

"Subway Love." *New Republic*, 20 May 1967, p. 26.

"The Angels." *New Yorker*, 26 January 1968, p. 34.

"The Naked Ape." *New Republic*, 3 February 1968, p. 28.

"The Origin of Laughter." *Atlantic Monthly*, 221 (June 1968), 105.

"Topsfield Fair." *American Scholar*, 37 (Summer 1968), 419.

"The Average Egyptian Faces Death." *New Republic*, 6 July 1968, p. 38.

"Dream Objects." *New Yorker*, 26 October 1968, p. 54.

"The Dance of the Solids." *Scientific American*, 220 (January 1969), 130–131.

"Report of Health." *New Yorker*, 22 February 1969, p. 40.

"Minority Report." *New Statesman*, 27 June 1969, p. 917.

MUSEUMS AND WOMEN

"The Sea's Green Sameness." *New World Writing*, no. 17 (1960), 54–59.

"Deus Dixit." *Esquire*, 64 (September 1965), 100–102. (Reprinted in *Esquire*, 80 [October 1973], 301–302.) (As "God Speaks" in *Museums and Women*.)

"Marching Through Boston." *New Yorker*, 22 January 1966, pp. 34–38.

"During the Jurassic." *Transatlantic Review*, no. 21 (Summer 1966), 47–50.

"Witnesses." *New Yorker*, 13 August 1966, pp. 27–29.

"The Pro." *New Yorker*, 17 September 1966, pp. 53–54.

"Your Lover Just Called." *Harper's*, 234 (January 1967), 48–51.

"The Taste of Metal." *New Yorker*, 11 March 1967, pp. 49–51.

"Museums and Women." *New Yorker*, 18 November 1967, pp. 57–61.

"Man and Daughter in the Cold." *New Yorker*, 9 March 1968, pp. 34–36.

"Under the Microscope." *Transatlantic Review*, no. 28 (Spring 1968), 5–7.

"Eros Rampant." *Harper's*, 236 (June 1968), 59–64.

"The Slump." *Esquire*, 70 (July 1968), 104–105.

"The Corner." *New Yorker*, 24 May 1969, pp. 38–41.

"The Day of the Dying Rabbit." *New Yorker*, 30 August 1969, pp. 22–26.

"I Am Dying, Egypt, Dying." *Playboy*, 16 (September 1969), 118–120, 250, 254–260.

"I Will Not Let Thee Go, Except Thou Bless Me." *New Yorker*, 11 October 1969, pp. 50–53.

"One of My Generation." *New Yorker*, 15 November 1969, pp. 57–58.

"The Hillies." *New Yorker*, 20 December 1969, pp. 33–35.

"The Deacon." *New Yorker*, 21 February 1970, pp. 38–41.

"The Orphaned Swimming Pool." *New Yorker*, 27 June 1970, pp. 30–32.

"The Carol Sing." *New Yorker*, 19 December 1970, pp. 36–37.

"Plumbing." *New Yorker*, 20 February 1971, pp. 34–37.

"The Baluchitherium." *New Yorker*, 14 August 1971, p. 39.

"Subliminating." *Harper's*, 243 (September 1971), 82–85.

"When Everyone Was Pregnant." *Audience*, 1 (November–December 1971), 35–36.

"Jesus on Honshu." *New Yorker*, 25 December 1971, pp. 29–30.

"Solitaire." *New Yorker*, 22 January 1972, pp. 26–27.

"The Invention of the Horse Collar." *Transatlantic Review*, nos. 42–43 (Spring–Summer 1972), 51–54.

PICKED-UP PIECES

"Briefly Noted." *New Yorker*, 9 September 1961, p. 155. (Review of Karl Barth's *Deliverance to the Captives*, part of "Religious Notes.")

"Accuracy." National Book Award acceptance speech, New York, March, 1964.

"Death's Heads." *New Yorker*, 2 October 1965, pp. 216-228.

"The Author as Librarian." *New Yorker*, 30 October 1965, pp. 223-246.

"Fall Books." *Motive*, 26 November 1965, 50-52. (As "Auden Fecit.")

"The Fork." *New Yorker*, 26 February 1966, pp. 115-134.

"The Mastery of Miss Warner." *New Republic*, 5 March 1966, p. 23. (Also in *Correction*, 26 March 1966, p. 40.)

"Briefly Noted." *New Yorker*, 9 July 1966, pp. 91-92. (Review of Paul Tillich's *On the Boundary* and *The Future of Religions*, part of "Religious Notes.")

"Briefly Noted." *New Yorker*, 20 August 1966, pp. 135-136. (Review of Martin Heidegger's *Discourse on Thinking*, part of "Religious Notes.")

"Promising." *New Yorker*, 29 October 1966, pp. 236-245. (As "A Short Life.") (Last part of original, review of Berry Morgan's *Pursuit*, omitted in *Picked-Up Pieces*.)

"Briefly Noted." *New Yorker*, 26 November 1966, p. 247. (Review of Karl Barth's *How I Changed My Mind*, part of "Religious Notes.")

"Briefly Noted." *New Yorker*, 10 December 1966, pp. 246-247. (Review of Norman Pettit's *The Heart Prepared*, part of "Religious Notes.")

"Two Points on a Descending Curve." *New Yorker*, 7 January 1967, pp. 91-94.

"Nabokov's Look Back: A National Loss." *Life*, 13 January 1967, pp. 9-15. (As "Mnemosyne Chastened.")

"Notes and Comment." *New Yorker*, 26 August 1967, pp. 19-20. (As "Voznesensky Met.")

"Behold Gombrowicz." *New Yorker*, 23 September 1967, pp. 169-176. (As "Witold Who?")

"Grove Is My Press, and Avant My Garde." *New Yorker*, 4 November 1967, pp. 223-238.

"Memories of Anguilla, 1960," *New Republic*, 11 November 1967, p. 21. (As untitled poem in "P.S.")

"My Mind Was Without a Shadow." *New Yorker*, 2 December 1967, pp. 223-232.

"Questions Concerning Giacomo." *New Yorker*, 6 April 1968, pp. 167-174.

"Letter from Anguilla." *New Yorker*, 22 June 1968, pp. 70-80.

"Writers I Have Met." New York *Times Book Review*, 11 August 1968, pp. 2, 23. (As "On Meeting Writers.")

"Indifference." *New Yorker*, 2 November 1968, pp. 197-201.

"Introduction." *Pens and Needles* by David Levine. Boston: Gambit, 1969, pp. v-viii.

"An American in London." *Listener*, 23 January 1969, pp. 97-99. (As half of "Notes of a Temporary Resident.")

"The Future of the Novel." Speech at Bristol Literary Society dinner, February, 1969. Published in *Books and Bookmen*.

"Albertine Disparue." *New Yorker*, 15 March 1969, pp. 174–180.

Translation of Jorge Luis Borges' "Labyrinth." *Atlantic Monthly*, 223 (April 1969), 72. (As part of "Three Translations.")

"Amor Vincit Omnia Ad Nauseam." *New Yorker*, 5 April 1969, p. 33.

"Views." *Listener*, 12 June 1969, pp. 817–818. (As half of "Notes of a Temporary Resident.")

"Cemeteries." *Transatlantic Review*, no. 32 (Summer 1969), 5–10.

"Notes." *New Statesman*, 27 June 1969, p. 917. (As "Notes to a Poem.")

"Love as a Standoff." *New Yorker*, 28 June 1969, pp. 90–95.

"Van Loves Ada, Ada Loves Van." *New Yorker*, 2 August 1969, pp. 67–75.

"Talk of a Sad Town." *Atlantic Monthly*, 224 (October 1969), 124, 128.

"Tributes." *TriQuarterly*, no. 17 (Winter 1970), 342–343. (As "A Tribute.")

"The View from the Dental Chair." *New Yorker*, 25 April 1970, pp. 133–136.

"Humor in Fiction." Speech at International P.E.N. conference, Seoul, South Korea, June, 1970. Published in *American P.E.N.*, 2, iii (1970), 18–33.

"For Louis, Childhood was Very Difficult." New York *Times Book Review*, 28 June 1970, pp. 4–5, 24. (As "His Own Horn.")

"Briefly Noted." *New Yorker*, 11 July 1970, p. 80. (Review of Paul Tillich's *My Travel Diary*: 1936, part of "Religious Notes.")

"Fool's Gold." *New Yorker*, 8 August 1970, pp. 72–76.

"Papa's Sad Testament." *New Statesman*, 16 October 1970, p. 489.

"Briefly Noted." *New Yorker*, 7 November 1970, p. 181. (As "Mary Unrevamped.")

"Black Suicide." *Atlantic Monthly*, 227 (February 1971), 108–112.

"The First Lunar Invitational." *New Yorker*, 27 February 1971, pp. 35–36.

"If at First You Do Succeed, Try, Try Again." *New Yorker*, 10 April 1971, pp. 143–153.

"Alienated Youth, Czarist-Style." *Life*, 6 August 1971, p. 11. (As "A Raw Something.")

"Bombs Made Out of Leftovers." *New Yorker*, 25 September 1971, pp. 131–139.

"Briefly Noted." *New Yorker*, 9 October 1971, p. 169. (As "Half-Mad and Maddening.")

"Phantom Life." *New Yorker*, 23 October 1971, pp. 176–179.

"Out of the Glum Continent." *New Yorker*, 13 November 1971, pp. 187–198.

"Henry Bech Redux." New York *Times Book Review*, 14 November 1971, p. 3. (As "Bech Meets Me.")

"Remarks on the Occasion of E.B. White's Receiving the 1971 National Medal for Literature on December 2, 1971."

Introduction to *Soundings in Satanism*, ed. F.J. Sheed. New York: Sheed and Ward, 1972, pp. vii–xii.

"The Enigmas," p. 181; "The Sea," p. 215; "The Labyrinth," p. 221, in Jorge Luis Borges' *Selected Poems* 1923-1967, ed. Norman Thomas di Giovanni. New York: Delacorte Press/Seymour Lawrence, 1972. (As "Three Translations.")

"Infante Terrible. *New Yorker,* 29, January 1972, pp. 91–94.

"The Crunch of Happiness." *New Yorker,* 26 February 1972, pp. 96–101.

"Satire Without Serifs." *New Yorker,* 13 May 1972, pp. 135–144.

"Is There Life After Golf?" *New Yorker,* 29 July 1972, pp. 76–78.

"From Dyna Domes to Turkey-Pressing." *New Yorker,* 9 September 1972, pp. 115–124.

"Remembrance of Things Past." *Horizon,* 14 (Autumn 1972), 102–105. (As "Remembrance of Things Past Remembered.")

"In Praise of the Blind, Black God." *New Yorker,* 21 October 1972, pp. 157–167.

"The Translucing of Hugh Person." *New Yorker,* 18 November 1972, pp. 242–245.

Introduction to *The Harvard Lampoon Centennial Celebration* 1876–1973, ed. Martin Kaplan. Boston: Atlantic Monthly Press, 1973. No page numbers.

"Polina and Aleksei and Anna and Losnitsky." *New Yorker,* 14 April 1973, pp. 145–154.

"Ayrton Fecit." *New Yorker,* 5 May 1973, pp. 147–149.

"A Sere Life; or, Sprigge's Ivy." *New Yorker,* 2 June 1973, pp. 119–122.

"Golf." New York *Times Book Review,* 10 June 1973, pp. 3, 20. (As "Tips on a Trip.")

"Milton Adapts Genesis; Collier Adapts Milton." *New Yorker,* 20 August 1973, pp. 84–89.

"Snail of the Stump." *New Yorker,* 15 October 1973, pp. 182–185.

"Coffee Table Books for High Coffee Tables." New York *Times Book Review,* 28 October 1973, pp. 4–6.

"Jong Love." *New Yorker,* 17 December 1973, pp. 149–153.

"Shades of Black." *New Yorker,* 21 January 1974, pp. 84–94.

"Mortal Games." *New Yorker,* 25 February 1974, pp. 122–126.

"Inward and Onward." *New Yorker,* 25 March 1974, pp. 133–140.

"A Messed-Up Life." *New Yorker,* 8 April 1974, pp. 137–140.

"Sons of Slaves." *New Yorker,* 6 May 1974, pp. 138–142.

"Why Write?" Speech in Adelaide, South Australia, March 1974. Published in *Southern Review* (South Australia), 7 (July 1974), 94–101.

"A New Meliorism." *New Yorker,* 15 July 1974, pp. 83–86.

"Saganland and the Back of Beyond." *New Yorker,* 12 August 1974, pp. 95–98.

"Alive and Free from Employment." *New Yorker,* 2 September 1974, pp. 80–82.

"Before the Sky Collapses." *New Yorker,* 16 September 1974, pp. 140–147.

"Motlier Than Ever." *New Yorker,* 11 November 1974, pp. 209–212. (As "Motley But True.")

"Through a Continent, Darkly." *New Yorker,* 24 March 1975, pp. 109–115.

"Farewell to the Middle Class." In *Suntory Fiction and Essays.* Tokyo: Suntory. This citation may be Updike's joke on bibliographers, for he claims the essay was hitherto published only in Japanese for a series of whiskey commercials advertising Suntory Whiskey. *See Picked-Up Pieces,* p. 13.

TOSSING AND TURNING

Bath After Sailing. Stevenson, Conn.: Country Squires Books, 1968.

"Post-Impressionist Wives." *Saturday Review*, 8 February 1969, p. 5. (As "Painted Wives.")

"Skyey Developments." *New Republic*, 8 March 1969, p. 28.

"A l'Ecole Berlitz." *New Republic*, 6 and 13 September 1969, p. 33.

"Business Acquaintances." *New Republic*, 4 October 1969, p. 28.

"South of the Alps." *Commonweal*, 17 October 1969, p. 72.

"Upon Shaving Off One's Beard." *New Yorker*, 16 May 1970, p. 37.

"On an Island." *Saturday Review*, 7 November 1970, p. 29.

"Sunday Rain." *Saturday Review*, 17 April 1971, p. 59.

"Marching Through A Novel." *Saturday Review*, 3 July 1971, p. 24.

"Wind." *Commonweal*, 21 January 1972, p. 373. (Reprinted by *Commonweal*, 16 November 1973, p. 175.)

"Sand Dollar." *Atlantic Monthly*, 229 (March 1972), 43.

"A Bicycle Chain." *New Yorker*, 15 April 1972, p. 48.

"Sunday." *American Scholar*, 41 (Summer 1972), 389.

"Insomnia the Gem of the Ocean." *New Yorker*, 16 September 1972, p. 40.

"To a Waterbed." *Harper's*, 245 (December 1972), 66.

"The Cars in Caracas." *New Yorker*, 30 December 1972, p. 27.

"Phenomena." *New Yorker*, 24 February 1973, p. 38.

"The House Growing." *New Yorker*, 23 July 1973, p. 34.

"Commencement, Pingree School." *New Republic*, 28 July and 4 August 1973, p. 28.

"Query." New York: Albondocani Press/Ampersand Books, 1974.

"The Jolly Greene Giant." *The Critic*, March–April 1974, p. 67. (Reprinted from *Punch*.)

"Notes to the Previous Tenants." *New Republic*, 30 November 1974, p. 20.

"Heading for Nandi." *New Yorker*, 16 December 1974, p. 42.

Cunts. New York: Frank Hallman, 1974.

Sunday in Boston. Derry, Pa.: Rook Press, 1975.

"Mime." *New Yorker*, 3 March 1975, p. 42.

"Golfers." *New Republic*, 5 April 1975, p. 30.

"Poisoned in Nassau." *Boston University Journal*, 23, iii (1975), 48.

"News from the Underworld." *American Scholar*, 44 (Autumn 1975), 584.

"Authors' Residences." *Harper's*, 251 (December 1975), 64.

"Dutch Cleanser." *Paris Review*, no. 17 (Winter 1976), 57.

"You Who Swim." *American Scholar*, 45 (Summer 1976), 374.

"Calder's Hands." *New Yorker*, 6 December 1976, p. 45.

"Leaving Church Early." *Ontario Review*, 5 (Fall–Winter 1976–77), 14–17.

"Dream and Reality." *New Yorker*, 24 January 1977, p. 34.

"Rats." *Atlantic Monthly*, 239 (February 1977), 34.

The following six poems were also published in a limited edition as *Six Poems*. New York: Aloe Editions, 1973. "Upon Shaving Off One's Beard," "A l'Ecole Berlitz," "South of the Alps," "Tossing and Turning," "On an Island," "Phenomena."

Index

The index does not include references to material in the footnotes and checklist.

Dali, Salvador: "The Persistence of Memory," 99
Dante: 34, 35, 40; *The Divine Comedy*, 34
Davenport, Guy: on *Museums and Women*, 163
Davis, D.M.: on *Assorted Prose*, 202
De Bellis, Jack: on "A Gift from the City," 81
Deemer, Charles: on *Museums and Women*, 165
Detweiller, Robert: *John Updike*, xix, 81, 97
Dillinger, John, 207
Dimaggio, Joe, 225
dinosaurs, 43, 182, 209
Dostoevsky, Fydor: 232; *The Gambler*, 233

Earp, Wyatt, 206
Edelstein, J.M.: on *Pigeon Feathers*, 93–94
Edwards, A.S.G., 106
Egypt, 177–178
Ehrenpreis, Irvin: on *Buchanan Dying*, 244–245, 247, 248
Eiffel Tower, 225
Eisenhower, Dwight David, 172, 208, 212
Eliot, George, 226
Eliot, T.S., 7, 28, 29, 61, 207, 213, 231, 232
Emmanuel, Victor, 147
England: 116, 140, 210; see Britain, London, Oxford

Faulkner, William: 221, 262; *Absalom, Absalom!*, 202; *New Orleans Sketches*, 205;

Yoknapatawpha, 262
Fearing, Kenneth, 28
Fenway Park, 223–226
Ferguson, Halty, 192
Fiji, 55
Fillmore, Millard, 251
Finn, Huckleberry, 76
Forney, John, 257
Fort Sumter, South Carolina, 256, 257
Fox, William Price: *Doctor Golf*, 186
France: 141, 146; see Cannes
Frost, Robert: 7, 208; "The Gift Outright," 206
Fuller, Edmund: on *Telephone Poles*, 21

Gantry, Elmer, 120
Garbo, Greta: *Camille*, 78
Gates, Anne: on *Midpoint*, 31
Germany, 17
Gesell, Arnold: *Infant and Child in the Culture of Today*, 15
Gilman, Richard, xii
Giotto, Bondone de, 85
Gombrowicz, Witold: *Ferdydurke*, xii, 237
Gower, Herschel, 106
Grass, Gunter: *From the Diary of a Snail*, 237
Graver, Lawrence: on *Picked-Up Pieces*, 204
Green, Henry, 39
Greenwich Village, 187
Grumbach, Doris: on *Museums and Women*, 163

Hamilton, Alice and Kenneth: 61, 181; *The Elements of*

John Updike, xix; on *Mid-point*, 31–32, 34
Hamlet, 251, 252
Hamsen, Knut, 232
Hannah, Barry, 232
Hansel and Gretel, 138
Harappa, 152
Harvard University, 46, 48, 49, 50, 57, 61, 157–158, 231
Hawkes, John: 220; *Second Skin*, 236
Hawthorne, Nathaniel: Aylmer, 149, 151; "The Birth-mark," 149, 151; *The Scarlet Letter*, 16
Hegel, 17
Hemingway, Ernest: 28, 157, 233; *Across the River and into the Trees*, 231; Nick Adams, 28
Herbert, George, 5
Heron, Patrick, 28
Heyen, William: on *Midpoint*, 31
Hicks, Granville: 95, 157; on *Assorted Prose*, 203; on *The Music School*, 135–136; on *Pigeon Feathers*, 92
Holt, Joseph, 254
Hooker, Richard, 71
Horton, R.G.: *The Life and Public Service of James Buchanan*, 251
Housman, A.E.: "To An Athlete Dying Young," 9
Howe, Irving, xii
Howells, William Dean, 188
Howes, Victor: on *Tossing and Turning*, 45
Hughes, Richard, 205
Huysmans, Joris Karl, 234

Hyman, Stanley Edgar: 95; on *Pigeon Feathers*, 93

Ilg, Frances: *Infant and Child in the Culture of Today*, 15
Ipswich, Massachusetts, 38, 39, 61, 133, 233
Ireland, John, 79
Italy: 146; *see* Rome

Jackson, Andrew, 245, 247, 251, 258
Jacobson, Josephine: on *The Music School*, 135
James, Henry: 76; *The Golden Bowl*, 202
Jason, 225
Johnson, Lyndon, 188
Johnson, Samuel, 27, 233
Jong, Erica: *Fear of Flying*, 239
Joyce, James: xiv, 14, 109–110, 232, 233, 238, 239; *Ulysses*, 14, 50, 221
Kafka, Franz: 93, 159, 180, 233, 238; "A Report to an Academy," 96
Kanon, Joseph: on *Museums and Women*, 165
Kauffmann, Stanley: xii, 130; on *The Music School*, 136
Kazin, Alfred, xii
Kelly, Walt, 211
Kennedy, John F., 208, 213
Kennedy, X.J.: on *Telephone Poles*, 20
Kerouac, Jack: 219, 234, 236; *On the Road*, 208
Kierkegaard, Soren: 29, 39, 119, 182, 183, 230, 239, 246, 250,

Musial, Stan, 225

Nabokov, Vladimir: 205, 230, 232, 233, 236-237, 239; *Ada*, 236-237; *Lolita*, 230, 236
Nash, Ogden, 7, 27, 57
Nasser, Gamal Abdel, 97
Nestor, 225
Nevin, Blanche, 249
Nevins, Allan: 252; *The Emergence of Lincoln*, 251
New Orleans, 212
New Republic, 81
New York (Manhattan), 38, 75, 77, 79, 80, 81-83, 87, 116, 209
New Yorker, 6, 8, 61, 63, 65, 94, 128, 135, 183, 192, 201-239 *passim*, 262, 263
New York *Times*, xvi, 27, 231
Newsweek, 201
Nile River, 177, 179
Nixon, Richard, 110, 206, 211

O'Hara, John, 229
Olinger, xvi, xvii, 22, 23, 35, 42, 46, 48, 49, 53, 57, 73, 75, 77, 85-87, 90, 101, 102, 103-105, 128-132, 133, 136, 137, 148, 151, 158, 159, 163, 165, 168, 171, 175, 180, 187, 192, 253, 262
Overall, Nadine: on *Olinger Stories*, 129
Oxford, England: 61, 70, 102, 140, 141, 145; *see* Britain, England, London
Oxford University Press, 76

Paris Review, 50

Patchen, Kenneth, 28
Peden, William: on *The Same Door*, 63
Pennington, New Jersey, 218
Pennsylvania: 42, 70, 75, 87, 99, 116, 151, 184, 192, 211, 232, 262; *see* Chapter Four
Peyton Place, xiii
Phillips, Robert, 181, 187
Pierce, Franklin, 251
Plath, Sylvia, 239
Plato, 26, 113
Plowville, Pennsylvania, 111, 217
Podhoretz, Norman: xiii, xiv-xv, xix; Updike's opinion of, xiv
Polk, James K., 251, 254, 255, 258
Polonius, 251
Pope, Alexander, 34, 39, 40
Pope Benedict, 85
Pound, Ezra, 31, 34, 40, 50
Pravda, 205
Prescott, Orville, 28
Pritchard, William: on *Museums and Women*, 165
Proust, Marcel: 226, 232, 233, 239; *Sodom and Gomorrah*, 81
Public Broadcasting System: "The American Short Story," 153
Pynchon, Thomas, xiii, 220

Rabinowitz, Dorothy: on *Museums and Women*, 163
Reid, Alastair: on *The Coup*, 261
Reising, R.W., 106
Rexroth, Kenneth, 28
Robbe-Grillet, Alain, 238
Roethke, Theodore, 239

Rohrbach, Peter: on *Museums and Women*, 165
Rolls Royce, 8-9, 15
Rome: 147; *see* Italy
Roosevelt, Franklin D., 217
Rougemont, Denis de, 192, 222
Rowland, Stanley J., Jr.: on *Pigeon Feathers*, 94
Rupp, Richard, 104, 123
Ruskin School of Drawing and Fine Arts, 61
Russia, 42, 177, 178
Ruth, Babe, 225

Salinger, J.D.: 72, 202, 205, 223, 236; *Franny and Zooey*, 202; the Glass family, 72, 202-203, 236
Samuels, Charles Thomas: 103, 130, 157, 158, 187; on *The Music School*, 135
Saturday Evening Post, 205, 217
St. Paul, 78, 83
Schlesinger, Arthur, Jr.: on *Buchanan Dying*, 245-248, 252
Scientific American, 34, 36
Selby, Hubert, Jr.: *Last Exit to Brooklyn*, 234
Selma, Alabama, 188
Seoul, South Korea, 232
Shakespeare, William: 40, 69, 70; *Cymbeline*, 180; *Macbeth*, 69, 70
Shepard, Alan, 186
Shillington, Pennsylvania, 19, 22, 35, 38, 39, 46, 48, 91, 111, 129, 133, 213-217, 233
Sillitoe, Alan, 205, 223
Slidell, John, 257

Soundings in Satanism, 230
South Carolina, 251, 255, 256, 257, 258
Spark, Muriel, 205, 220, 223
Spectorsky, A.C.: on *The Same Door*, 62-63
Spenser, Edmund, 34, 36, 37, 40
Steiner, George, 185
Stevens, Wallace: 14, 41, 221; "The Comedian as the Letter C," 33, 35, 40; "The Man on the Dump," 41; "Sea Surface Full of Clouds," 12, 17; "To the One of Fictive Music," 133
Stitt, Peter: on *Telephone Poles*, 7-8, 27
Suderman, Elmer F.: on *Museums and Women*, 163
Sullivan, Walter: on *Assorted Prose*, 201, 202
"Summertime," 72

Tanner, Tony: xiii; on *Museums and Women*, 164
Tappan Zee Bridge, 225
Tarbox, xvii, 11, 35, 42, 46, 53, 57, 73, 130, 133, 136, 137, 143, 145, 148, 151, 157, 159, 163, 164-165, 168, 171, 174, 179, 180, 187, 192
Taylor, Larry: *Pastoral Patterns in John Updike's Fiction*, xix
Taylor, Zachary, 251
Tennyson, Alfred, 108
Texas, 171
Thompson, Kate, 243, 251, 254
Thoreau, Henry David, 159, 165
Thurber, James, 181, 205, 221, 229, 231
Tillich, Paul, 119, 202

CHARACTERS